COMMERCIAL PHOTOSHOP®
with Bert Monroy

D1533604

Contents at a Glance

COMMERCIAL PHOTOSHOP®
with Bert Monroy

800 East 96th Street, 3rd Floor, Indianapolis, Indiana 46240
An Imprint of Pearson Education
Boston • Indianapolis • London • Munich • New York • San Francisco

Commercial Photoshop® with Bert Monroy

Copyright © 2004 by New Riders Publishing

All rights reserved. No part of this book shall be reproduced, stored in a retrieval system, or transmitted by any means—electronic, mechanical, photocopying, recording, or otherwise—without written permission from the publisher, except for the inclusion of brief quotations in a review.

International Standard Book Number: 0-7357-1388-X

Library of Congress Catalog Card Number: 2003112023

Printed in the United States of America

First printing: December 2003

08 07 06 05 04   7 6 5 4 3 2 1

Interpretation of the printing code: The rightmost double-digit number is the year of the book's printing; the rightmost single-digit number is the number of the book's printing. For example, the printing code 04-1 shows that the first printing of the book occurred in 2004.

Trademarks

All terms mentioned in this book that are known to be trademarks or service marks have been appropriately capitalized. New Riders Publishing cannot attest to the accuracy of this information. Use of a term in this book should not be regarded as affecting the validity of any trademark or service mark.

Adobe, Photoshop, and Illustrator are registered trademarks of Adobe Systems, Inc.

Warning and Disclaimer

Every effort has been made to make this book as complete and as accurate as possible, but no warranty of fitness is implied. The information is provided on an as-is basis. The authors and New Riders Publishing shall have neither liability nor responsibility to any person or entity with respect to any loss or damages arising from the information contained in this book.

PUBLISHER
Stephanie Wall

PRODUCTION MANAGER
Gina Kanouse

SENIOR DEVELOPMENT EDITOR
Jennifer Eberhardt

SENIOR PROJECT EDITOR
Lori Lyons

TECHNICAL REVIEWERS
Dan Margulis
Wayne Palmer

COPY EDITOR
Keith Cline

INDEXER
Lisa Stumpf

MANUFACTURING COORDINATOR
Dan Uhrig

INTERIOR DESIGN AND COMPOSITION
Kim Scott

COVER DESIGNER
Aren Howell

COVER IMAGE
Bert Monroy

MARKETING
Scott Cowlin
Tammy Detrich
Hannah Onstad Latham

PUBLICITY MANAGER
Susan Nixon

Table of Contents

About the Author

Bert Monroy was born and raised in New York City, where he spent 20 years in the advertising industry as an art director and creative director for various agencies as well as his own.

Upon discovering computers with the introduction of the Macintosh 128 in 1984, he embarked on a new digital career. He embraced the computer as an artistic medium and is considered one of the pioneers of digital art. Bert's work has been seen in every major magazine. His work has also been featured in scores of books, including *Making Art on a Macintosh*, *The Photoshop WOW Book* (all editions), *The Illustrator WOW Book* (all editions), *The Art of Digital Painting*, and *Photoshop A to Z* in Japan.

Bert co-authored *The Official Adobe Photoshop Handbook*, which was the first book on Photoshop and the only one for almost 2 years. It won various awards. He also co-authored many other books, including *Photoshop Channel CHOPS*, co-authored with David Biedny and Nathan Moody. His first solo effort was released in 2000 by New Riders. It was called *Bert Monroy: Photorealistic Techniques with Photoshop and Illustrator*. Upon the release of Photoshop version 7, Bert released *Photoshop Studio with Bert Monroy*. These last two titles concentrate on the techniques he has established over the years in the creation of his fine art works.

He has appeared on many television shows both in the United States and Japan, and for the past 2 1/2 years has been a monthly regular on *The Screen Savers* show on TechTV.

Bert is an accomplished teacher and lecturer who has served on the faculty of the School of Visual Arts (NYC), Center for Creative Imaging (ME), Dynamic Graphics Educational Foundation (IL), California College of Arts & Crafts (CA), and he lectures at many other institutions and conferences around the world. He currently teaches at San Francisco State University.

Bert now lives in Berkeley, California. He continues to serve his installed base of clients, including Apple Computer, Adobe Systems, Pioneer Electronics, Fujitsu, SONY, AT&T, Chevron, and American Express. Bert has also done a considerable amount of film work for Industrial Light & Magic, Pacific Data Images, and R/Greenberg Assoc.

Acknowledgments

Writing a book like this is impossible without a good team behind you, and I am proud and thankful to have had such a team behind me. The few words expressed here can in no way be enough to express my gratitude for the help and support that I received in the production of this work.

First I would like to thank Jennifer Eberhardt for being such a good editor. What I really want to thank her for is the patience she displayed, especially when deadlines came and went without being met.

Along with Jennifer are the rest of the folks at New Riders who have always proved to be a professional and dedicated bunch. They are a true pleasure to work with. And with New Riders is the gang at Peachpit Press, who have always made me feel like part of their family.

A special thanks goes to Steve Weiss, who kept this project alive since we first conceived it years ago.

Dan Margulis. What can I possibly say about the best tech editor on the planet? Tough! Honest! Fearless, in letting me have it straight. He took the time in spite of his hectic schedule to go thoroughly through everything with a fine-toothed comb.

My wife, Zosia. She spent countless hours reading the dribble I put on paper and somehow, miraculously, turned it into English. A close second to Dan on not letting me get away with anything that was not close to perfect.

I truly want to thank Mark Hamburg for a few reasons. First, for the glowing foreword he wrote that brought a little tear to my eye. Second, for his friendship through the years, but most of all for being so instrumental in the development of Photoshop, a tool that is so much a part of my life. He and that collection of wizards at Adobe know how to do it right.

Of course, if you are thinking of Photoshop, how can you not think of Tom and John Knoll? A special thanks to them for giving birth to the ultimate dream tool for so many of us.

I want to thank the gang at TechTV for being such a wonderful bunch of folks to work with.

Thanks go to Carl Munoz, a friend and client, who took time out to dig up all those images I did for him for his wine accessories catalogs.

Thanks to my old friend John Melo, who pushed me into the graphic arts industry when we were young. He would not take no for an answer. I am glad he didn't.

Thanks to all my clients, many of whom I have the pleasure to call friends.

A special thanks must be given to Bill Schoenberg, my nephew Mark Surawski, Chip, and the rest of the guys who make up my weekly hiking party. Without that distraction to look forward to, I probably would have gone off the deep end.

Finally, I want to thank all my friends and family. I have been blessed with some really great people, and I love you all.

Tell Us What You Think

As the reader of this book, you are the most important critic and commentator. We value your opinion and want to know what we're doing right, what we could do better, what areas you'd like to see us publish in, and any other words of wisdom you're willing to pass our way.

As an editor for New Riders Publishing, I welcome your comments. You can fax, email, or write me directly to let me know what you did or didn't like about this book—as well as what we can do to make our books stronger. When you write, please be sure to include this book's title, ISBN, and author, as well as your name and phone or fax number. I will carefully review your comments and share them with the author and editors who worked on the book.

Please note that I cannot help you with technical problems related to the topic of this book, and that due to the high volume of email I receive, I might not be able to reply to every message.

Fax: 317-428-3280

Email: **jennifer.eberhardt@newriders.com**

Mail: Jennifer Eberhardt
        Senior Development Editor
        New Riders Publishing
        800 East 96th Street, 3rd Floor
        Indianapolis, IN 46240 USA

Foreword

A Reality Built in Photoshop

Technically speaking, this is not an Adobe Photoshop book. It has material on Adobe Illustrator and on using 3D modeling programs and on a variety of other topics. But Bert has a lot to say about Photoshop, and my interactions with Bert over the years have been centered around Photoshop, so this is a Photoshop-centric foreword.

I did not know it at the time, but my first experience with Bert's work was a poster that he worked on for Ann Arbor Softworks' FullWrite Professional, a Macintosh word processor from the late 1980s. I worked on FullWrite, and the poster boldly proclaimed, "We're going to change serious writing. Forever." I am writing this foreword, however, with Microsoft Word, so clearly "forever" does not last as long as it once did.

Bert's work has lasted and deepened and grown. He has been involved with Photoshop at a variety of key points in its evolution.

Bert's involvement with Photoshop actually goes back well before my own. He was using beta copies and pre-beta copies while I was still at Ashton-Tate. He was one of the first significant non-Adobe proponents of Photoshop and was part of the moderately elite collection of people who really grasped the power provided by the calculation commands. It was not a private elite, however, and Bert was happy to share his techniques with anyone who cared to learn.

Calculations or channel operations (ChOps) were how people did sophisticated compositing work in Photoshop before the advent of layers. Bert will show you that even with layers, channels still matter. Because of his earlier work, however, he was one of our early guinea pigs when developing layers in Photoshop 3. We put him in a room with a one-way window and watched as he tried to figure out how it all worked. We learned that some things in our implementation at that time—about 10 months before shipping—made sense and some things distinctly did not. Bert then became someone we could go back to and ask, "Is this better?"

On Adobe Photoshop 7, Bert again played a key role. This time he served as our target user for the new painting engine. We looked to him for feature requests and suggestions in building the engine and he contributed a number of brushes to the final product.

Many people think of Photoshop as a tool for working on photographs. Bert has shown that it is also a viable tool for creating photo-realistic images essentially from scratch. The images don't look exactly like photographs, but neither do they look like paintings in the traditional sense (although Bert routinely refers to them as paintings). He may use photographs, but they are raw material for completing broader designs. This is particularly true in his personal work, but even in the commercial work documented here, the real world is at best a place to find raw materials for a synthetic reality.

Bert combines years of experience and a detailed approach to make images that astonish people when they realize what they are looking at. He shares that approach here with you. Seeing behind the curtain, however, makes the results no less astonishing.

—*Mark Hamburg, Fellow, Adobe Systems Incorporated*
15 September 2003

Introduction

I am a commercial illustrator. I create the visuals you see on magazine covers, advertisements, posters, and such. Though there are many steps and technologies that go into the creation of a commercial illustration such as pencil roughs, 3D software and the like, Photoshop plays the key role in bringing it all together.

I have written and co-written many books on the subject of Adobe Photoshop. I co-wrote the very first book ever written on Photoshop. My last two books focused on my use of the program as an artistic medium for the creation of images from scratch. This book deals with a different side to my use of Photoshop—my primary tool of the trade.

I will try to give you an insight into the ways in which Photoshop can be of tremendous value during the various stages of the creative process, from conceptualization to the finished art. Whether your direction is print, 3D, gaming, the web or film and video, Photoshop is an important integral part of the production process.

You might recognize some of the images throughout the book. Some were done quite some time ago. In this book, however, I have taken the liberty of updating the techniques to conform to the current version, Photoshop CS. As I look back at some of these works, it made me laugh at how much easier things have become. With each new version of the software, new feature sets make the creative process easier and much more rewarding.

While thumbing through the book, there might be a few images that might make you think to yourself "I'll never have to do something like that." But what I think is important for you to know is that it is not the end result that is important—it is the steps that got me there. I always stress that in the creation of my art it is not the finished painting that I love but rather the process that leads to it. That process or journey, as I like to refer to it, is what this book is about.

This book will take you through steps that not only will make your job easier, but will structure your approach to a project. And hopefully to overcome any limitations that currently hold you back from letting your imagination run wild.

I get many people writing me saying they feel so overwhelmed or intimidated by the complexity of Photoshop. Overwhelming—I can understand—there is a lot there. Intimidation—that's something you must not let get to you. What you must try to feel is determination and a desire to explore. It can't hurt you! I know of no one who has been injured by Photoshop. Maybe a slight headache every now and then. But nothing life threatening.

I also get a lot of people asking me if there is a lot of money to be made as an artist. I have only one answer to that one. To really succeed in a career, you have to follow your heart. Don't let money be the main motivator. You have to do whatever it is you do for a major portion of the day. If you hate what you do, then you will end each day feeling unfulfilled. Sure, you might say, the money makes it worthwhile! Not really. Maybe at first, but in the long term, personal satisfaction is far more important. Do what you do because you love it! If you love what you do, you will do the best you can and there will always be someone ready to pay you for that. I hit the bed at night and start thinking of what I can do tomorrow. I'm not saying you have to be a workaholic, just someone who loves their work.

There is a vast landscape of possibilities placed before you waiting to be discovered. A wondrous world limited only by your imagination. What does this tool do? Click on it! Find out! Learning is a wonderful and rewarding experience. Photoshop rewards you with a feature set that can open up so many avenues for creativity.

This book will give you a few road maps, but the journey is yours to take. Buckle up and let her rip!

Getting Started

With this chapter we begin our journey into the complex and fascinating world that is Photoshop. This chapter covers the development of a concept from the initial sketch to the final layout. I introduce you to my personal methods of organizing the elements for an illustration and the work habits that I have established throughout my years as a commercial illustrator.

This chapter also serves as a refresher course on the basics of the program. I know many of you consider yourselves Photoshop savvy and think that you know all the basics. Take a moment and read through this chapter anyway. You might find a few things you didn't know.

First, I want to review certain commands that will be used over and over in these pages: alpha channels, Clipping Groups, the Pen Tool, Layer Styles, and Adjustment layers.

Channels and Alpha Channels

Every image is made up of channels that contain the tonal and color information for that image. Unless you add more, a grayscale image consists of a single channel, an RGB file three channels, and a CMYK file four channels. In a color file, you can display the channels on the monitor with the keyboard shortcut Command (Control)-1 to display the first (red, or cyan) channel, Command (Control)-2 to display the second (green, or magenta), and so on, with Command (Control)- ~ available to display the composite color. Many people like to keep track of the individual channels with the Channels palette (Figures 1 and 2).

Each channel can be accessed independently, which can prove very advantageous in certain situations. Understanding the functions of these color channels is crucial when making color corrections or other modifications to an image.

I tend to work in an RGB color space the majority of the time. First of all, red, green and blue are the primary colors of light. Working on a computer monitor, which uses light to display color, it makes perfect sense to me to work in that color space. Another reason is that some of the features, such as certain filters, will not work in the usual alternative, CMYK.

The original file is an RGB, and the final image is CMYK for print. This is a personal preference. Most people will work in CMYK from the start, and that also makes perfect sense because that way they will be choosing colors that work and will print properly. I do not find working in RGB a problem because Photoshop does warn you when you are picking colors that will not translate properly into CMYK.

Let's look at how the RGB channels usually stack up and the way they interact. Figure 3 has a shot of some vegetables. There are some bright reds and deep greens against the stark white of a colander.

1 This is an RGB file showing the individual channels and the Channels palette.

2 This is a CMYK file showing the individual channels and the Channels palette.

3 This is a RGB file containing a variety of contrasting colors.

The lighter an RGB channel, the more of that color will hit our eye. So, in the tomatoes and red peppers, the red channel will be quite light. The darker the other two channels are, the more saturated the dominating color will be. Because these red vegetables are of rather a pure color, one would expect the green and blue channels to be rather dark.

The green areas in this image aren't nearly as saturated as the reds are. The peppers are definitely what we'd call a dull green. For such a color, the dominating channel—here, the green—will only be a little lighter than the other two.

4 The red channel shows a dramatic difference in tonality between the red tomatoes and peppers and the dark green peppers.

This image doesn't have any blue areas, so there aren't any areas where blue is light and the other two dark. There are, however, two prominent intermediate colors: the purple eggplant, and the yellow pear tomatoes. Such colors have two light channels and one dark one. In purple, the green is dark and the red and blue light; in yellow, the red and green are light and the blue dark.

What we perceive as contrast may just be drama, not detail. That's what's happening in the red channel (Figure 4.) The difference between the very light tomatoes and the dark peppers is stark. It almost hides the fact that the green channel is generally better detailed. The green (Figure 5) has more definition in both peppers and tomatoes. In fact, the only area in which the red is better is in the light green lettuce behind the bowl on the left.

This is par for the course. The best definition in any object is usually found in the channel that hugs the middle: one that's neither too light nor too dark. In the tomatoes, the red is too light and the blue too dark, so the green has the best tonal range. The green peppers are so dark that the green is still the best even though it's the lightest of the three channels. It's a mid-tone, whereas the red and blue are both much darker.

The blue channel is the darkest of the three in almost every image. It also can be home to a good deal of noise—an objectionable, irregular pattern of stray pixels. And it has little impact on the contrast of the image, because we aren't as sensitive to blue light as we are to red or, especially, green. Professional retouchers therefore rarely try to milk contrast out of it and instead concentrate on the red and green.

5 The green channel doesn't have as many light and dark areas in the tomatoes and peppers. Therefore, it has better definition than the red channel does in these areas.

6 The blue channel is almost always the darkest of the three RGB channels. Often it is also home to disagreeable amounts of noise.

Knowing these little tidbits about the RGB color space makes correcting images an easier task. Take for example the Despeckle filter (Filter > Noise > Despeckle). Most people apply it, or some substitute such as Gaussian Blur or Dust & Scratches, to remove film grain or other noise. The downside is that the image tends to get blurred. If you apply one of these filters to the blue channel only, you get a much bigger bang for the buck, with much less degradation, because the noise or grain is disproportionately in that channel as opposed to the other two.

Similarly, with experience you will learn which channel is the best bet for enhancing certain types of images. If it's a picture of a face, the green will usually be the best-detailed channel, because the red will be too light and the blue too dark. If you're trying to emphasize the cloud pattern in a blue sky, however, the red channel is a better option, because the green and blue will be too light to hold much detail.

Although an RGB file has a minimum of three channels and CMYK four, users can add additional ones, occasionally as different colors (most commonly to house masks and other tidbits needed for retouching). These are called alpha channels. Although Layer Styles have simplified many of the processes that earlier required the use of alpha channels, the channels still have very powerful functions.

With the exception of spot color channels, alpha channels contain no color information—in fact, they are purely grayscale channels. They are used as specialized, reusable selections or masks. Reusable because they reside within the file and will be there every time the file is opened. Selecting part of the image with any of the selection tools, such as the Lasso, is a temporary state. When you deselect it, the selection is gone. If that selection is saved to an alpha channel, you can recall it at any time. Throughout the book I often use the phrase "the selection was then saved to an alpha channel."

When you have selected an area of an image, you have segregated that area for some action that will affect that area exclusively. When the area is selected, you can colorize it, filter it, scale it, or perhaps duplicate it. Anything you want to do will be done to that area while leaving the unselected areas of the image untouched.

Selecting can be done with any of the selection tools, including the Lasso Tool, Rectangular Marquee Tool, and Magic Wand Tool. Color Range, found under the Select menu, enables you to make selections based on sampled colors, specific colors, highlights, midtones, shadows, or colors that are out of Gamut. As previously stated, these selections are temporary. After the selection is made, choosing Save Selection from the Select menu stores the selection to an alpha channel (Figure 7) or, less commonly, to an entirely new document.

How the Alpha Channel Works

Let's do a little exercise together to see how an alpha channel works. In Photoshop, open an existing RGB image that you have, such as the one in Figure 8. Make sure you have the Channels palette open (Windows > Channels).

7 Save Selection is the menu choice to create an alpha channel from something currently selected in an image.

8 This image will serve as an example for the function of an alpha channel. Open an image of your own to follow along. It does not have to look like this one; any image will do.

9 With the Rectangular Marquee Tool, a small rectangle is selected.

Using the Rectangular Marquee Tool, select a small rectangle, such as the one in Figure 9. Choose Save Selection from the Select menu.

The dialog box that pops up enables you to name the channel (Figure 10). Also note that under Document you could send this to a new document (Figure 11). This means that you send the selection into an alpha channel in a separate document. This gives you the opportunity to have literally thousands of alpha channels that pertain to an image without them actually being stored with the image. For now, keep the current file as the Destination Document.

The bottom portion of the dialog box is discussed later. For the purpose of this exercise, let's just click OK for now.

Notice that the new alpha channel now appears in the Channels palette (Figure 12).

Click the alpha channel in the palette to make it active.

The "marching ants" of the marquee should still be visible. Note that the area within the marquee is white, whereas everything else is black. White is the selected area. Anything that is white in an alpha channel exposes the image to alteration just as the normal selection process does. Black protects the image from any alteration just as the unselected portions of an image are protected (Figure 13). This particular channel has no gray areas, but if it did, they would create a partial selection. That is, a gray area would be affected by any change, but not so much as a white area would. Only totally black areas would be unaffected. The lighter the gray, the stronger the exposure to change would be.

10 This dialog box allows you to name the alpha channel and select its destination.

11 By choosing New for Document, you can send the selection to an alpha channel in a different document.

12 The new alpha channel appears in the Channels palette.

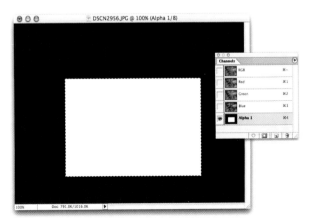

13 The selected area appears white in the alpha channel.

Go back to the RGB image by clicking RGB in the Channels palette. Deselect.

In professional retouching, it's often necessary to reselect the same area that was previously selected at some point in the process. I'd hate to have to go back and re-create a rectangle at exactly this size and exactly this location within the image. Hence, the alpha channel: a ready-made selection, always at your disposal. When you need to activate it as a selection, the conventional way is to use Select > Load Selection. All alpha channels—and for that matter, all other open grayscale documents with the same pixel count as the present document—will be available in this dialog box for loading.

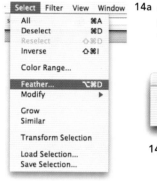

14a A feather can be added to a selection after the selection is established, from the Select menu.

14b A feather radius is entered into this dialog box that pops up when Feather is chosen from the Select menu.

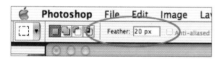

15 A feather radius can be applied to the selection tool prior to using it to select.

Personally, I find it easier to just Command (Control)-click the icon of the particular alpha channel in the Channels palette. Do that now and you will find your original selected area is back.

Now, let's explore the function of gray areas in an alpha channel. Go to the RGB composite channel. Make another selection, but this time give it a feather (Select > Feather) of about 20 (Figures 14a and 14b).

NOTE
A feather can be applied prior to selecting by assigning a feather radius to the selection tool in the options bar for the tool (Figure 15).

Use Save Selection as before.

Looking at the alpha channel this time, you will see a soft-edged selected area (Figure 16). These grays can be of tremendous value when you want to apply alterations gradually to an image.

To illustrate this, let's start from scratch, without any selection or alpha channel. Open an image and apply a filter. For present purposes, I used Filter > Stylize > Find Edges. We see that the entire image has been filtered (Figure 17).

Undo the filter.

What we want to do now is to reapply the filter so that it doesn't affect the left side of the image at all, but is completely effective on the right side. In between we want a gradual transition.

16 A feathered selection will appear in the alpha channel as a soft-edged selection.

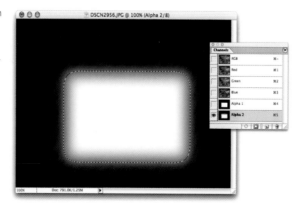

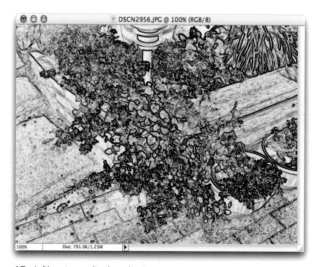

17 A filter is applied to the image.

Click the Make New Channel icon at the bottom of the Channels palette. This creates a totally black alpha channel because nothing was selected in the image. It also makes it the active channel (Figure 18).

With the Gradient Tool, apply a gradient to the alpha channel with black on the left and white on the right as seen in Figure 19. Yes, that's right, the tools work in the alpha channels. You can paint in them, erase, or even put other images into them. Remember they are not in color and have nothing to do with the image other than providing a means for selecting.

Go back to the RGB composite by Command (Control)- ~ or by clicking RGB in the Channels palette and load the new gradient alpha channel as a selection (Command-click the alpha channel in the palette).

The "marching ants" indicating a selected area will now be present, but they won't give an entirely accurate view. In Figure 20, they show a misleadingly hard edge to the selection because they outline only areas that are more than 50% selected, which is basically the right half of the image. But in fact, there is a partial selection almost all the way across to the left side of the image. The selection just fades out along the way.

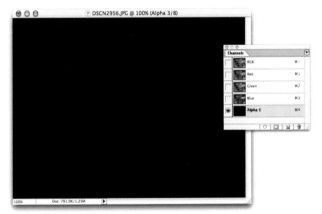

18 A new alpha channel is created without a selection. The result is a totally black channel.

20 The "marching ants" that display a selected area over an image are visible from the 50% gray area to the white area of the alpha channel.

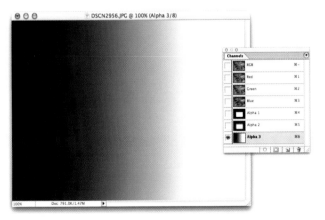

19 A gradient is applied to the alpha channel.

Apply the same filter as before, Filter > Stylize > Find Edges. Notice that the effect is total on the right whereas nonexistent on the left with a gradual transition in between (Figure 21).

Similarly, if you cancel this filter and instead try changing colors, pressing the Delete key, or dragging a painting tool across the image, you will observe the same effect provided you haven't also deselected the alpha channel. Whatever operation you perform will have more of an impact on the right side of the image and a diminishing effect as you go further left.

Figure 22 illustrates what is happening through the alpha channel. Where it is black, the filter is not being applied to the image below. Where it is white, the image below is getting 100% of the

21 The filter is applied as before but this time through the alpha channel selection. The effect is gradual because the alpha channel contained a gradient.

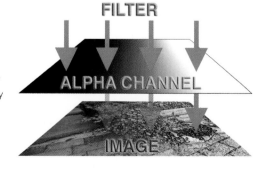

22 Here we see the filter effect, represented by the red arrows, applied through the alpha channel and affecting the image.

filter. The grays in between apply the filter based on their level of gray: 50% gray applies 50% of the filter.

Alpha channels are very important to keep around in commercial applications because clients have a tendency to make changes. Imagine selecting a simple blue sky. Easy! Put some cloud formations in it. Then the client says, "I want a different sky." Not so easy to select that sky now; if you made an alpha channel when you originally selected the sky, however, reselecting is a snap.

Remember that "New" option under Destination in the Save Selection dialog box? This means you can store the channels in another file. When you choose Load Selection from the Select menu, you can choose a channel from the file where you stored your channels to select an area in the image, provided that the mask file is open at the time you want to select from it.

It is always advisable to keep a PSD (Photoshop native format) work file in your archive. This way you will have all the paths, layers, and alpha channels for future use. When you change the format of a file for output or to send it to the client, you will want to discard the alpha channels.

NOTE
When you change the format of a file, some formats, such as EPS, automatically discard the alpha channels.

To load an alpha channel from a separate file as a selection, choose Load Selection from the Select menu. At this point, allow me to briefly explain the bottom portion of the dialog box—Operation. This section of the dialog box is active only if something else is currently selected in the image when you are about to load a channel as a selection. This gives you the option to have the new selection created by the Load Selection command interact in some fashion with the area currently selected.

NOTE
If another document is opened that matches the dimensions and resolution of the file you are saving the selection from, that second file's name also appears under the Destination submenu.

You will find alpha channels in use in many different situations throughout this book. They are very powerful tools, and it is to your advantage to master them.

Layers

Even though layers have been around since version 3 of Photoshop, and even though many readers probably know most of their functions, in view of their importance throughout the text I still feel the need for a basic discussion here.

A Photoshop document can have as many layers present in the file as memory permits. Each one of these layers can contain parts of the overall image. These layers can be manipulated in as many ways as you desire without affecting the rest of the image. There

are many ways to control the interaction of a given layer with what is underneath it, and the ordering of the layers can be changed at any time. A layer that sits above another layer in the Layers palette will be seen in front of the lower layer. Figure 23 shows a layer containing a green rectangle that has been created over a layer that contains a red oval. By moving the position of the green rectangle layer in the palette so that it is below the layer with the red oval, it will appear to be behind it (Figure 24). Layers are repositioned in the palette by simply clicking them and dragging them to where you want them to be. As a layer is moved within the palette, a thick black line appears between the other layers, indicating the position where the layer will be placed when released.

Elements of an image can be separated from the overall image so that they can be altered in some way. They can, for example, be scaled or colorized or filtered separately from the rest of the image. The drawback is that the original image is permanently changed. If the selected area is sent instead to a separate layer, changes are applied to that layer only while the original image remains untouched. This proves especially valuable when trying to create a collage of multiple elements. It is crucial to be able to reposition elements to achieve a balanced composition without leaving holes in the background every time you move an element.

Using the Move Tool, you can move the contents of the layer anywhere you want (Figure 24a).

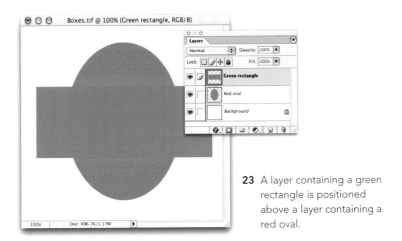

23 A layer containing a green rectangle is positioned above a layer containing a red oval.

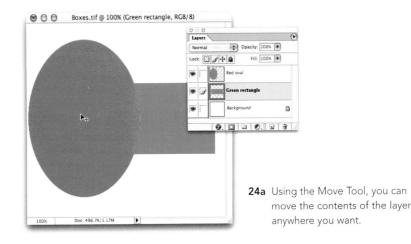

24 The layer with the green rectangle is moved in the palette to a position below the layer of the red oval. The result is that the oval appears above the rectangle in the image.

24a Using the Move Tool, you can move the contents of the layer anywhere you want.

25 New layers can be created by clicking the New Layer icon at the bottom of the palette. Existing layers can be duplicated by dragging them in the palette and over the icon.

25a The Lock icons enable you to lock portions of the layer.

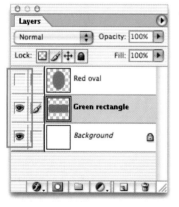

26 Turing the Eye icon on makes the layer visible. Turning it off makes it invisible.

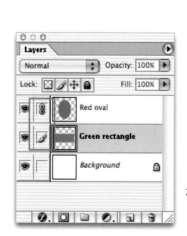

27 Checking the "Link" box will link multiple layers so that they can be moved or modified together.

You can duplicate an existing layer by dragging it over the Make New Layer icon at the bottom of the palette (Figure 25).

Four icons display next to Lock at the top of the palette (Figure 25a). These enable you to lock portions of a layer to prevent alteration. The first is Transparency. With this locked, you can paint only within pixels that already exist in the layer. You will not be able to make any additions to the transparency area that is displayed by a checkerboard pattern. Throughout this book I refer to this many times.

The second protects the existing pixels from any modification. The third locks the position of the elements in the layer so that they can't be moved. The fourth, lock icon, locks all of them at the same time.

Clicking the Make New Layer icon will create a new, blank layer.

You can rename layers by double-clicking the name in the palette. Turning the Eye icon off for a layer makes it invisible (Figure 26).

You can modify multiple layers at the same time if you link them. With a particular layer selected in the palette, you can link other layers to it by clicking in the small box to the right of the box with the eye (Figure 27). The modifications are somewhat limited to movements and transformations such as scaling and rotating.

Layers also prove very useful as multiple undos. Yes, History is for that purpose, but History will not work tomorrow morning when you reopen the file. Layers enable you to change your mind.

28 Adjustment layers can be chosen from the Layer palette.

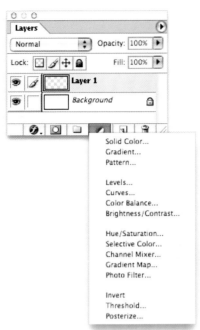

Adjustment Layers

Adjustment layers allow economical, editable application of certain valuable Photoshop commands, such as Curves, Levels, Selective Color, and Hue/Saturation. You can have multiple Adjustment layers in a document. Even if there are layers on top containing retouching or other major changes, the Adjustment layer can still be changed. No permanent change to the base image occurs until the job is flattened for final output.

Like regular layers, the modifications made with these Adjustment layers can be changed or removed entirely at any time. Adjustment layers can be made by either choosing them from the Layer palette (Figure 28) or the Layer menu (Figure 29).

The Adjustment layer comes in with an automatic Layer Mask (Figure 30). We'll discuss this in more detail in a moment. For now, this mask is white—that means it will affect the entire image. If something is selected at the time you create the Adjustment layer, the mask reflects that selection by displaying it in white, whereas the protected area is in black (Figure 31).

29 Adjustment layers can also be chosen from the Layer menu.

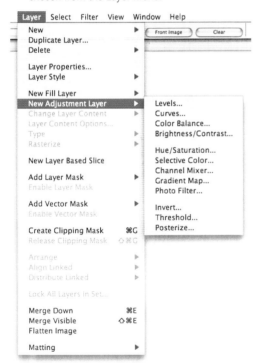

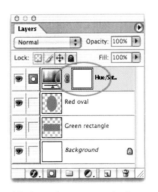

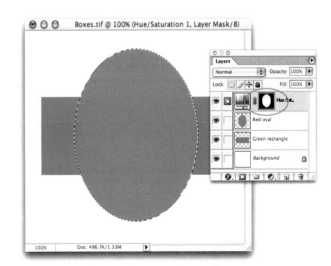

30 A mask is automatically set for the entire image with an Adjustment layer.

31 The mask for the Adjustment layer reflects anything that is selected at the time the layer is created.

Layer Masks

A Layer Mask is applied to a layer to allow portions of the layer to be seen. A Layer Mask is applied either from the Layer palette (Figure 32) or the Layer menu (Figure 33).

32 A Layer Mask can be assigned through the Layer palette.

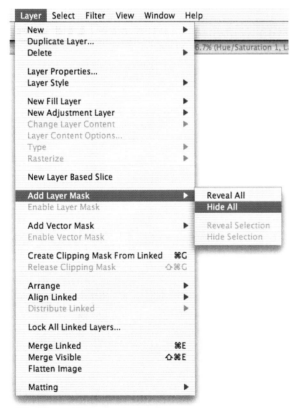

33 A Layer Mask can also be chosen from the Layer menu.

In the Layer Mask, where the mask is white, you can see the contents of that layer. Where the mask is black, the contents of the layer are hidden. Where the mask is gray, we see a combination of the masked layer and the layers underneath it. The lighter the gray, the more we see the contents of the top layer; the darker the gray, the less we see of it.

This is analogous to the way an alpha channel operates, but with a different end result. White in the alpha channel exposes the image to an effect. White in the Layer Mask exposes the image to be seen. Black in the alpha channel protects the image from change. Black in the Layer Mask hides the image from view.

Like alpha channels, all Photoshop tools work within the mask, so you can create gradients, paint strokes, or many other special effects into them. Figure 34 shows two layers with Layer Masks assigned to them. The Layer Mask for the layer called Red Oval has a gradient that is causing the oval to disappear gradually toward the bottom of the image. The Layer Mask for the layer called Green Rectangle has a black stroke drawn through it that is making that portion of the rectangle transparent.

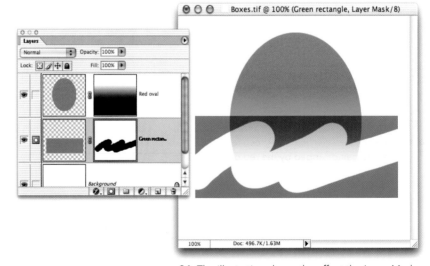

34 The illustration shows the effect the Layer Masks are having on their respective layers.

The Clipping Group

Another cool function of layers is the Clipping Group, which you will come across many times in this book. In this case, one layer is used as a mask for other layers. All the layers above the base layer of the group that are grouped with it will be seen only through the active pixels of that base layer. Where there are no pixels in the base layer, the layers above will be invisible. The base layer, or the one being used as a mask, uses its transparency information as the mask.

To illustrate this concept, Figure 35 shows a layer containing a red oval. This oval will act as a mask for the layer with the green rectangle in Figure 36. Using the transparency information (checkerboard area) of the red oval layer, the areas of the green rectangle that fall within that transparency area will be hidden as seen in Figure 37.

To create these Clipping Groups, click between the layers you want to group in the Layer palette while pressing the Option key (Alt on a PC).

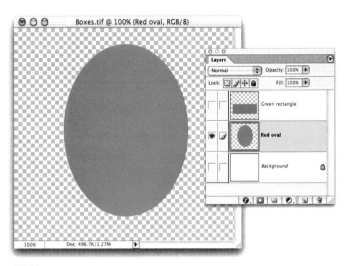

35 The transparency area.

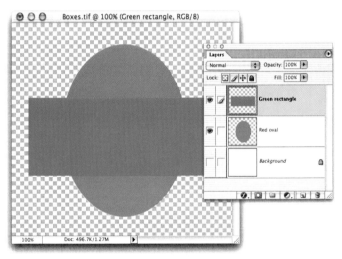

36 Here we see the layer with the green rectangle prior to being clipped by the red oval.

37 The Clipping Group is created causing the green rectangle to be visible only through the live area of the red oval.

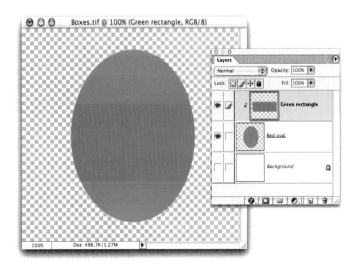

Layer Styles

This is an enormously useful feature for creating all sorts of special effects. Throughout the book you will see this feature employed many times to add depth, create glows, and so on; and, because they reside on layers, Layer Styles can be modified or turned off at any time without affecting the original image.

There is an almost infinite variety of Layer Styles. They are often used in conjunction with the kinds of alpha channels I've just discussed, or with the Calculations dialog box that I'm about to get to. For these reasons, instead of seeing examples here, you'll see specialized Layer Styles in action throughout this book. The item that the Layer Style will apply to must be selected out and placed on its own layer. Then, you can choose Layer Styles from the Layers palette (Figure 38) or from the Layer menu (Figure 39). My favorite way is just to double-click the layer in the Layers palette.

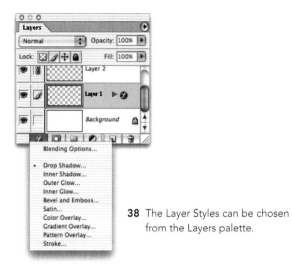

38 The Layer Styles can be chosen from the Layers palette.

39 The Layer Styles can also be chosen from the Layer menu.

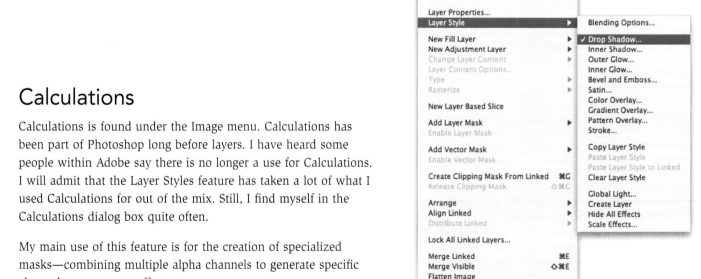

Calculations

Calculations is found under the Image menu. Calculations has been part of Photoshop long before layers. I have heard some people within Adobe say there is no longer a use for Calculations. I will admit that the Layer Styles feature has taken a lot of what I used Calculations for out of the mix. Still, I find myself in the Calculations dialog box quite often.

My main use of this feature is for the creation of specialized masks—combining multiple alpha channels to generate specific channels to create an effect.

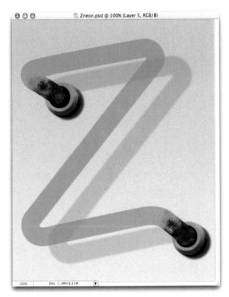

40 The neon in this image needs depth.

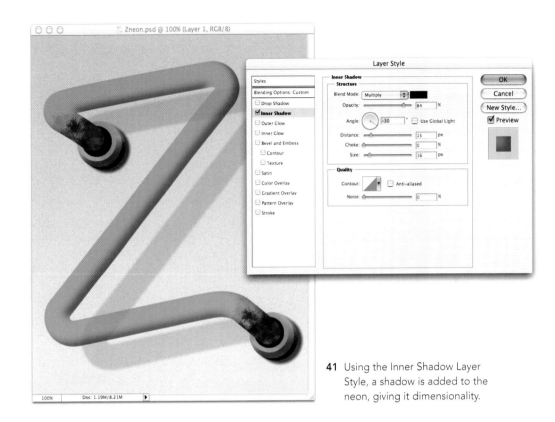

41 Using the Inner Shadow Layer Style, a shadow is added to the neon, giving it dimensionality.

Take for instance the illustration of an unlit neon tube in Figure 40. I suggest you take a moment to skim through the section of Chapter 8 called "Make Your Own Neon." It will give you a step-by-step of how to create a neon tube. Here, however, we are just trying to grasp a concept. Using a Layer Style of Inner Shadow would make it easy to add the depth to simulate the roundness of the tube (Figure 41).

The problem comes in when you need to add more than one color to that inner shadow. Figure 42 shows the same tube, but this time, besides the inner shadow, it needs to reflect the stripes on the wall behind it. I've put these lines in for the sake of argument, to create a theoretical problem and to show you how I would solve it. This requires a special mask through which the effect is applied.

42 The neon in this case requires a bit more work than is possible with a Layer Style, because the added feature of the red stripes requires a reflection of those stripes to be visible within the glass of the neon.

43 The layer that contains the neon tube is made into a selection.

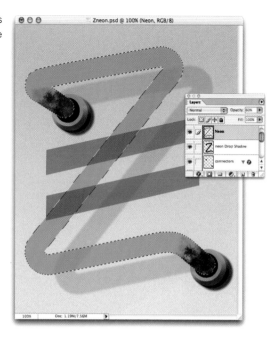

An alpha channel is created for the neon tube by selecting the tube. If you looked at Chapter 8 on how to make a neon, you know that the tube exists in its own layer. Making it a selection is just a matter of Command-clicking (Control-clicking on a PC) it in the Layers palette (Figure 43). With the tube selected, you send it to an alpha channel by choosing Save Selection from the Select menu.

You duplicate the alpha channel by dragging it over the Make New Channel icon at the bottom of the palette (Figure 44).

The round nature of the tube makes shadows and reflections gradually dissipate as they travel along its surface. To simulate this effect, the duplicate channel is blurred (Filter > Blur > Gaussian Blur) as seen in Figure 45. The amount of blurring should be slight. Too strong and the effect is lost. Too sharp and you lose the sense of roundness.

44 The alpha channel for the neon is duplicated by dragging it over the Make New Channel icon in the palette.

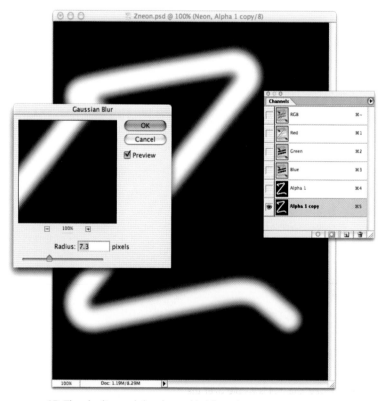

45 The duplicate alpha channel is blurred.

I would now like to see how these two alpha channels interact with one another, but I have to do something to distinguish one from the other before viewing them simultaneously. So, I double-click the second, blurred channel in the Channels palette. This brings up the viewing options box for the channel (Figure 46). I change the viewing color to blue, rather than the default, red. While I am at it, I name the channel to better distinguish it from the other.

Now, I click the eye icon next to the first, unblurred channel (Alpha 1). This enables me to see both alpha channels at once. And, because one channel is represented as blue and the other as red, the composite preview is purple (Figure 47).

With the Move Tool, I repositioned the blurred channel slightly up and to the left so that it appears as a shadow as seen in Figure 47a. Because the original channel is viewed in red, the blue of the blurred channel can be easily seen overlapping.

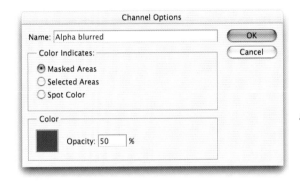

46 The color for viewing the alpha channel over other channels is changed to differentiate it from the unblurred channel.

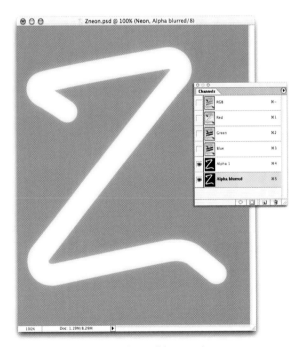

47 The blurred channel is visible over the original alpha channel.

47a The blurred channel is moved to form an overlap over the original alpha channel. This overlap will serve as the area of shadow for the tube.

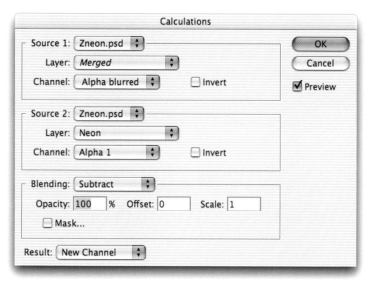

48 The Calculations dialog box enables you to combine channels in a variety of methods for the purpose of creating specialized masks.

Here is where Calculations comes in (Image > Calculations). The original, sharp-edged channel is placed in Source 2 and is subtracted from the blurred duplicate channel that has been placed in Source 1 (48). The result is sent to a new channel (Figure 49).

Which channel is placed in Source 1 or Source 2 will have a totally different effect on the result. Experiment on your own.

The new alpha channel is loaded as a selection and makes a perfect mask through which alterations can now be applied to the neon tube as seen in Figure 50. Through that alpha channel, I painted in the red stripes to represent the reflection of the stripes on the background.

49 Here you see the result of the Calculation that exposes the edge of the neon.

50 The art with the neon showing a shadow and a reflection of the stripes behind it.

The Pen Tool

Try and count how many times I use the Pen Tool in this book. Many! In my opinion, it is *the* most powerful tool for the creation of images. The Pen Tool is the Photoshop tool for creating vectors. It is my main tool for drawing, selecting, and creating masks.

At first sight it comes across a bit complex and difficult to use. Mastering it, however, could be one of the best things you do in Photoshop because it is the most flexible and powerful selection tool found in the application.

When I teach a class, I always ask my students, "Who does not use the Pen Tool?" Most often, at least half the hands go up in the air. No surprise! The Pen Tool is one of the most misunderstood and underutilized ways in Photoshop to select elements of an image—right up there with the alpha channel. The main reason for the neglect is that its use is quite different from any other Photoshop selection tools. In fact, the only people who seem to find the Pen Tool intuitive are users of Adobe Illustrator or other vector-art apps that have similar tools.

The Pen Tool made its debut in the very first version of Adobe Illustrator. It met with much resistance from the artistic community because it did not conform to the way people were used to working with graphics tools on a computer. Artists were used to the conventional clicking and dragging with any tools to produce a line or shape. Clicking and dragging with the Pen Tool produces an anchor point with a handle. It is not until a second click is performed (producing a second anchor point and handle), that any line is actually created. What those little handles do has confused many to the point where they abandon the use of the tool altogether. In what direction should they be dragged? How long should they be? What is this thing?

Let's take a close look at this wonderful tool. The Pen Tool creates what is known as a *path*. A Photoshop document can store up to 32,000 of these paths, which can be edited. They can generate selections at any point. Paths take up almost no memory. Having a few thousand of them will not make a noticeable difference in the storage size of your image.

You can make paths available to the Pen Tool in two ways. In the options bar for the Pen Tool, the two choices are at the left, next to the Tool Preset Picker (Figure 51). Even though there are three choices, only the first two apply to the Pen Tool. The first creates what is called a Shape layer (Figure 52). This is a Vector layer that is filled with the current foreground color and uses the path created as a mask. Consult your manual for a full description of this function, which will not appear in the exercises in this book.

The second choice (Figure 53) is the one I use the most. It creates paths.

The paths created with the Pen Tool can be stroked automatically with any of the other tools—even the Eraser Tool can follow a path. The Pen Tool proves very handy when trying to get a long, smooth flowing line such as the one in Figure 54. Using the Paintbrush Tool by itself to make that shape would have you doing it and undoing it many times, and still you might not get it right.

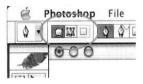

51 The method that the Pen Tool will use is chosen from the options bar.

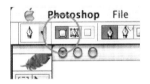

52 The first choice is for creating Vector layers.

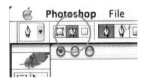

53 The center choice is for creating paths. This is similar to the Path Tool in Adobe Illustrator.

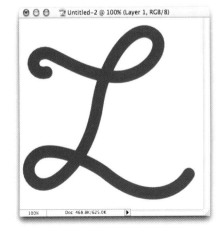

54 A smooth line such as the one shown here is difficult to create in a single stroke with a mouse or stylus.

With the Pen Tool, the path is created and then stroked with the Paintbrush Tool. Figure 55 shows the path that was created with the Pen Tool.

Stroking the path can be done in couple of ways. One way is by choosing Stroke Path from the Path palette submenu (Figure 56). This will pop up a dialog box (Figure 57) that enables you to determine which tool will be used to perform the stroke. The other way is to have the particular tool with which you want to stroke the path already selected, and then click the Stroke Path icon at the bottom of the Path palette (Figure 58).

You can fill the paths with a color by either choosing Fill Path from the Palette submenu or by clicking the Fill Path icon at the bottom of the palette (Figure 59). One thing to keep in mind when filling a path is that the fill will happen from the starting to the ending anchor point. In the case of the "L" shape in the example we have been viewing, we have an open path where the starting and ending points do not meet. This will cause an undesirable fill effect. Figure 59a shows a comparison of paths and how they fill. The letter on the upper left is a single, open path. The fill adds the color from starting to ending point. By contrast, the shape on the upper right is a closed shape that produces a better fill result.

The Pen Tool enables you to make difficult and precise selections. There are many times when selecting a part of an image is difficult or far too labor intensive for the other selection methods and tools. The Pen Tool is how I select most of the elements for alteration throughout this book. As with the other selection tools in Photoshop, a feather radius can be assigned to the selection beforehand. This makes the selected area into a soft-edged shape.

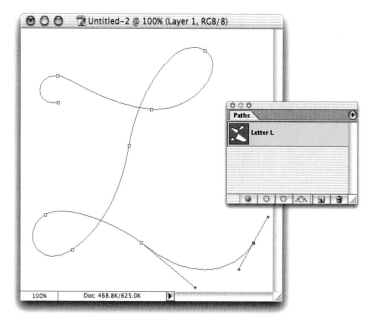

55 The path for the shape in Figure 54 was created with the Pen Tool.

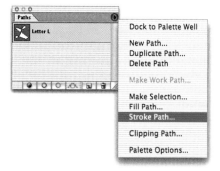

56 Stroking the path can be done from the Path palette submenu.

57 In this dialog box, you can choose which tool will be used to stroke the path.

58 Stroking the path can also be done by clicking the Stroke Path icon at the bottom of the Path palette.

You can make a path a selection in a number of ways. You can select Make Selection from the Path palette submenu. This brings up a dialog box where attributes such as the feather amount can be input. You also can drag the path over the Make Selection icon at the bottom of the Path palette (Figure 60). It also can be done by Command-clicking (Control-clicking on a PC) the path in the Path palette. If you use either of the last two methods, the resulting selection takes on any attributes previously assigned in the Make Selection dialog box (for instance, a feather radius).

If an area of the image is currently selected, making a path a selection enables you to have the path interact with the currently selected area (Figure 61). The path can override the current selection and make a new selection based on its shape and attributes. It can use its shape and attributes to add to, subtract from, or intersect with the current selected area.

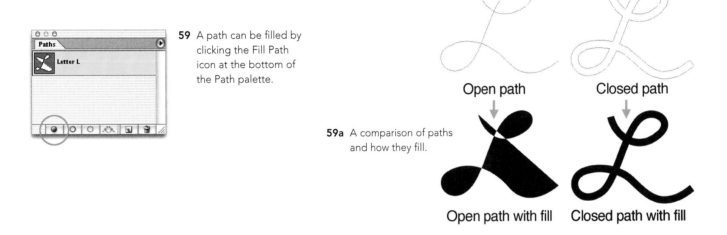

59 A path can be filled by clicking the Fill Path icon at the bottom of the Path palette.

Open path   Closed path

59a A comparison of paths and how they fill.

Open path with fill   Closed path with fill

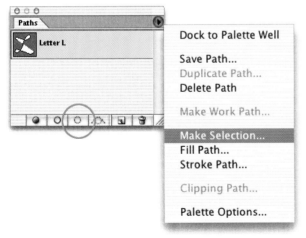

60 A path can be made into a selection from the Path palette submenu or by clicking the Make Selection icon at the bottom of the Path palette.

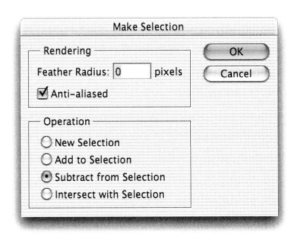

61 When making a path a selection, if there is currently something else selected, you can choose how the path will interact with that current selection.

How Does the Pen Tool Work?

To make a comparison to traditional tools of the trade, the Pen Tool is the equivalent of using any tool such as a brush, pencil, or art knife with a set of "French curves." If you are not familiar with the French curve, it is just a plastic shape used as a guide for any tool to create a flowing, curved line (Figure 62). The use and limitations of working with these French curves is the perfect analogy to help you understand the methodology involved in making the most of Photoshop paths. The main challenge when using French curves is selecting the specific curve that will give you the longest and most accurate sweep.

It is often necessary to switch shapes or change the position of the French curve to follow a particular sweep. With the Pen Tool, a similar approach is vital. You must try to create the longest distance between two points and keep the paths as simple as possible with as few control handles. The more points you have in a path, the longer it will take Photoshop to process it. This is especially true, and may even cause output problems, in the case of a Clipping Path (covered later in this chapter).

A path is often used to surround an element in an image. It can also be a shape created to serve as a new element in an image. The path is made up of "anchor points," which determine the starting and ending point of each line segment (Figure 63). These anchor points can have "handles," which produce curved lines or "Bezier curves." An anchor point that has no handles makes a corner (or sharp) point, which produces straight lines. Figure 64 shows a comparison of the two types of lines produced by the two different anchor points. The path on the left is made up of corner points that make the resulting lines straight. The path on the right has handles for the anchor points. That path is made up of Bezier curves.

Keep in mind a few simple rules when using the Pen Tool. The most important is to click and drag in the direction that your line (path) will be traveling. Figure 65 shows a path where handles of two anchor points are pulled in the same direction (up and to the right). The handle that is pulled out is not the one that actually

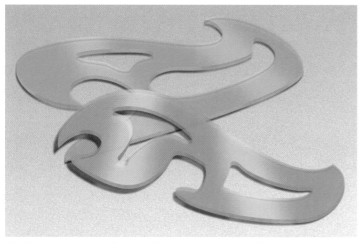

62 French curves are plastic guides used to control tool movement over a paper or canvas.

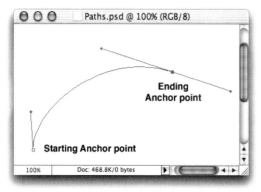

63 Here we see a path that is formed by starting and ending anchor points.

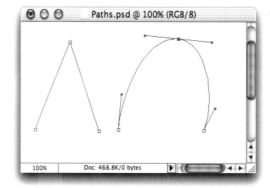

64 The path on the left is made up of straight lines because the anchor points are corner points with no handles. The path on the right is made up of curves because the anchor points have handles.

determines the angle of the line. It is the handle that faces the line that is controlling the curve. The handle you are pulling is locked to the one on the other side, so how you pull that handle is creating the handle that counts. Figure 66 shows a curve being created. The point at the lower left is the starting anchor point. The anchor point on the upper right is the second. When that second point is clicked and dragged, the handle is pulled out in the direction the curve is traveling. As this handle is being pulled, a second handle is being made behind the point, facing the line. When the mouse button is released, the line is complete. It is that second handle, the one facing the line, that controls the path's shape. Grabbing and moving that handle affects the line.

The click and drag action produces a handle. This handle is *not* the line itself, but just the method by which a path is controlled. The actual line of the path is created when the second anchor point is created. The result is a line between the two anchor points.

The rule mentioned previously, as most rules, has exceptions. Sometimes you might want to pull the handle in the opposite direction from that which the line is following. These moves produce lines that exaggerate the curve or have the line curve back on itself. Figure 67 shows how the handles work when pulled in different directions.

The length of the handle determines the height or depth of the curve. Figure 68 shows the effect of the length of handles on two similar line segments.

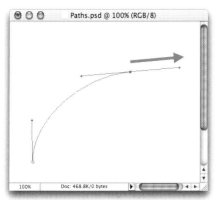

65 The handle of the anchor point is pulled in the direction the line is traveling.

66 The handle being pulled as an anchor point is created is controlling the handle that faces the line. That second handle is the actual handle being used to determine the path's shape.

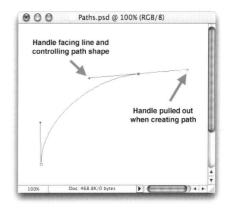

67 Handles pulled in different directions have different effects on the lines being produced.

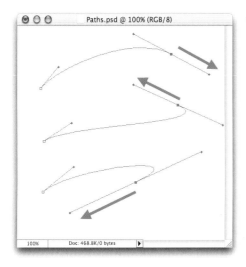

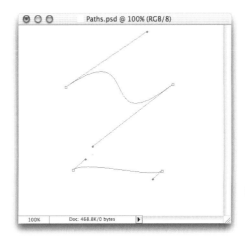

68 The length of the handles determines the depth of the line.

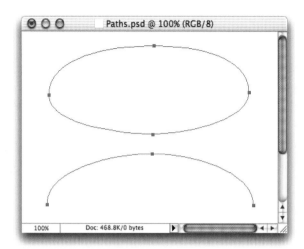

69 At top we see a closed path making a complete oval. Below it is an open path making an arc.

The click and drag procedure is applied for each additional point until an entire shape is completed. The shape can be a closed path. This means that the shape is one complete form such as a ball. The path can be an open path. This means that the starting and ending points do not meet. This can be used to create an arc. Figure 69 shows a closed path and an open one.

A path is closed when after creating a shape the final anchor point is clicked directly over the original, starting anchor point.

There are times, however, when the next point must follow a different curve. In this case, it is necessary to create a new handle from the last anchor point to follow this new curve. Pressing the Option key (Alt on a PC) while clicking and dragging the anchor point produces a new handle, which can be set to an entirely new angle (Figure 70). It is important to note that you click and drag from the *anchor point* and not the handle of the point. If you click the handle, it will produce a new anchor point in that position. Figure 71 shows the effect on the line with an unaltered handle and with a new handle.

70 With the Option (Alt) key pressed, a new handle is pulled from the anchor point.

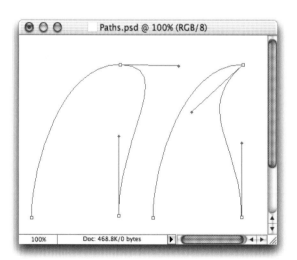

71 The path on the left is continuing the path with the handle unaltered. The path on the right has a new handle pulled from the anchor point to change the direction of the next line from the anchor point.

Outlining Objects

Still don't get it? The best way to make sense of all this is to actually see it put to use.

Figure 72 shows a coffee cup sitting on a wooden table. You need to select that cup to put it into a new background.

The first point is made at the left bottom of the cup. Why did I start there? Why not?

I pulled a slight handle up toward the top of the cup where my next point will be. I gave it a handle because, as you can see in Figure 73, the side of the cup has a slight roundness to it. Had the side of the cup been perfectly straight up, a corner point without a handle would have worked fine.

In Figure 74, the next point has been added at the top rim of the cup with a handle that matches the handle on the first point.

72 This coffee cup needs to be selected.

73 The first anchor point is placed on the lower-left edge of the cup.

74 The second anchor point is created.

75 The handle for the anchor point is extended to create a stronger curve to cover the rim of the cup.

76 The path for the top rim of the cup is made up of two anchor points.

77 The handle is adjusted for the anchor point to correct the path for alignment.

The next point is at the other side of the rim. Because the shape of the rim has a stronger curve than the side, the handle is pulled out further to allow for the stronger curve (Figure 75).

In Figure 76, the next point has been added at the opposite side of the rim. Notice that the line is not perfectly aligned with the top of the cup. As stated earlier, the paths can be modified at any time. In Figure 77, the handle has been adjusted with the Direct Selection Tool to align the path with the rim.

Taking a closer look at Figure 77, you will notice that the handle pointing down from the anchor point is so long it goes beyond the place where the next point needs to be put. Pressing the Option (Alt) button and clicking and dragging from the anchor point, a new handle is brought out to set up the next curve (Figure 78).

The next anchor point is positioned at the top of the cup handle (Figure79).

The handle moves away from the cup. The handle must follow the angle of the curve. Again, pressing the Option (Alt) button and clicking and dragging from the anchor point, a new handle is brought out to set up the next curve (Figure 80).

The next anchor is placed at a juncture on the cup handle where the slope peaks (Figure 81).

The next anchor point is placed where the cup handle starts to slope downward (Figure 82).

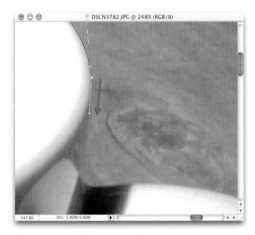

78 A new handle is pulled from the anchor point.

79 The next anchor point is created at the juncture where the cup handle meets the cup.

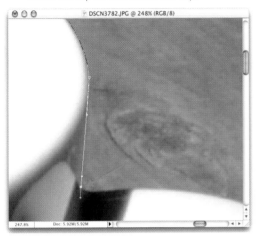

80 The handle is adjusted for the anchor point.

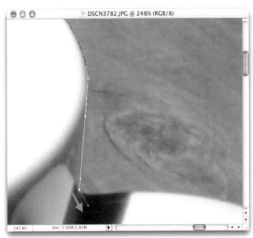

81 A new anchor point is created to travel along the edge of the cup handle.

82 The next anchor point is created.

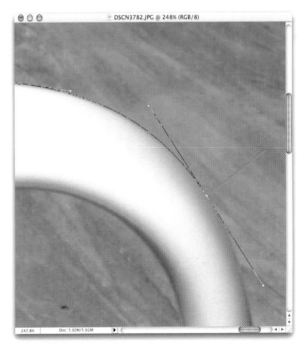

83 The next anchor point is created rounding the bend in the cup handle.

Figure 83 shows the anchor point that rounds out the bottom of the cup handle.

In Figure 84, the final anchor point for the cup handle is placed at the juncture where the handle meets the cup. Here again the previous handle is too long to properly align the path to the edge of the cup. In Figure 85, the handle from the previous anchor point is shortened to adjust the path.

In Figure 86, the small loop of the place where the handle meets the cup is created with a new anchor point.

In Figure 87, the path continues toward the bottom of the cup.

84 The final anchor point for the cup handle is created.

85 The handle is adjusted to correct the path.

In Figure 88, an anchor point has been placed at the center of the bottom edge of the cup. There is a sharper curve at the bottom of the cup than exists in the rim at the top. There is also a smoother connection to the sides than the sudden change of direction seen at the top, so placing an extra anchor point at the bottom gives us a little more control over the curvature of the bottom edge of the cup.

In Figure 89, the path is closed by clicking the last anchor point over the starting anchor point.

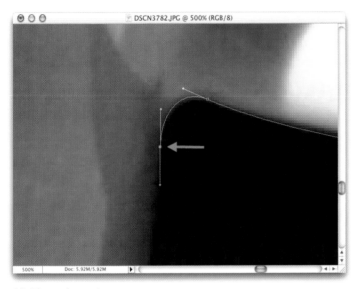

86 The path continues.

87 An anchor point is created at the bottom edge of the cup.

88 An anchor point is created at the center of the bottom of the cup.

89 The path for the outer edges of the cup is completed.

Figures 90 through 93 show the path being created for the finger hole in the handle of the cup.

Figure 94 shows another of those instances where a handle needs to be adjusted. In Figure 95, the handle has been shortened to soften the curve.

In Figure 96 the handle of the anchor point is almost perpendicular to the path. This helps to create the tiny indent of the cup's edge without the need of additional points to make that curve.

Figure 97 closes the path.

In Figure 98, the path is saved and named.

90 The path for the finger opening in the handle of the cup begins.

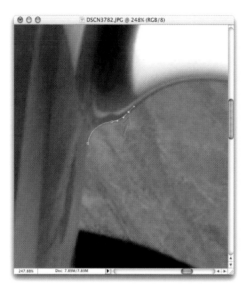

91 The path for the handle of the cup continues.

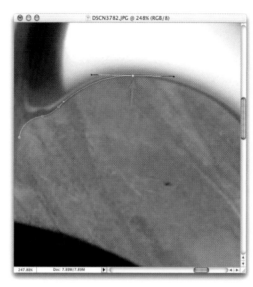

92 The path for the handle of the cup follows the curve of the cup handle.

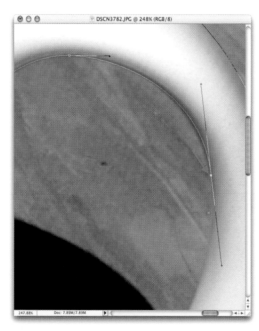

93 The path for the handle of the cup follows the bottom curve.

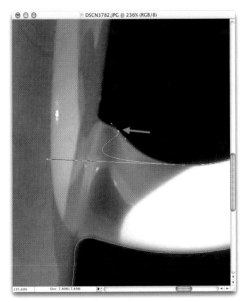

94 The path for the handle needs to be adjusted.

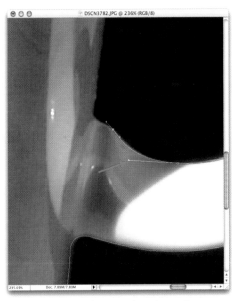

95 The handle is shortened to obtain the proper curve.

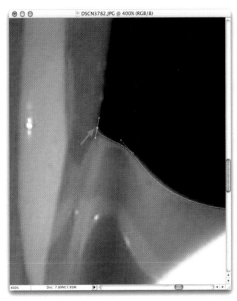

96 The path continues along the small loop where the cup handle attaches to the cup.

97 The path is complete.

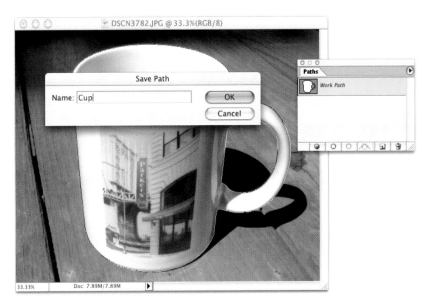

98 The path gets saved and named.

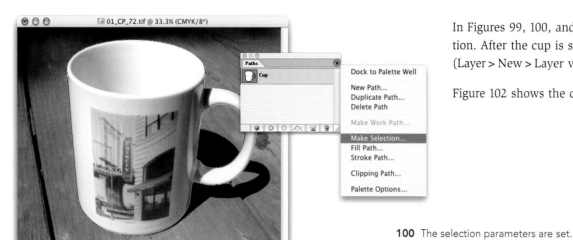

99 The path is made into a selection.

In Figures 99, 100, and 101, the path is made into a selection. After the cup is selected, it is sent to a new layer (Layer > New > Layer via Copy).

Figure 102 shows the cup in its new background.

100 The selection parameters are set.

101 The cup is selected.

102 A new background is added to the final image of the cup.

As mentioned before, having the fewest possible points on a path speeds processing and ensures smoothness. Figures 103a and 103b show a comparison of a good path to one that has too many points.

If a path has too many points, you can eliminate unnecessary points by clicking them with the Delete Anchor Point Tool found under the Pen Tool in the Tool palette. If a path is selected, passing the Pen Tool over an existing anchor point will temporarily, automatically convert the Pen Tool into the Delete Anchor Point Tool.

The Pen Tool is very forgiving—if you don't get it right the first time, you can always adjust it later. After a path is created, you can click any line segment with the Direct Selection Tool and drag it to a new shape or click the anchor points of that segment and the handles will appear. Dragging the handles adjusts the line to the desired shape. During the adjustment period, if you find it impossible to get the proper line with the existing points, you can add more. By the same token, if you think you have too many, you can delete some. Placing the Pen Tool over an existing path turns it into the Add Anchor Points Tool. Placing the tool over an existing anchor point converts the tool into the Delete Anchor Points Tool. Placing the tool cursor over an existing anchor point while pressing the Option (Alt) key will turn the tool into the Convert Anchor Point Tool. This one enables you to change a curved line into a straight line and vice versa.

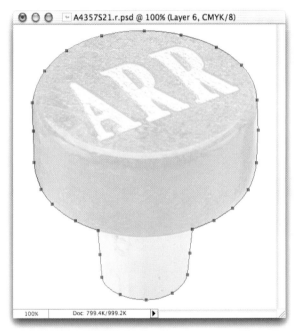

103a The path in this image has far more anchor points than are needed to surround the element.

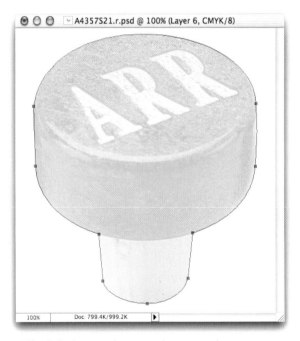

103b Only the crucial positions have an anchor point, making this an ideal path.

These last three tools mentioned can also be chosen from the Tool palette under the Pen Tool (Figure 104).

A path saved in Photoshop can be made up of multiple line segments or individual shapes. If there is more than one shape to a path, it is considered a single path, and any actions performed to it affect all elements uniformly. If one particular shape within a path made up of multiple shapes is selected, as in Figure 105, any action performed is applied to that path shape exclusively as seen in Figure 106.

If any shape intersects another, the area where they intersect acts as a compound path, creating a hole in the shape. Figure 107 shows two shapes that have been filled with a color. Figure 108 shows the same two shapes, but one has been moved to create an overlap that acts like a hole when filled with a color.

The bottom line is that the Pen Tool is an extremely useful tool when working with Photoshop. Spending the time to master it will be very rewarding.

Alas, there are some limitations to this tool within Photoshop. To get around these limitations, I turn to the birthplace of the tool, Adobe Illustrator. Chapter 2 shows exactly what I mean.

104 Additional tools that can be used to modify paths can be found under the Pen Tool in the Tool palette.

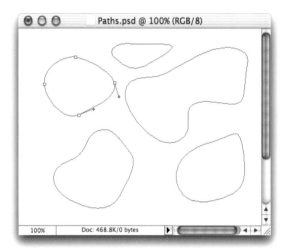

105 Here we see a path made up of multiple shapes. The one on the upper left is selected.

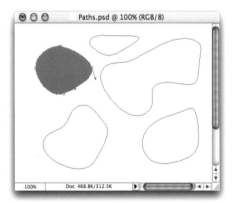

106 Filling the path with red affected only the shape that was selected, leaving the other shapes that made up the total path untouched.

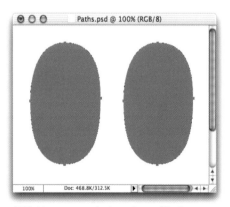

107 Here two paths have been filled.

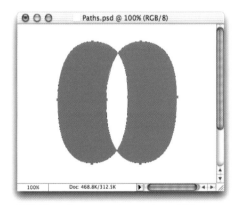

108 Here the two paths overlap, which causes a negative area where the overlap occurs. This overlap area is not filled when the path is filled with a color.

The Clipping Path

If you want an image to appear silhouetted in your page layout program, you must create a Clipping Path for it in Photoshop. A silhouette means that the image will have no background of its own, allowing other images or text to be seen behind it. Thumb through any catalogs or magazines and you will see many instances where some element on the page sits without a background.

Figure 109 shows a coffee mug photographed against a stark white background. If this coffee mug were to appear against a white background on a sell sheet such as the one shown in Figure 110, there would be no problem with the current background. The cup appears silhouetted even though nothing has been done to the background.

The same image on a sell sheet that has an existing image for its background will cause a problem, such as the one seen in Figure 111. This is where the Clipping Path comes in handy.

Creating the path for use as a Clipping Path is what was just covered in the section "Outlining Objects."

Sometimes there is an easier way to create paths. Anything that is currently selected can be turned into a path by clicking the Make Work Path from Selection icon at the bottom of the Path palette (Figure 112).

In the particular case of this coffee mug in Figure 109, creating the path can be quite simple because the image is easy to select using any of the other selection tools. Using the Magic Wand Tool, the white areas of the background are selected as seen in Figure 113.

109 This coffee mug has been photographed against a white background.

110 The cup appears silhouetted against the background.

111 The cup maintains the white of its background.

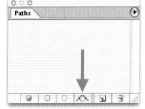

112 The Make Work Path from Selection button in the Path palette converts any selected area in the image into a path.

Inverse is selected from the Select menu (Figure 114). This selects the opposite areas, the coffee mug as the selection. The selection is then made into a path by clicking the Make Work Path from Selection icon at the bottom of the Path palette (Figure 112).

It is not always perfect and it might need a little adjusting here and there. If you are meticulous, then it always needs adjusting. At that point, it is a path—the Pen Tool can adjust it.

To turn the path into a Clipping Path, you choose Clipping Path from the Path palette submenu (Figure 115).

A dialog box appears, in which you can choose which path to use as the Clipping Path (Figure 116). The Clipping Path is then embedded into an EPS file, and now it can also be saved in a TIFF file for high-quality, resolution-independent masking of bitmapped images when placed into page layout programs or drawing software. This is perhaps the most typical use of Photoshop paths for most users.

The cup with its Clipping Path then looks like the sample in Figure 117.

113 The white areas of the coffee mug image are selected with the Magic Wand Tool.

114 The coffee mug becomes the selection.

115 A Clipping Path is chosen from the Path palette submenu.

116 Which path to be used as the Clipping Path is chosen from the Clipping Path dialog box.

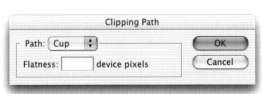

117 The cup is properly silhouetted against the background image.

118 The File Browser window can be accessed via the Window menu or the options bar as seen here.

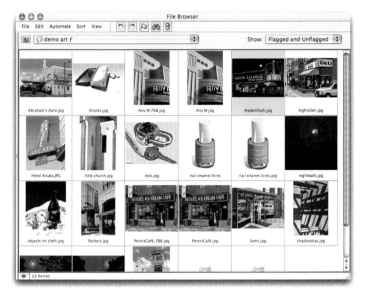

119 This is the File Browser displaying only thumbnails.

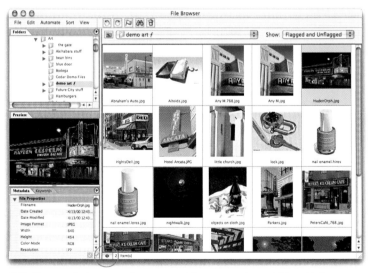

120 The toggle button at bottom enables you to view additional information for a selected image in the File Browser. At the upper left of the window, you can browse through all the volumes on your computer.

File Browser

First introduced in version 7, the File Browser has evolved and become more powerful. This feature greatly enhances the chore of organizing the workflow process. It enables you to browse through your files, view information, assign Keywords, and perform searches. You can even open documents from within the File Browser. Yes, it even opens files (although it works independently from the Open command).

The File Browser can still be accessed via the Windows menu, but now you can instantly open it via the options bar for all the tools (Figure 118).

The File Browser sits on the desktop as any other window or palette within Photoshop. Many functions that formerly required you to go to the desktop to do can be performed within this window. Files can be moved, renamed, and even rotated. The rotation is applied to the thumbnail within the palette and is automatically applied to the file when it is opened.

Figure 119 shows the basic window displaying the contents of the currently selected folder. Clicking the toggle button on the lower left of the window expands the palette to display the information pertinent to any selected file (Figure 120). You can select the order and method of viewing from the categories seen in Figures 121a and 121b.

121a How documents are viewed in the File Browser can be set.

121b The viewing criteria for the File Browser can be set.

You can choose to see all the details for every image at the same time (Figure 122).

As stated previously, many functions can be applied within the File Browser. Figures 123a, 123b, and 123c show the drop-down menus for the File Browser, where these functions can be selected.

On the lower left of the dialog box, there are tabs for viewing the metadata (Figure 124). This provides a look at the metadata that digital cameras embed in the image at the moment of exposure, such as F-stop, ISO ratings, and so forth. The second tab enables you to view and assign keywords to an image that can be used in the search process (Figure 125).

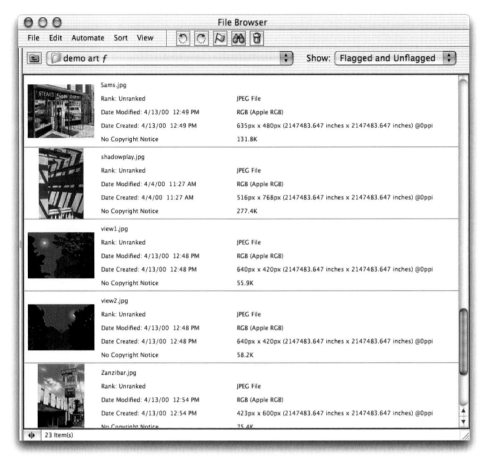

122 The details can be chosen as a viewing option.

123 The drop-down menus give you many functions and options for altering images without having to open the documents.

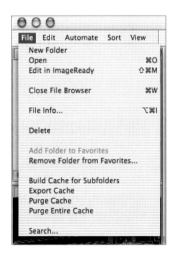

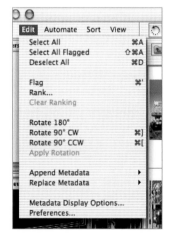

The File Browser has come in very handy for me in the preparation of all the files for this book. I have been able to organize and eventually edit all the screen grabs without leaving Photoshop where the work is performed. Because the figures are named by their placement within the text, there is no way I can tell what they are until I open them. Going into the Open dialog box does show a preview, but scrolling through 80 files is time-consuming. The File Browser gives me the preview of all the contents in a folder. In some cases, I need to see details of a dialog box and am able to see them in the preview without having to open the file.

Another big time saver for me is having the File Browser open on one screen while working in Microsoft Word on another. This enables me to see the figures as I write the description, without having to go back and forth between programs.

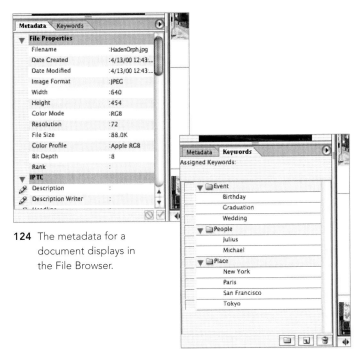

124 The metadata for a document displays in the File Browser.

125 Keywords can be assigned in the File Browser.

Getting Organized

Keeping track of a job can be very difficult, especially if many components are involved. The computer is designed to help people get organized, but it does not do it on its own: *We* have to be organized.

What the computer does is give us the means by which we can bring order to our workflow.

On my computer desktop I have a main folder I have labeled Work.

Upon getting a call from a potential client, I immediately create a folder for that client in the Work folder.

In that folder, I create a folder titled Correspondence. Any and all emails I receive from this client immediately get saved into that folder.

Before starting any actual work, I create another folder in the client folder called Comps. This is where I will save all the various layouts created for the job.

If the job calls for it, there will be an additional folder created—one called Reference, which will contain any images that will be used to convey the idea. The images that the client sent me as reference for the Las Vegas scene discussed later in this chapter are an example of what would go into this folder.

The main folder in this lot is the one called Art. This one will contain all the elements of the finished work. It will contain subfolders, one of which is always called Pieces. This is where I store bits and pieces of the art, such as Illustrator files or scans that are used in the final art. Needless to say, they are in appropriate folders: Scans and so forth. I always keep these in their original, Photoshop format in case I need them again.

There will be a folder called Early Versions. I save files with different numbers along the way. Job_so-and-so.ver01 might have 40 layers that can be merged and 30 alpha channels that can be deleted. Instead of losing them, I save the file with a version number. I merge the layers, dump the channels, and save it with the next number, Job_so-and-so.ver02, and continue. This way I have access to the original elements if I ever need to make a change. Have I ever had to? Every time!

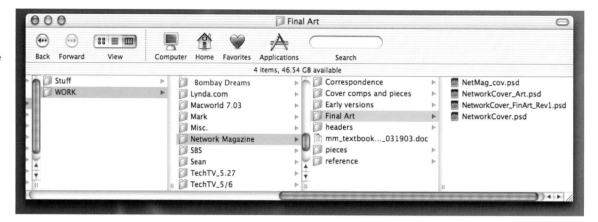

126 The Work folder on my main machine is broken down into a series of folders that make it easy to keep track of a job while it is in the studio.

When all the work is completed, I flatten the file and save it as Job_client.FinalArt into a folder called Final Art.

At that point the files start getting a new suffix, Job_client.FinalArt.Rev1. Figure 126 shows the window for my Work folder on the desktop.

If you stay organized, through my methods or your own, things should go smoothly. But, you must be organized!

Email, the web, fax machines, and technology in general have transformed the job of a commercial artist into a global enterprise.

Having an online portfolio enables you to instantly show your work to a potential client on the other side of the world. Ideas can be exchanged in real time, making it easy to get things done without the normal delays once associated with the graphic arts industry. On 9 out of 10 jobs I do, I never even see the client. It is all done electronically.

Starting the Job

Now that the basics are out of the way, it's time to get into what this book is really about: using Photoshop for commercial work.

It all starts with the call from the client requesting a job to be done. As an illustrator, by the time the job gets to me, the client has a pretty good idea of what they are looking for. The art director has

come up with the basic concept and presented it to their client for approval. I then receive the layout in sketch form as a fax or attached to an email or on a CD with a bunch of reference materials in an overnight package.

Figure 127 is one such layout that was sent to me as an email to create the cover for a magazine. The concept was a brightly lit marquee of a Las Vegas casino announcing the winners for the magazine's annual "Product of the Year" campaign. Las Vegas is where the conference is held and the awards are given out.

I also was supplied with an image for reference (Figure 128). Based on the layout, I started to create a design in Adobe Illustrator that closely matched what they were looking for.

Figure 129 shows the comp that I sent to the client for his approval prior to starting the final art. The approval process is very important because clients can change their minds very quickly. In most cases, I am not dealing with the final client or recipient of the art but rather the ad agency or design studio that subcontracted me to do the art. They have to get approvals from their client before giving me the go-ahead.

Sure enough, the sketch I had provided was not what they had in mind. Even though it looked a lot like the original layout, it needed something else. They wanted the marquee to fill the page. They also wanted a specific look to the lettering. I was sent another image for reference (Figure 130). Now I had a better idea of what they were looking for.

Based on this new direction, I proceeded to create a new layout that fit more what they were looking for. Figure 131 shows the second round comp. I also decided to make this one in color so that it would be easier for the client to visualize where I was intending to go with this.

This one they approved, and I was given the green light to create the final art. Chapters 2 and 6 outline some of the techniques I used to create the art.

127 This comp was sent to me to convey the concept for a magazine cover.

128 This image was supplied by the client to give me an idea of the look they wanted.

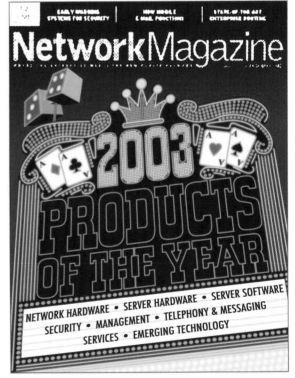

129 This is the first rough layout that I sent to the client for approval (prepared in Illustrator to match the look of Figure 128).

130 A second image was sent to me to better convey the look of the letters the client wanted on the sign.

131 The second layout I sent the client (which met with their approval).

132 The client faxed a rough layout giving direction for the creation of my illustration.

Sometimes the client gives me a lot of freedom to improve on their design. Figure 132 shows a sketch that was sent to me by a client. He made some pencil roughs on a legal pad (note the lines of the paper). This sketch was faxed to me. The concept was for a program for telecommunications. They wanted the package to show a modem. The modem was to be racing down a road as if it were a car.

I took the layout a step further and suggested that the actual boundary of the ad be lessened so that the modem/car could take up the open space and appear to be leaping out of the ad.

I created a layout sketch in Adobe Illustrator (Figure 133) to show this new concept.

After I received client approval, I took the same Illustrator file and imported it into Adobe Photoshop, via Copy and Paste, where I completed the illustration (Figure 134). I imported the paths present in the Illustrator file into Photoshop as paths. I then used each of the paths to select areas to be filled with color and texture.

133 In Illustrator, I created a layout showing the proposed placement of the elements in the illustration. I faxed this to the client for approval.

134 The Illustrator file became the basis for the final art. The paths were imported into Photoshop as paths where color, detail, and texture were added.

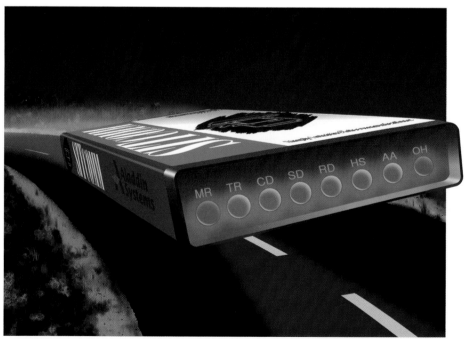

Another Example of Progression of an Idea

Figures 135 and 136 show more examples of the process of visualization. In this case, an ad agency needed art for a billboard. Their client was expanding by taking over a facility next door to their current site. The ad agency wanted to make it look as if the store was upgrading, as in adding RAM to a computer.

The client sent me a rough sketch showing me the general concept. I felt the image needed a little more impact. Also, I thought the straight-on nature of the layout would make it difficult to distinguish the pins and socket holes that were the main idea of the image. I added a little perspective to make it easier to make the pins and socket of the computer-type upgrade stand out. It also put them in the foreground, bringing more attention to them. I also thought the added angles would give the image more depth and movement. When I was finished, I sent my version back to the client for approval.

With the final "okay," I went ahead and started the final art (Figure 137).

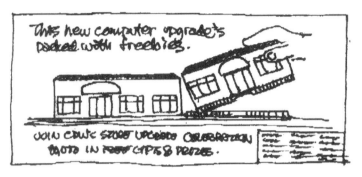

135 I received a faxed sketch from the client.

136 The layout was produced in Illustrator and was faxed back to the client for approval.

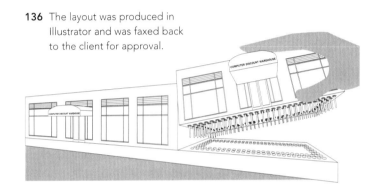

137 The final illustration

The Adobe Illustrator Connection

Illustrator is a vector application used to create...well...illustrations. Photoshop is a raster application that works better with...photos, or computer-generated graphics that look like photos.

In principle these are two very different programs. In practice they work hand in hand. Sometimes a job can be performed in only one program. Sometimes it can be done in either. And in some cases— as discussed in this chapter—it's best to use a combination.

Photoshop Versus Illustrator

Photoshop is a raster- or pixel-based program. A Photoshop file has a predetermined, user-defined width and height. The resolution set for the file determines how many pixels are along the horizontal and vertical dimensions. These pixels contain information whether they are white or any of the other million colors available to them. This is why Photoshop files can take up so much room on your hard disk.

An Illustrator file, on the other hand, is a vector–based program. It is simply a set of numeric values that determine what the image is in size, color, and placement on the page. The workspace is huge without taking up valuable RAM because the workspace, or page, has no information of its own. Only the elements created within the space have information.

An element created in Illustrator can be resized as large or small as you want, and as many times as you want. It will never lose quality. A Photoshop element distorts if resized too large. It loses information if reduced in size. Try reducing something to 10% of its original size, and then try to increase its size by 500%. Garbage! That's what you'll get.

Illustrator has some very useful features that have not found their way into the Photoshop feature set (for example, the Scissors Tool and the Blend Tool). This chapter covers some of these useful features and functions as well as demonstrates the ways in which Illustrator and Photoshop work together.

The Pen Tool in Photoshop has evolved through the years into a powerful feature. Its functionality has come a long way from earlier versions, and now it resembles more closely its cousin in Illustrator. A few functions still remain that require the use of the Illustrator Pen Tool. For example, the Transform Again feature for the Pen Tool is lacking in Photoshop. Not that Photoshop would ever replace Illustrator. Illustrator is a completely different type of program.

Illustrator is the ideal place for planning your illustration. You can play with different objects to your heart's content without losing quality or taking up RAM, no matter what the final size of the image will be.

You can import all the vectors created in Illustrator into Photoshop via Copy and Paste. The amount of information in a vector is so small that relying on the Clipboard for transfer is fast and easy. When you paste something from Illustrator into Photoshop, you are given a choice of how that information will be read. It can be As Pixels, which means any attributes you have assigned in Illustrator, such as fill color and line weight, will be rasterized as such in

Photoshop. The second choice is As Path. This means the vector will be a path just like the ones created with the Pen Tool in Photoshop. These paths work exactly the same as any other paths in Photoshop. The third choice is As Shape Layer. This will create a shape layer that is filled with the current foreground color using the path as a mask.

One of the features I use quite often in Illustrator is one that some people mistakenly think is obsolete—the Blend Tool. In early versions of Illustrator, it was used to create gradients by creating a blend from one colored shape to another shape of a different color. At one point the Gradient Tool was introduced and replaced the Blend Tool for creating gradients, and in doing so eliminated the cumbersome, older method that added more data than necessary. However, this did not spell the end of the Blend Tool because the way it works is useful for other instances. It creates morphs, or interpolations, between two objects. This proves useful in many situations—for example, when creating the in-betweens needed for animations.

The Transform Again function, which enables you to repeat the last action performed, helps to automate certain steps. This chapter starts with an example of how it works.

Transform Again

Some time ago I was commissioned to produce the art for a poster that involved a considerable amount of imagery (Figure 1). The main concept revolved around one of those large goblets that usually contain tasty tropical drinks. In this case, the goblet was to enclose a bunch of fun activities. Some of the images to be composited were existing photographs, but a few items needed to be created from scratch. Otherwise, I would have had to spend a huge amount of time researching the right image to fit the layout.

NOTE
Compositing is discussed at greater length in Chapter 4.

1 Poster art for Bay Networks.

The straw visible inside the goblet was one of these from-scratch elements. In Illustrator, I created the basic shape for the straw and filled it with a light yellowish-gray color (Figure 2). Close to the top of the straw's edge I created a small shape to begin to simulate a candy cane stripe that would travel the length of the straw. This shape was filled with a red color (Figure 3). Pressing the Option (Alt) key to make a clone and the Shift key to constrain its movement, I dragged a copy of the stripe shape down to form a second stripe (Figure 4).

The idea now was to create as many additional stripe shapes as necessary to get to the bottom of the straw, to create the illusion of one continuous stripe going down the entire length of the straw. By pressing Command-D (Control-D on a PC), Object > Transform > Transform Again, the action of making that clone below the original gets repeated. Pressing it again and again repeats the action as many times as needed to cover the entire length of the straw (Figure 5).

After the entire straw was completed, all the elements were selected and grouped (Object > Group) into a single object. This grouped object was then copied and pasted as a new layer into the Photoshop file. Once there, it was rotated to the angle needed for the overall image. It was in Photoshop that the necessary highlight and shadow were added to give the straw dimensionality. These could have been added in Illustrator but, in my opinion, it was easier to do it in Photoshop where it is going to end up anyway.

In Photoshop, a Layer Style of Inner Shadow was applied to the layer with the straw that was soft and conformed to the direction of the overall lighting of the image (Figure 6). There were modifications done to the Layer Style to position the shadow on the right side and spread it enough to create a strong edge.

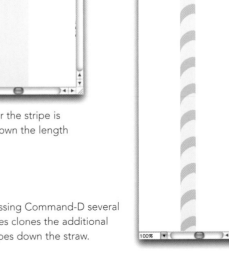

2 With the Pen Tool, a shape is created to serve as the straw.

3 A shape to represent the stripe that decorates the straw is created and filled with red.

4 The shape for the stripe is duplicated down the length of the straw.

5 Pressing Command-D several times clones the additional stripes down the straw.

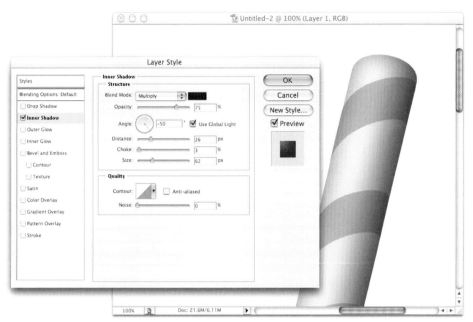

In a third layer, I created a highlight with a soft-edged Paintbrush (Figure 7). The layer was turned into a clipping group with the layer of the straw (Option-click between the layers to be grouped) as seen in Figure 8.

6 Using a Layer Style, the shadow at the edge of the straw is added.

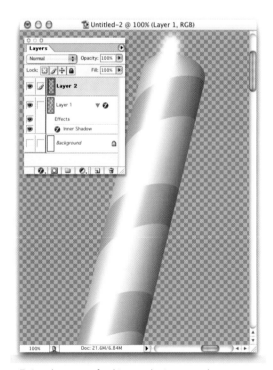

7 In a layer, a soft white stroke is created to serve as the highlight on the straw.

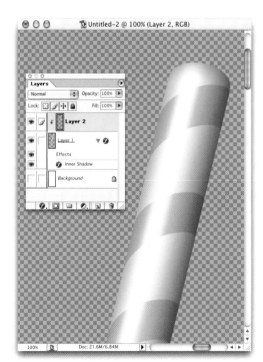

8 The layer of the highlight is turned into a clipping group with the layer of the straw.

9 A 360-degree circle serves as the shape for the paper umbrella.

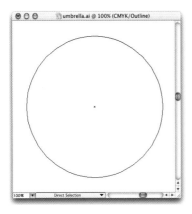

10 A tall and narrow rectangle serves as the spoke on the umbrella.

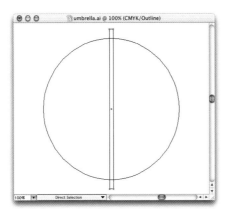

The little paper umbrella in the drink was also created in Illustrator. I started with a basic circular shape as seen in Figure 9. I then added a long narrow rectangle to act as the small wooden spokes found in such party favors (Figure 10). The center of the rectangle was directly over the center of the umbrella shape. I then created four more spokes with the Rotate Tool. A circle consists of 360 degrees. I intended to have a total of five spokes, each of which would intersect the umbrella in two places. Consequently there would be 10 intersections, which needed to be 36 degrees apart.

Being careful to hold the cursor at the exact center of the shape, I activated the rectangle and called up the Rotate menu, choosing Copy (Figures 11 and 12). With the new rectangle still active, the other three spokes, shown in Figure 13, were generated quickly by Transform Again. I simply used its keyboard shortcut, Command-D, three times.

I went to a local bar and picked up a real paper umbrella for reference on what they have as ornamental designs. I then copied these additional details for the umbrella as filled shapes as seen in Figure 14. When the entire umbrella was completed, I distorted it (Effect > Distort & Transform > Free Distort) to follow the angle I needed for the image (Figure 15). New vector shapes were then created that would eventually be used in Photoshop to make selections where highlights and shadows would be applied to the umbrella (Figure 16).

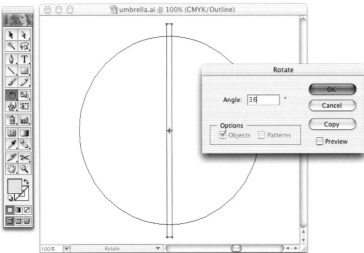

11 The Rotate Tool is applied to the rectangle and a 36-degree angle is chosen.

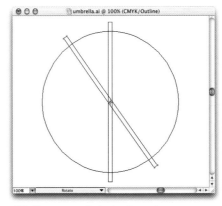

12 The rectangle is duplicated at a 36-degree angle.

13 Pressing Command-D three times created the rest of the spokes.

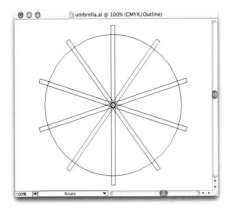

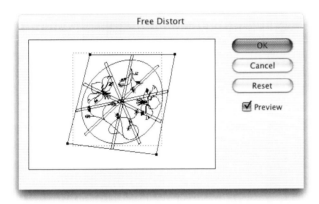

15 The overall shape of the umbrella is distorted to conform to the perspective in the image.

The small cap at the top of the umbrella was a couple of shapes that were used in Photoshop to select and fill to complete the look of the finished party favor (Figure 17). The cap is a simple cylindrical shape. (In the "The Scissors Tool" section of this chapter, you can find steps for creating shapes similar to the cap.)

14 With the Pen Tool, the additional decorations are added to the umbrella.

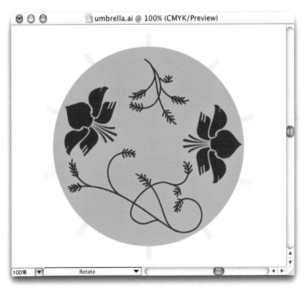

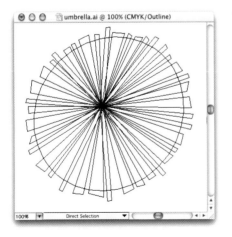

16 Additional shapes were created. These would later be used in Photoshop as selections to add shading.

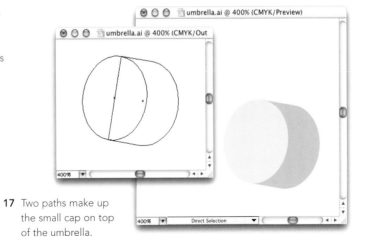

17 Two paths make up the small cap on top of the umbrella.

The Blend Tool

By creating and distributing shapes evenly between two objects, the Blend Tool simplifies many tasks that would normally require a lot of calculation and experimentation.

Billboard

I was commissioned by an ad agency to create the art for a billboard that announced the expansion of a computer store in Chicago. The client faxed me the high-quality sketch of Figure 18 to work with. The idea was to create the effect of the expanded building being inserted into a socket, as though it were additional RAM for a computer.

I thought that adding a little angle to the image would improve the impact and make it easier to see the socket/pin connection. In Illustrator, I created the comp that I sent to the client (Figure 19). Note that the pins and socket holes are clearly visible in the foreground of the image.

The farthest pins and holes are smaller than the ones closer to us to create the perspective typical of a three-dimensional image. Creating the pin and hole was easy. Figure 20 shows the Illustrator shapes that went into each. Notice that the hole is made up of two ellipses. The outer one is the shape of the socket and filled with the color of the socket board. The inner ellipse was filled with black to

serve as the hole within the socket. I also created two subshapes inside the pin. The larger one was filled with a dark color to represent a shadow. For the smaller one, I chose a lighter color to represent the reflection off the shiny metal of the pin.

I moved the pin to one end of the building's underside and placed a hole opposite it at ground level. This established the starting positions for the future blend. Duplicating both and reducing their size and placing them at the other end established the end positions (Figure 21). With the starting position selected, double-clicking the tool in the Toolbox pops up its Options dialog box. I chose Specified Steps for the Spacing. I then entered the number of additional pins and holes that I needed (Figure 22).

Clicking a specific anchor point on the pin on one end and the same relative anchor point on the pin at the other end automatically created all the pins in between (Figure 23). In this example, the appropriate point to click on in the second shape was obvious, but it isn't always. Choosing the correct point is critical for accurate blending. For example, it would ordinarily be crazy to click a point on the bottom of the first shape and the top of the second. This would cause Illustrator to create intermediate shapes that appear to turn a somersault as they move across the blend (Figure 24). The correct method, choosing two points that correspond with each other, creates the smooth blend of Figure 25.

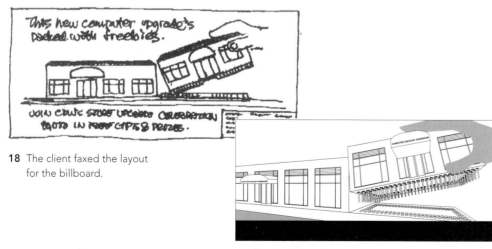

18 The client faxed the layout for the billboard.

19 I altered the perspective of the original layout, making it easier to get the pin/socket connection across.

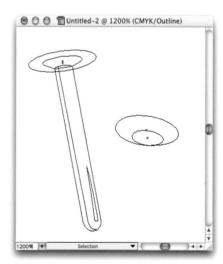

20 Several paths went into the creating the basic shapes for the pins and holes.

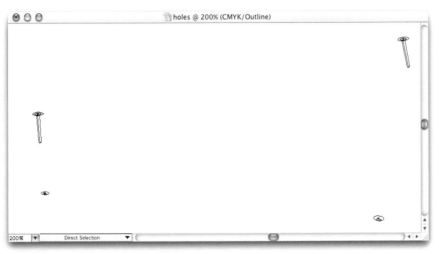

21 A pin and hole are placed at each end of the building bottom and ground to establish their position within the space.

22 In the Blend Tool dialog box, the number of steps for the blend is entered.

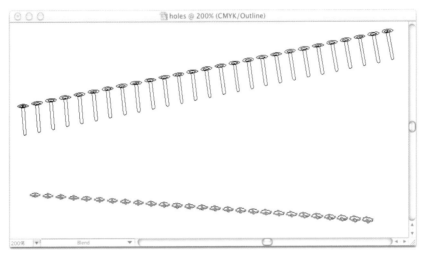

23 The pins and holes in between were created and distributed evenly between the starting and ending shapes.

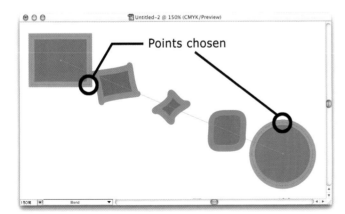

24 These two shapes are blended using anchor points that are at opposing positions to each other.

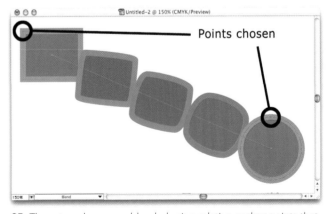

25 These two shapes are blended using relative anchor points that correspond to each other in position.

NOTE

NOTE

If a shape is made up of multiple objects, as in the case of both the pins and holes in the billboard illustration, the objects must be grouped (Object>Group) for all of them to be blended together. If they are not grouped, you must perform the blend for each individual object. As long as the number of blend steps and position of the starting and ending objects are the same, all subsequent steps generated by the blend will be in register to each other.

The completed rows were duplicated and resized to form the additional rows of pins and holes for the overall connector socket look (Figure 26).

Grafix Cover

The same blend technique was used to create the keyboard on the lower left of the Grafix brochure cover in Figure 27. Figure 28 shows a single key plus another that has been duplicated and reduced in size. I used the Blend Tool to make the intermediate keys as shown in Figure 29. Like most keyboards, this one has several wider keys, such as the Return key. To create these, I selected the right endpoints of my generic key shape, and pulled them away from the left side to create the stretched key (Figure 30).

26 The additional rows were duplicated and resized for perspective.

27 I created this cover for the Grafix show in New York City.

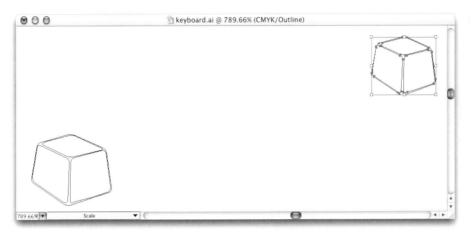

28 The key on the keyboard was made up of several paths, and then grouped. The first key was duplicated, reduced in size, and moved to serve as the last key in a row.

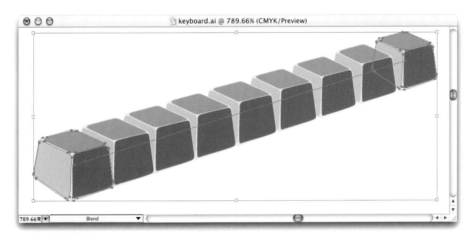

29 The intermediate keys were made by using the Blend Tool, which created and distributed the keys evenly between the first and last keys.

30 Some of the keys are larger in size. These were made by stretching portions of the original key shape to create longer keys and bars.

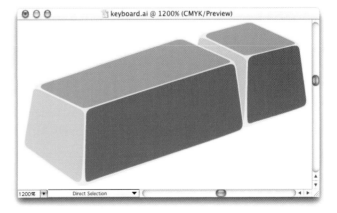

Outline Path

Sometimes the sheer complexity of an image makes it easier to tackle it within Illustrator. The flexibility of the Pen Tool in Illustrator allows for more manipulation of the paths than the Pen Tool in Photoshop. Figure 31 shows a folder that an ad agency commissioned me to create for Chevron. This image is full of complex detail, with a multitude of small items such as hoses and bolts. The paths needed to create them are best constructed with the Illustrator Pen Tool, because the Photoshop Pen Tool lacks the critical Outline Path feature.

31 This is the art for a folder done for Chevron.

A simple hose such as the one in Figure 32 is an easy task in Illustrator. I created an S-shaped path for the main shape of the hose (Figure 33). By choosing from the menu Object > Path > Offset Path, I created the full hose (Figure 34). In situations like this, I hope you will reject the lazy option of hitting the S-shape of Figure 33 with a wide stroke and calling it quits. Because the tractor is at a slight angle away from our view, the hose gets slightly narrower as it recedes into the background. Having one continuous path for the entire hose enables me to thin out its farthest sections (Figure 35). It may be slight in the case of this particular illustration, but the technique could prove quite useful in areas where there is more perspective.

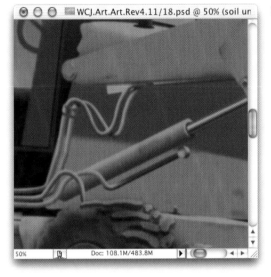

32 There was a considerable amount of detail in the parts that make up the heavy equipment.

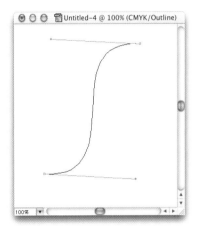

33 A single path serves as the basis for the hose on the tractor.

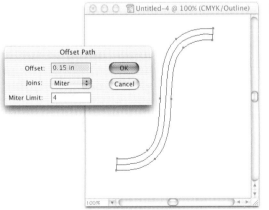

34 The Offset Path function creates the outside shape of the hose.

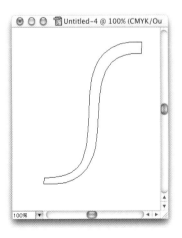

35 The path is altered to add dimensionality.

36 Additional details of the equipment show disc-shaped objects and cylinders.

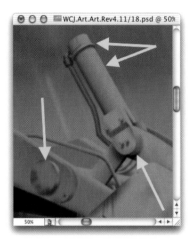

37 A basic elliptical shape serves as the top to a cylinder.

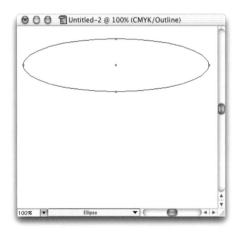

The Scissors Tool

Sometimes it is necessary to cut a path at a specific point to make some alteration. The Illustrator Scissors Tool is ideal for this kind of work—and no such tool exists in Photoshop.

Machine Details

Figure 36 shows another detail of the machinery where thick, disc-shaped metal parts are visible. Figure 37 shows the basic ellipse that makes up the top of the disc. I created what will serve as the bottom of the cylinder by duplicating the disc further down (Figure 38). Using the Scissors Tool, I cut the bottom ellipse in half (Figure 39). To create the sides of the cylinders, as seen in Figure 40, I extended the top by continuing the path with the Pen Tool.

NOTE

Clicking an open anchor point with the Pen Tool enables you to continue the path. When continuing a path, placing the cursor over the remaining open path closes the path.

I used the same technique to create the steel drums on the right side of the image in Figure 31.

I then imported these paths created in Illustrator into Photoshop, where I used them to make selections. To these selections, I added color and texture.

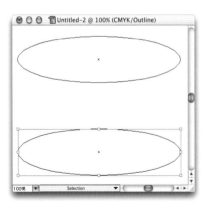

38 The ellipse is duplicated to the bottom of what will become a cylinder.

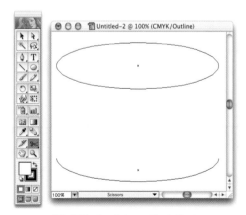

39 With the Scissors Tool, the top portion of the bottom ellipse is cut off at the two side points.

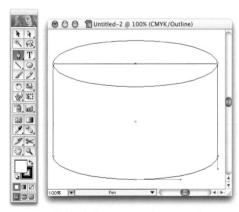

40 With the Pen Tool, the cut ellipse is continued to extend it to the top ellipse, thus making a cylindrical-looking shape.

41 This soda can was created for a poster about recycling.

Soda Can

The soda can of Figure 41 looks quite complex, but its basic shape was created using the technique of extending an ellipse. Figure 42 shows the original paths and the result of the Scissors and path-extension technique.

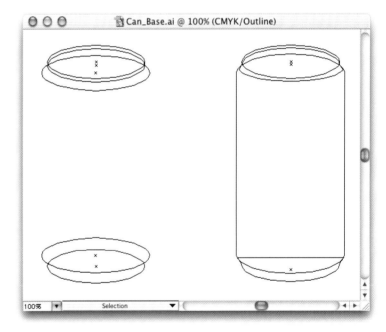

42 The can was created by cutting and extending ellipses.

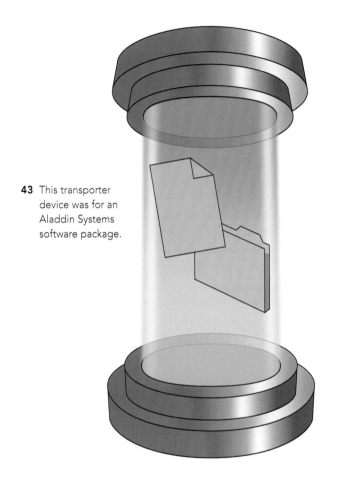

43 This transporter device was for an Aladdin Systems software package.

Aladdin Transporter

The Scissors technique also played a big role in the construction of Figure 43, a document transportation cylinder that I created for Aladdin Software. Figure 44 shows the ellipses before and after cutting and extending. I duplicated and flipped the top shapes of the transporter to create the bottom portion (Object > Transform > Reflect on a Horizontal Axis) as seen in Figure 45.

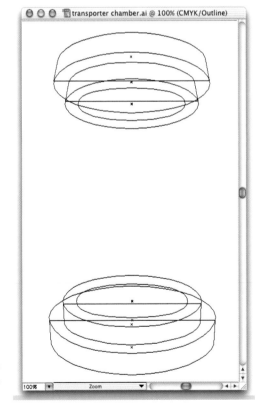

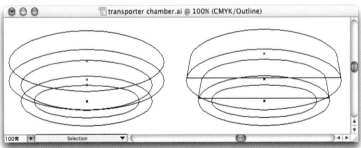

44 On the left are the original ellipses, and on the right are the shapes after cutting and extending.

45 The reshaped ellipses were copied and flipped vertically to form the bottom portion of the transporter.

Illustrator as the Main Drawing Tool

Sometimes I use Illustrator as the place where I sketch out the elements to play with their composition and come up with the overall look and feel of an illustration. You might compare Illustrator to the pencil lines on the canvas, whereas Photoshop is the actual paint.

Because of the flexibility of Illustrator, I sometimes create all the elements in Illustrator and then rely on Photoshop just to add effects.

Network Magazine Cover

Figure 46 shows a cover illustration I did for *Network Magazine*. In this case, I created the vast majority of the elements for the image in Illustrator and did the final rendering in Photoshop. The repetitive nature of the elements in the sign and the flexibility needed for adjusting shapes easily are where Illustrator outperforms Photoshop. Let's take a look at the production process.

46 This is a cover illustration for *Network Magazine*.

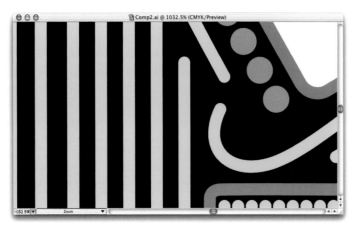

47 Paths were stroked with a specific size and color to simulate neon tubes.

47a The Round Cap feature made the ends of the lines rounded, as are real neon tubes.

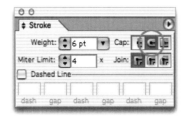

48 Circular shapes were filled with specific colors to represent light bulbs.

The subject matter—neon signs and light bulbs—made Illustrator the program of choice for this illustration. Neon signs are made up of curved tubes repeated many times. The same is true for light bulbs—circular shapes repeated over and over again.

Because the sign would be a mirror image of itself on both sides, I started the sign as a flat sign without perspective. This made it easy to create shapes and just flip copies of them to fill the opposite side. Each neon tube is made up of a single-line path stroked in the size and color needed to simulate the various neon tubes on the sign (Figure 47). I selected the Round Cap feature (Figure 47a) to round out the ends of the lines, as would be the case in real neon tubes. I filled the bulbs with circular shapes of different sizes (Figure 48).

To make the neon tubes on the side edge of the marquee, I created a single, vertical stroked path. I then duplicated the path and moved it slightly to the right (Figure 49). Pressing Command-D (the shortcut for Transform Again) five times produced the additional tubes, in position to complete the set (Figure 50).

49 The neon tube is duplicated to the right of the original.

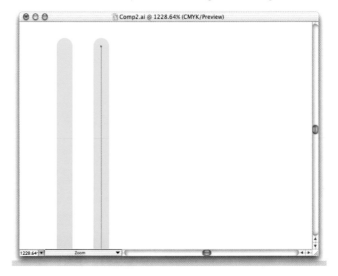

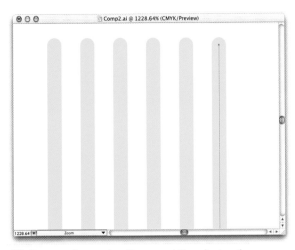

50 Repeatedly pressing Command-D replicates the previous step, making additional tubes.

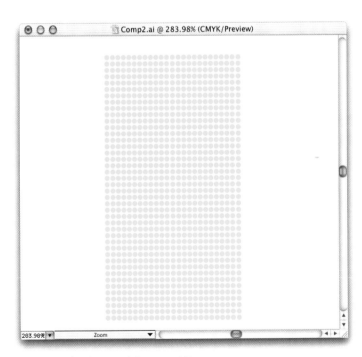

52 Using the Copy and Command-D function, a large block of light bulbs is created to fill the neon letters.

Grabbing the individual points on the tubes enabled me to twist and resize them to fit into the design as seen in Figure 51.

The light bulbs visible inside the main letters were a little different. I first created a large block of bulbs (Figure 52). I duplicated the block and centered it into the shape of each letter. I then deleted the unnecessary bulbs to form the interior lights (Figure 53).

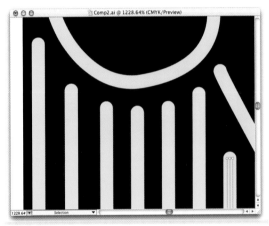

51 The individual paths are adjusted to create different heights to conform to the design.

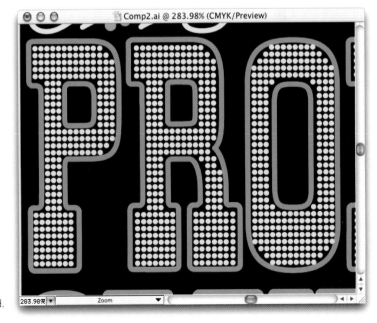

53 To fill the letter shapes, certain bulbs are deleted.

54 The text is created using an existing font.

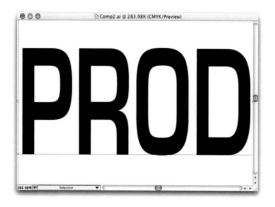

55 The text is converted to outlines.

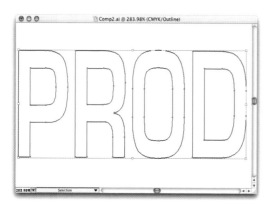

I did not have the particular font that the client was looking for. I had fonts that were similar, but I was wasting too much time looking for a perfect match, so I decided to create it. Only a few letters were needed, so I didn't need an entire alphabet. I took a font that had the basic shape I was looking for. In Illustrator, I typed out the text I needed (Figure 54) and created outlines (Type < Create Outlines). That converted the text to paths as seen in Figure 55. I created a basic shape for the oversized serifs as seen in Figure 56. I cut the paths for the various letter forms and inserted the serifs (Figure 57). I selected and joined the end anchor points for the serifs and the letters (Object > Path > Join). I duplicated the final shapes and placed them in position to form the sign. Then I assigned the strokes the appropriate stroke size and color to complete the neon effect.

I figured it would be easier to create the four aces than to scan an actual set of cards. A single card shape was created with a rounded corner rectangle (Figure 58). The letter A was typed in an appropriate font and converted to outlines as previously described. A rotated duplicate of it went to the lower-right corner (Figure 59). I drew the simple suit icons (Figure 60) using the Illustrator Pen Tool.

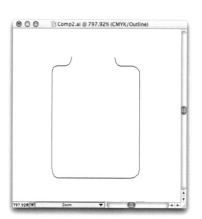

56 A path is made to serve as the oversized serifs for the letters.

57 The serif shape and the shapes of the letters are joined to form single letter forms.

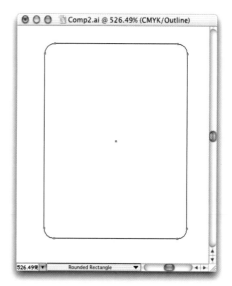

58 The basic shape of the cards is made from a rounded corner rectangle.

After filling the suit icons with red or black and stroking them, I rotated the completed cards and placed them in position on the marquee (Figure 61).

After completing all the elements, I had to distort the entire graphic to conform to the angle needed for the perspective view—as if the sign is being seen from the ground level looking up. I do so by selecting all the shapes (Select > All), grouping them (Object > Group), and using the Free Distort filter (Filter > Distort > Free Distort) as seen in Figure 62.

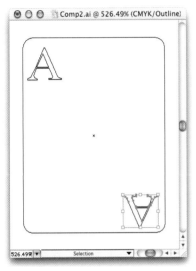

59 The letter A is created with the Text Tool. It is converted to outlines and duplicated and rotated to the bottom of the card.

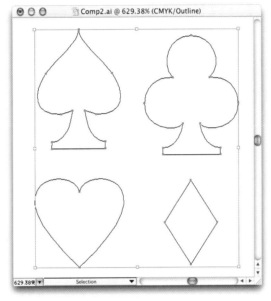

60 Various shapes were made to represent the four suits of a deck of cards.

61 The cards were altered and placed in position on the sign.

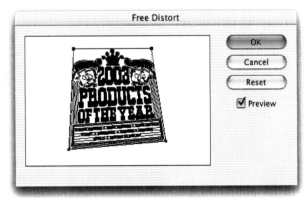

62 All the paths are grouped and distorted to fit the angles needed for the perspective view of the cover.

63 The paths for the cards were used again and offset slightly to make the neon shapes in the sign.

I used the paths for the cards again and offset them slightly to create the neon tubes in the sign (Figure 63). I simplified the second set of paths for the neon, as in the case of the letters. A single stroke was needed for the neon tubes of the letters rather than the full outline of the entire font. The ends of the tubes also had to change direction to create the effect of the neon tubes being connected to the sign.

I had to give these same connection points for the tubes to the card shapes and suit icons. Using the Scissors Tool, I cut the main paths for the cards and icons in the appropriate places to create the extension for the connectors.

64 Many bulbs are visible under the marquee.

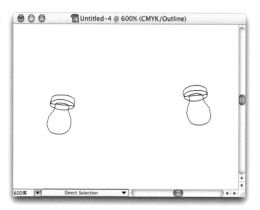

Now that the angle of the marquee was established, I created the light bulbs underneath it (Figure 64). I used the Blend Tool technique to place a single bulb at one end of the base as seen in Figure 65. I then duplicated the bulb, reshaped it to conform to the perspective, and resized and placed it at the opposite end of the base. Then I made a blend between the two bulbs to create all the bulbs in between, shifting in size and shape as they travel along the bottom edge. The additional bulbs seen on the cover art (Figure 66) were not created in Illustrator. I needed to add additional details, such as glows, in Photoshop, where it is easier to create these effects, prior to duplication for the bulbs receding toward the rear. The receding bulbs would be added in Photoshop. Chapter 6 discusses that technique.

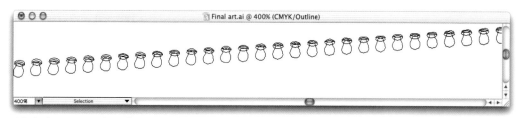

65 Paths were made to form a single bulb and fixture. It was then duplicated and altered to appear on the opposite side of the marquee.

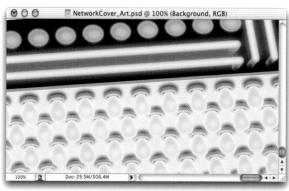

66 The additional bulbs going back in the distance were created in Photoshop.

67 A whisk broom for the package art of the Aladdin Systems Spring Cleaning™ software package.

Spring Cleaning Software Package

Figure 67 shows an example in which I used paths stroked with different colors and line weights to simulate the bristles on a dust broom for Spring Cleaning, an Aladdin Systems software package.

I created all the paths for the art in Illustrator. Figure 68 shows the paths.

I separated the paths into individual layers for color groups. Figure 69 shows four of these color groups. In Figure 69, you also see a central stroke of a lighter color.

I then stroked the paths with a line weight of 6 points and a specific color. After that, I copied and pasted the paths in front (Edit > Paste in Front). I altered this second set of paths—reducing the stroke weight to 3 points and lightening the color. This gave the effect of a highlight running along the individual shafts of straw.

I then imported the paths into Photoshop as pixels. Because I had gone through all the trouble of assigning colors and stroke weights in Illustrator, I wanted Photoshop to use these parameters.

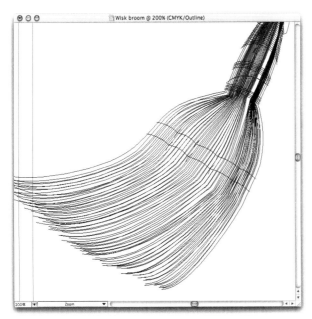

68 All the paths for the whisk broom were created in Illustrator.

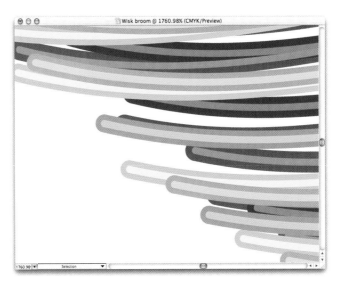

69 This close-up of the completed paths in Illustrator shows that the paths are really two paths on top of each other. The paths on top are half the thickness and lighter in color than the paths underneath them.

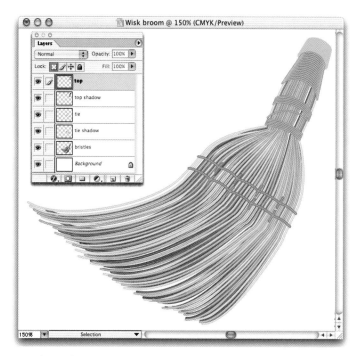

I placed the individual groups of paths for the straw, metal top, and string tie into separate layers in the Photoshop file (Figure 70).

I then used Photoshop to add details. Figure 71 shows the straw bristles. Using the Burn Tool, I darkened the right edge of the broom. I also darkened the area where the string tie belongs.

Figure 72 shows the paths that make up the metal fittings at the top of the broom in their original state in the Illustrator file.

70 The paths were imported into Photoshop and placed in separate layers for the individual parts.

71 With the Burn Tool, areas of the straw are darkened for depth.

72 The Illustrator file for the metal parts of the broom.

In the same manner as for the straw, I modified the metal to add depth. I locked the Transparency for layer containing the metal parts of the broom. Using combinations of the Dodge, Burn, and Paintbrush tools, I added the highlights and shadows to the metal (Figure 73).

The highlights and reflections on the top are paths filled with different tones.

Figure 74 shows the final metal combined with the other elements. I added a shadow behind the metal parts to add the sense of depth.

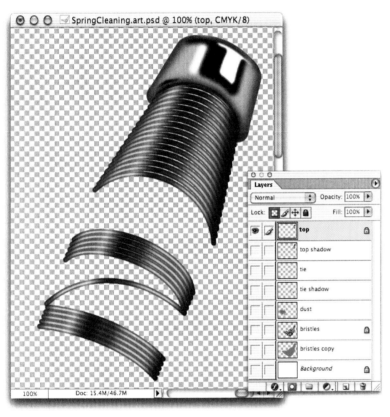

73 The metal parts of the broom are given highlights and shadows with combinations of the Dodge, Burn, and Paintbrush tools.

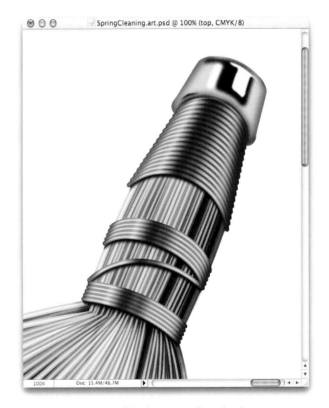

74 The metal parts of the broom combined with the other elements plus a shadow

Retouching

Retouching is the creation of new detail, or the modification or elimination of existing detail, in an image. The purpose of retouching can be to enhance what is there, eliminate something undesirable, or even change the mood of the image entirely. Retouching can be as simple as removing scratches, hairs, and other unwanted blemishes, or as complex as adding detail that was never present in the original photograph. Almost every Photoshop professional is called upon to do some type of retouching from time to time.

Prior to using computers for my work, I relied on professional retouchers who painstakingly retouched images by hand. The cost in time and money was quite high—high enough that many a time the client would go with a bad shot rather than spend the extra money to get the perfection that the job really deserved.

Photoshop has made retouching more manageable and accessible to the average user. That little fix that would have required much labor a few years ago is now a simple matter of selecting and modifying.

In this chapter I take you through the process for many of the retouching jobs that I have tackled. I also hope to impart some of the reasoning behind the choices made in the process of taking what many times seems like a perfectly good shot and changing it.

NOTE
Chapter 1 covers the basics of Photoshop, layers, selections, and so on. Refer to it if you need additional information on how some of the steps for the following examples were done.

1 The carrying case for this corkscrew is too far away from the product to be effective in the final layout.

2 Using the Pen Tool, I created a path to select the pouch.

Composition

Sometimes it all looks great in the camera back, but when the image hits the layout we discover that it needs to be tightened a bit. Figure 1 is a perfect example of this kind of situation.

The product is a wine bottle opener. It comes with its own handy little carrying pouch. The pouch, however, is positioned a little too far from the bottle opener. The composition needs to draw the eye to a single element. The pouch, that far behind, looks a bit detached from the scene, almost as if it were an afterthought to stick it in the shot.

Repositioning an Element

The fix was fairly simple. With the Pen Tool, I created a path that surrounded the pouch (Figure 2). Then I turned the path into a selection (see Chapter 1 on paths) and separated the pouch into its own layer (Layer > New > Layer Via Copy).

I moved the new pouch layer closer to the central focus of the image. Figure 3 shows the new position of the pouch with the original pouch visible behind it. The pouch has moved closer by almost half of its own width. Now it's positioned so that it touches the tip of the bottle opener, thus making all the elements work as a group.

3 The pouch, duplicated into a separate layer, is repositioned closer to the product. Note that the original pouch is still visible, creating a doubling effect.

4 With the Clone Tool, parts of the original pouch are covered by the wood texture of the tabletop.

The eye was turned off for the layer with the repositioned pouch. I created a new layer between the Background layer and the layer with the repositioned pouch. In this layer, using the Clone Tool, I cloned the wooden texture to hide the original pouch (Figure 4). I selected the Use All Layers mode for the Clone Tool to allow it to use the information in the Background layer to add the wooden texture in the blank layer that housed the retouching.

I did a little extra work with the Healing brush to eliminate unsightly parts of the film, such as scratches on the tabletop. The reflection of the bottle opener on the table (seen in Figure 1) looks more like a scratch in the wood than a reflection, so I removed it. Figure 5 shows the final image.

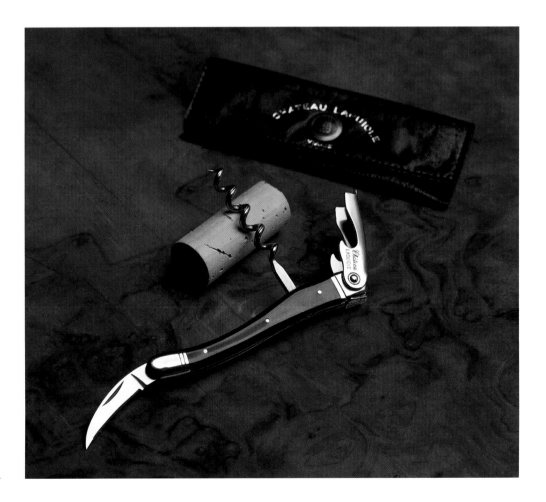

5 This is the final retouched image.

Repositioning Parts of the Total Image

Figure 6 is another case where there is too much space between all the elements in the image.

I copied a slice of the left side of the picture, enough to contain the two leftmost bottles and their stoppers, and sent it to its own layer (Figure 7). Then I repeated the same process for the rightmost bottle and stopper (Figure 8). The edges of both selections were feathered slightly so the seams would not be noticeable when the sides were repositioned closer to the central bottle (product). This process could also be accomplished by duplicating the Background layer and creating a Layer Mask to hide the sides that need to be hidden when the elements are brought closer to the center.

Figure 9 shows the sides repositioned inward toward the product, giving the total image more unity. There is a psychological effect to consider in images of this type—if there is too much space between all the elements, it causes a sense of chaos where all the elements are fighting for attention. This could have the subconscious effect of turning off viewers, causing them to ignore the ad.

6 In this image, there is too much room between all the elements in the scene.

7 The left side of the image was copied to a separate layer.

8 The right side of the image was copied to a separate layer, too.

9 The two sides were brought inward to tie them closer to the central figure.

10 The cap, which is the product being advertised, is difficult to spot because it blends into the background.

Defining Edges

Upon careful study of the new composition, it becomes clear that there is not enough separation between the cap on the product and the background (Figure 10). Considering that the cap itself is the focus of this advertisement, this is highly undesirable.

Using the Pen Tool, I select the cap and place it into its own layer (Figure 11).

I applied a Layer Style of Inner Shadow to add a little contrast to the top and right edges and better definition to the cap (Figure 12).

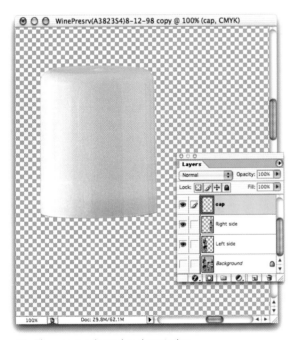

11 The cap is selected and copied to its own layer.

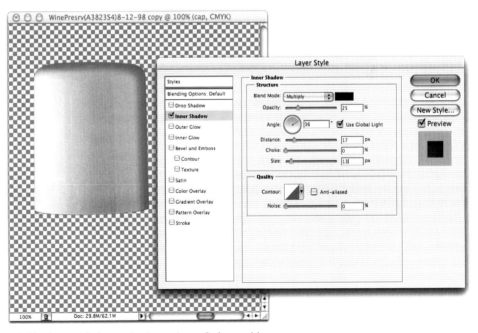

12 The layer with the cap is given a Layer Style to add definition to the edges.

Cleaning Up Text and Logos

The problem with the cap, although certainly worth fixing, pales into insignificance compared with the next issue: The product name is partially obliterated by a reflection. This is the kind of thing that irritates advertisers to no end (Figure 13).

Fortunately in this case, the letter *P*, which needs to be fixed, appears on the top line of the product name where it is clean and free of the unwanted reflection. Selecting the letter and duplicating it over the other two is all that this image required to repair it. Figure 14 shows the repaired label.

Repositioning an Element with Transparency

Figure 15 shows one last example of the need to reposition elements. Notice that all the elements overlap with the exception of the wine glass. The actual product is the CD and its case. The wine bottle and glass are props. The glass is too far to the side and distracts attention from the product.

With the Pen Tool, I selected the glass (Figure 16) and sent it to its own layer (Figure 16a).

In a new layer, I put the Clone Tool to use. Cloning areas of the background layer covers the area where the original glass sat (Figure 17).

The layer that contains the separated glass is repositioned so that it overlaps the bottle (Figure 18).

13 The name of the product is partially obliterated by a reflection of light.

14 Copying the letter *P* twice from the top line and positioning it over the damaged letters below repairs the label.

15 In this image the wine glass is too far removed from the other items.

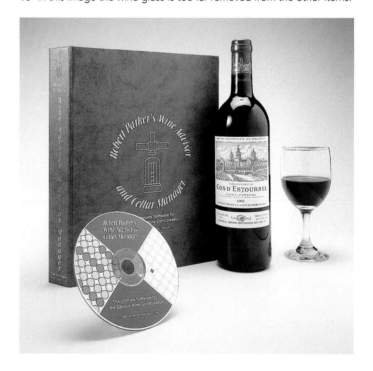

16 The glass is selected with the Pen Tool.

This last move creates two problems, one of which is much easier to fix than the other. First, the glass is made of clear glass, so you should be able to see the bottle through it. Second, and much worse, the shape of the glass is rounded. This shape will cause anything being seen through it to be distorted. This is one of those situations that could easily be overlooked by the person doing the retouching. An understanding of how things work will tell you that something is wrong with this picture. The best way to learn how these things work is to study reality. Take a glass and place it in front of a bottle and study what happens.

To solve both of these situations, I selected the portion of the bottle that rests behind the glass and sent it to its own layer. That layer is processed through the Pinch filter (Filter > Distort > Pinch) to create the necessary distortion (Figure 19).

16a The wine glass is copied to its own layer.

17 With the Clone Tool, the original glass is eliminated.

18 The glass is repositioned to tighten the composition.

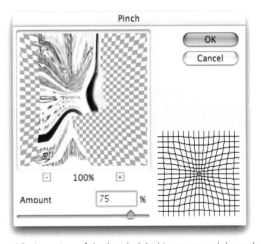

19 A section of the bottle label is processed through the Pinch filter to simulate the distortion of seeing it through a curved piece of glass.

I placed the layer with the pinched label in front of the layer with the glass, and clipped it with the layer of the glass as a Clipping Group. Finally, I lowered its opacity so that it appears lighter, as would be the case when seen through a glass of this type (Figure 20).

One final modification was needed—the overall image was a bit light, lacking the luster to make it stand out on the page. I created a new layer and merged all the other layers into it.

NOTE

When you press the Option (Alt) button and choose Merge Visible from the Layers palette's drop-down menu, all the layers merge into the currently selected layer while leaving the original layers intact. That is why a new layer was created in this preceding step. It housed the composited layers without losing any of the original layers.

I then put this new layer into Multiply mode to add depth and richness to the base image (Figure 21). I lowered the opacity slightly to reduce the amount of this effect.

NOTE

Multiply literally multiplies the brightness values for the pixels in the layers below it, thus having a darkening effect.

20 The layer with the distorted label is clipped with the layer of the wine glass.

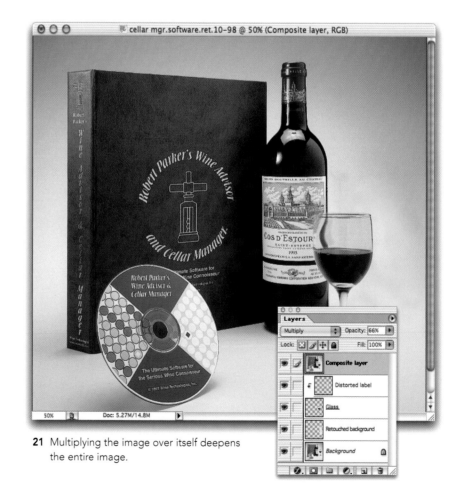

21 Multiplying the image over itself deepens the entire image.

Adding and Fixing

Sometimes the image needs a little something else to add interest or to make it more dynamic. Figure 22 shows an image of two water goblets that were to be offered in a mail-order catalog. The client liked the shot but felt that it would be better with liquid in one of the glasses. Good point, although raised rather later than one would like. Reshoot? No way! Photoshop and a little skill and the problem is solved.

Adding Content

In a new layer, I created a shape with the Pen Tool and filled it with a solid color (Figure 23). The particular color was of no consequence because this layer was to serve as the base layer for a Clipping Group.

NOTE

This could be a good place to use a Vector layer. The Vector Mask of the layer can be modified at any point. As the base for a Clipping Group, this has an advantage. However, painting or erasing within a regular layer will also enable you to change the shape of the Clipping Group.

22 This image shows two empty goblets. It would be better to show one of them containing a liquid.

23 A shape is created in a separate layer to simulate the liquid.

24 This image shows a set of goblets that have liquid in them.

I searched through the client's vast library of stemware images and finally found a similarly shaped glass containing white wine and with an interesting reflection. (Figure 24, third glass from left). I selected that wine and copied it over as a new layer to my working file of the water goblets. Then I made it into a Clipping Group (see Chapter 1) with the layer in which I had drawn the gray liquid shapes (Figure 25).

There was one problem, however; these were water goblets and the liquid I imported had the obvious color of a white wine. A few Adjustment layers were all that was needed to change the color of the wine into the clear look of water.

Because I wanted to affect only the liquid area and not the entire image, I needed to make a mask for the Adjustment layer. I made the layer of the liquid shape into a selection. I did so by just Command (Control)-clicking on the layer in the Layers palette. This automatically created the mask for the Adjustment layer when the layer was created.

I opted for a Hue/Saturation and Curves adjustment to do the trick (Figure 26).

25 The liquid from one image was imported into the image being retouched. The layer of the liquid shape then clipped it.

26 Curves and Hue Saturation were used to alter the color of the wine in the goblet.

I was working this image in CMYK. Feeling that the wine was slightly to the orange side of yellow, in the Curves dialog box I pulled back a bit on the magenta (Figure 27) and a considerable amount on the yellow (Figure 28). In the Hue/Saturation dialog box, the only adjustment I made was to lighten the layer just a tad (Figure 29). These are not formulas, so do not expect these settings to be exactly what your particular situation might require. All images are different and need to be addressed on an individual basis.

The job was not finished yet. The close-up in Figure 30 shows the highlight on the right edge of the glass stops abruptly at the edge of the liquid.

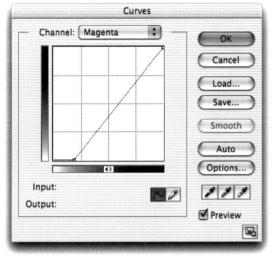

27 The magenta was reduced in the Curves dialog box.

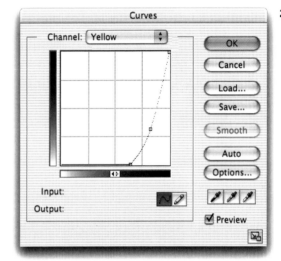

28 The yellow was greatly reduced.

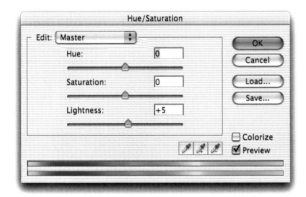

29 The settings for the Hue/Saturation were minor but enough to change the wine into water.

30 The highlight is cut off abruptly where the liquid begins.

I selected and copied the tiny highlight from the Background layer into its own layer. Using the Layer > Arrange command, I moved it in position in the Layers palette to be above the layer with the liquid and all the Adjustment layers for it. I lowered the opacity to allow the reflections in the liquid to show through. Figure 31 shows the new layer.

Figure 32, a close-up of the unretouched goblet on the left, shows another inconsistency. There's a fairly large reflection that should also logically be present in the newly filled goblet on the right. Therefore, using essentially the same procedure as for the small highlight on the right, I copied the reflection from the goblet on the left, pasted it into a new layer, and positioned it over the retouched version on the right.

31 The highlight was separated into its own layer and placed above the layer with the liquid.

32 The goblet on the left has a highlight that is missing on the goblet on the right.

33 The highlight has been restored.

34 The final retouched image.

Adding Highlights

Figure 35 shows a monogram that you can have etched onto your wine glasses. The problem with this shot is that there is neither depth nor form to the base of the glass. The introduction of a few highlights is all that would be needed to solve the problem.

Using the Pen Tool, I created a shape to simulate a reflection of light on the face of the base of the glass (Figure 36). An actual reflection of this type is not a flat shape. It tends to soften in some areas—in effect it contains varying gradients. To obtain this gradated effect, I made the path a feathered selection and saved it to an alpha channel (Figure 37) where I could play with it a bit.

35 This is a shot showing a monogram etched onto the base of a wine glass.

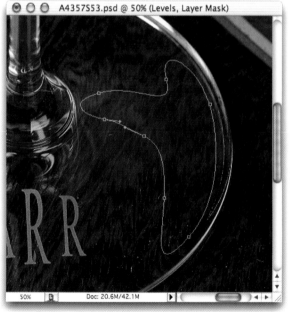

36 With the Pen Tool a shape is created to simulate a reflection of light.

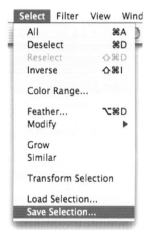

37 Save Selection creates an alpha channel.

In that alpha channel, I blurred parts and darkened or lightened others until I had the look I wanted (Figure 38). I used the Blur, Dodge, and Burn Tools to do all the alterations. The same treatment was applied to a similar shape for the left side of the base. The alpha channels were then made into selections and placed in a new layer to contain the reflections. I then filled the selections with white. I lowered the opacity to a point where the reflections looked realistic. Figure 39 shows the base with the reflections added.

The monogram needed to be accented a bit to make it stand out. After all, this is the main subject of the image. Using the Pen Tool, I selected the letters and copied them to their own layer (Figure 40).

Using the Levels command (Image > Adjustments > Levels), I adjusted the highlights and mid-tones to brighten the letters (Figure 41).

38 In the alpha channel, the shape created by the Pen Tool is modified using the Dodge, Burn, and Blur Tools to look more like a realistic highlight.

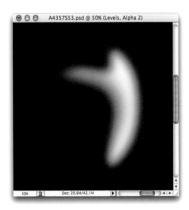

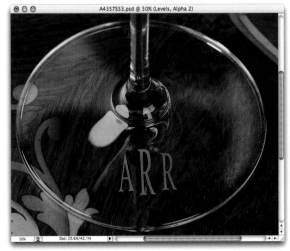

39 The highlights were added to both sides of the base.

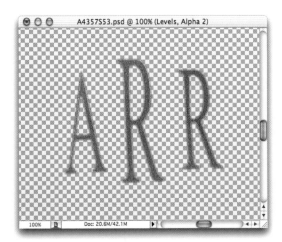

40 The letters of the monogram were copied to their own layer.

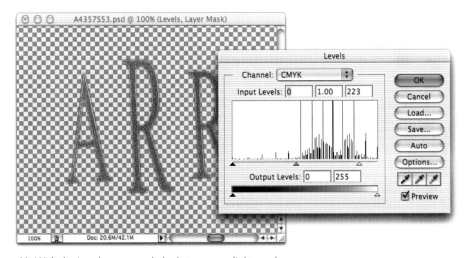

41 With the Levels command, the letters were lightened.

I applied a Layer Style of Inner Shadow to add a small highlight to the edge to further accent the letters. I changed the color to white and the mode to Screen so that the effect would be the opposite of a shadow and act as the desired highlight (Figure 42).

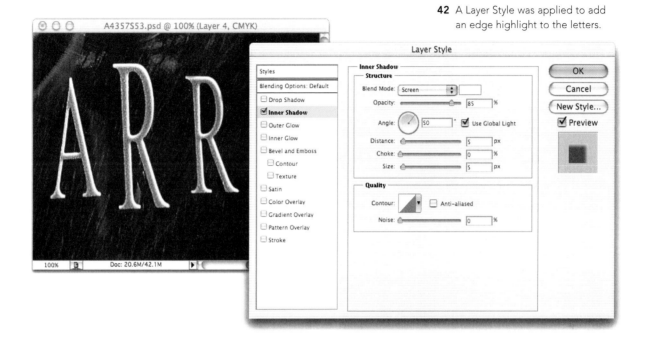

42 A Layer Style was applied to add an edge highlight to the letters.

Cleaning Up

One last fix necessary to make the shot perfect was to eliminate all the dust and scratches on the antique tabletop that caught the light (Figure 43).

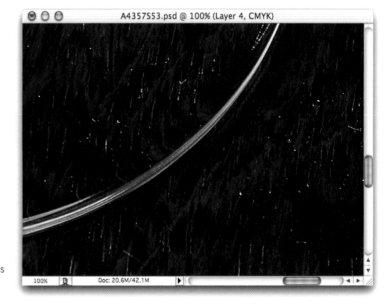

43 Here we see all the blemishes on the tabletop.

In a separate layer, using the Clone Tool in Use All Layers mode, I eradicated the blemishes. Figure 44 shows the layer with all the cloned parts, whereas Figure 45 shows the completed, clean tabletop. Figure 46 shows the completed image.

NOTE
This last step could also be accomplished with the Healing brush. With the Healing brush, however, the job of eliminating the blemishes would have to be done in the actual layer containing the blemishes. That might cause a problem if subsequent editing were needed.

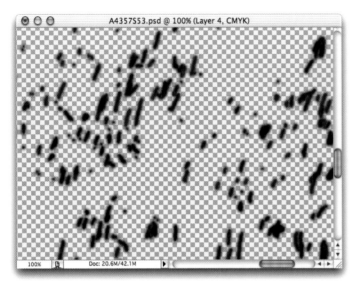

44 This layer contains all the clone bits to cover the blemishes on the tabletop.

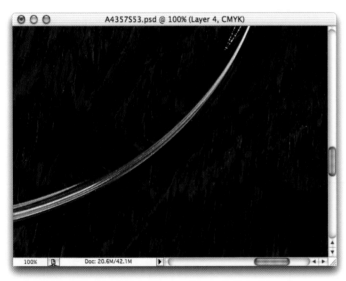

45 Here we see the tabletop clear and free of all the blemishes.

46 The completed image.

Adding Elements

The wine rack we're trying to sell in Figure 47 looks fine at first glance, except to the client, who is upset that one of its major functions is invisible. This rack is supposed to store not just wine bottles, but also wine glasses, just under the top shelf. Unless the rack has some glasses there, however, nobody will guess that such a feature exists. Consequently, I was asked to put in the glasses that should have been in the original photo but weren't.

I started by using the Pen Tool to isolate one of the wine glasses resting on top of the rack (Figure 48). I copied the glass to a new layer and used the Clone Tool to eliminate the wine inside the glass (Figure 49).

47 Here we see a wine rack with a major detail missing. There is a wine glass rack below the counter but without glasses in it; you can't tell it is there.

48 The glass was selected with the Pen Tool.

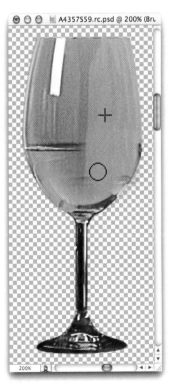

49 With the Clone Tool, the wine inside the glass was eliminated.

50 The retouched glass is placed in the rack under the counter.

I turned the glass upside-down (Edit > Transform > Flip Vertical) and then positioned it in place in the rack. The opacity was lowered to reveal the wall and wooden brace of the wine rack behind the glass. In a separate layer, I added an additional light reflection. Figure 50 shows the completed glass. Two more glasses were added to the rack to make it look utilized. There were still a few touches that were needed—such as removing the overlap at the top over the counter.

Attention to detail is crucial in imaging to make everything look as flawless as possible. Close inspection of the overall shot shows two glasses on the counter top of the rack with wine in them, yet the bottle is still capped (Figure 51).

Selecting the shape of the bottle top and cloning from the lower section of the bottle solved that problem (Figure 52).

Figure 53 shows the completed image as it appeared in the catalog.

51 The wine bottle is unopened, but the shot shows two filled wine glasses.

52 The lower portion of the bottle was cloned to make the bottle appear open.

53 The final image.

Removing Unwanted Items and Enhancing Others

Sometimes the photo stylist can take things a bit too far. When the client got the shot shown in Figure 54, his first words were, "What the hell is that?" pointing to the straw tie on the bottle. I was immediately asked to remove it and while I was at it, make the wine spill from the glass at left look like wine. The point was to make it look like a serious stain on the cloth napkin, to give the product, a stain remover, a tougher job.

Eliminating Unwanted Props

I started by creating a layer for all the retouching of the straw tie. Using the Clone Tool in Use All Layers mode, I carefully cloned areas of the background over the ties as seen in Figure 55. Portions of the bottle were also cloned over the parts of the tie that over-lapped the bottle as seen in Figure 56.

54 The original shot has far too much styling.

55 With the Clone Tool, the straw tie is eliminated.

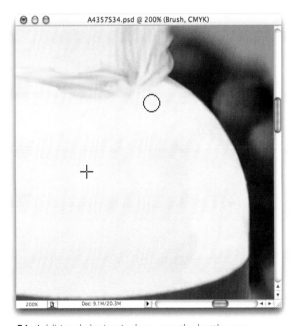

56 Additional cloning is done over the bottle area.

57 The cap on the smaller bottle was selected with the Pen Tool.

58 The cap from the smaller bottle is copied over to cover the damaged cap on the larger bottle.

Adding Definition

Most of the cap on the larger bottle was indistinguishable and blown out by the lighting. This was an easy fix. With the Pen Tool, I selected the cap on the smaller bottle (Figure 57) and copied it over to cover the poorer cap of the larger bottle (Figure 58).

Emphasizing Color

The stain was the next thing to tackle (Figure 59).

I created a new layer. In this new layer, I created shapes by painting them with a Paintbrush Tool, using a color that was suitable to represent red wine, which in real life is a purplish red (Figure 60). The layer with the wine was put in Overlay mode over the image to enhance the color and thus make it look more like spilled wine (Figure 61).

NOTE

Layers set to Overlay mode screen back light areas and multiply dark areas onto all layers below (see the Glossary for a full description of this mode). Hard Light and Soft Light modes operate similarly, but I found that Overlay mode was the best choice in this situation. Your particular problem might work better with a different mode, so experimentation is the way to go.

Figure 62 shows the final image with all the corrections in place.

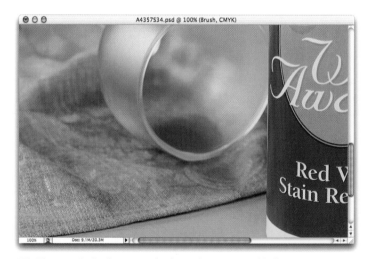

59 The stain lacks the strength of a real stain. It could almost just be a little dirt.

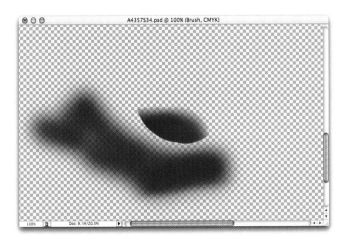

60 In a separate layer, the wine stains were created with the Paintbrush Tool.

61 The layer with the stains was put in Overlay mode to saturate the color of the stained cloth and liquid inside the glass.

62 The final image.

Changing the Mood

Figure 63 shows the original shot of a wine cooler taken in a photographer's studio. The wall is badly damaged and the overall shot lacks punch. There is no definition to the interior of the cooler, and the strong reflection of the floor on the door is too distracting. This is definitely one of those shots in desperate need of a Photoshop fix.

Creating a Mask

The first thing to do was to separate all the elements in the scene from the background. Using the Pen Tool, I carefully selected the straight solid portions of the image—the cooler, table, and countertop—turned the paths into a selection, and sent them to an alpha channel (Select > Save Selection) as seen in Figure 63a.

NOTE

With an area selected, it can be saved to an alpha channel by clicking the Save Selection as Channel button at the bottom of the Channel palette.

63 This scene set up in a photographer's studio needs some retouching.

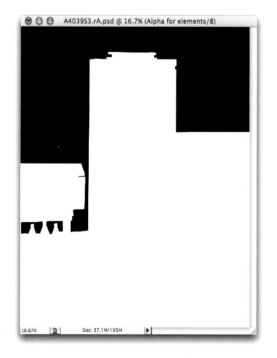

63a The alpha channel containing the solid shapes of the image.

64 The plant needed to be selected, but its shape was too complex for easy use of the Pen Tool.

The more complex areas, such as the plant and items on the table seen in Figure 64, required a little extra work. In this case, I looked at the different color channels to search for the one that contained the most contrast. The red channel had the most contrast, so I duplicated it into an alpha channel (Figure 65). I did so by just dragging the red channel in the Channel palette over the Create New Channel icon at the bottom of the palette.

In the new alpha channel and using the Curves dialog box (Image > Adjustments > Curves) with the Pencil mode (Arbitrary) selected, I repositioned the tones to force the lighter values of the background to white and the darker values of the plant to black (Figure 66). I pressed the Smooth button in the Curves box to soften the edges of the plants to eliminate any stair-stepping that occurs by a sharp contrast between the black and white.

Some gray tones still remained from the shadow area around the plant. I killed these easily with the Paintbrush Tool, using white as the foreground color.

65 The red channel was duplicated into an alpha channel.

66 Using Curves, I increased the contrast to separate the plant from the background.

There were now two alpha channels. Figure 67a contained the rectangular elements, and Figure 67b the plant and other irregularly shaped items. There's a whole slew of ways to merge these channels in Photoshop. My personal method, and you are free to substitute your own, was as follows. With Figure 67a active, I loaded Figure 67b as a selection (Select > Load Selection; Figure 67c) and filled it with white (Figure 67d).

NOTE

Using Calculations enables you to merge channels in a variety of different combinations. This is a more effective method but requires more in-depth knowledge (see Chapter 1).

67a The alpha channel for the hard-edged elements in the scene.

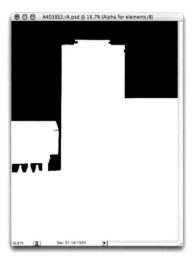

67b The alpha channel for the complex elements in the scene.

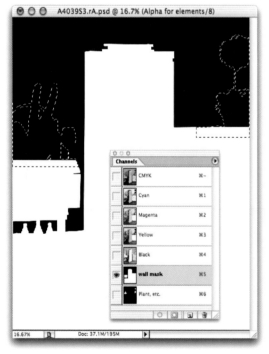

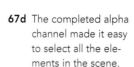

67c The alpha channel of the complex elements was made into a selection over the alpha channel with the rest of the scene.

67d The completed alpha channel made it easy to select all the elements in the scene.

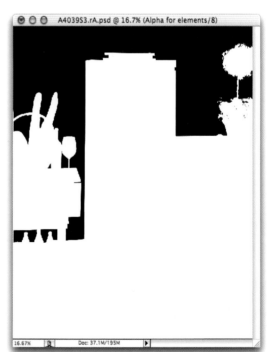

68 The elements in the scene were separated from the background into their own layer.

When the alpha channel was complete, I used it to select all the elements in the image (Select > Load Selection) and copy and place them on their own layer (Figure 68).

In a new layer between the Background layer and the layer with the elements of the scene, a color was filled to represent the new wall (Figure 69). I then gave the layer a texture to make it look real. I chose the Texturizer filter (Filter > Texture > Texturizer) in Sandstone mode for the effect (Figure 70).

69 A layer was filled with a color to replace the original wall.

70 The layer of the wall was texturized.

71 This layer contains the shadow for the table on the left side of the image.

Adding Shadows

Restoring the shadow cast by the various elements in the scene was next. In a new layer for each shadow, I created some black tones with the Paintbrush Tool. Figure 71 shows the layer for the shadow behind the table at left, and Figure 72 shows the shadow of the cooler. I lowered the opacity for each of the shadow layers. Figure 73 shows the shadows in place on the wall behind the scene.

Adjusting with Adjustment Layers

The interior of the cooler was too dark and had no definition (Figure 74). I selected the rectangular shape of the visible interior and copied it to its own layer where an Adjustment layer of levels was applied to lighten the contents (Figure 75).

72 This layer contains the shadow for the cooler.

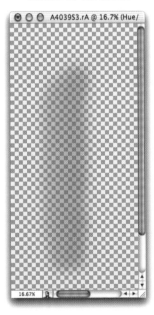

73 Here we see the shadows in place.

74 The interior of the cooler is overly dark.

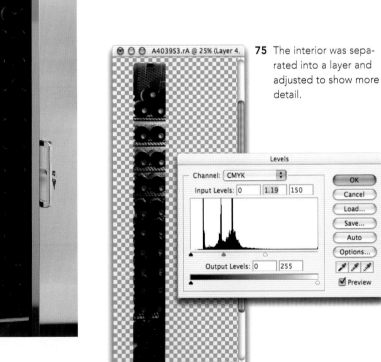

75 The interior was separated into a layer and adjusted to show more detail.

Other areas were selected and given adjustment layers. The cabinet to the right of the cooler was too bright and took attention away from the cooler, so I toned it down, as seen in Figure 76. I muted the color by adding a slight tint of blue to make it blend into the overall background. For this modification, I used a Hue/Saturation Adjustment layer. The wine glass was also toned down (Figure 77) because it was now against a darker wall than originally created. Because the original wall was white, the white shone through the glass. Now that the wall was darker, the brightness of the wall through the glass needed to match the new tones in the wall.

Using the Dodge Tool

The nameplate visible at the top right of the cooler was too dark and hard to read (Figure 78). A little touch-up with the Dodge Tool helped to bring out the details and brighten the metal and make it look shiny (Figure 79). The tool was set to Highlights because it was the light tones in the log that I wanted to exaggerate.

77 The wine glass is altered to match the new, darker wall behind it.

76 The cabinet is toned down to lessen its prominence in the image.

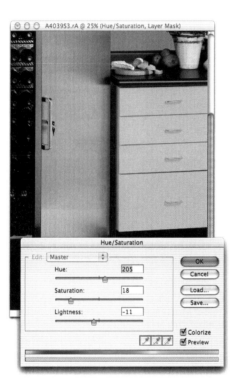

78 The nameplate of the product was too dark and illegible.

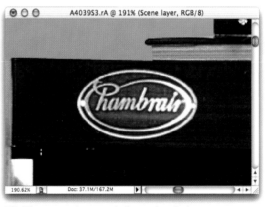

79 The nameplate was lightened with the Dodge Tool.

Eliminating a Reflection

The reflections on the door were the next to be addressed. They were too strong. Figure 80 shows the dark mass of the floor reflected along the edge and front of the door. In a new layer, I cloned upper portions of the door to cover the part where the reflection appeared (Figure 81). I applied a Layer Mask to fade out the top part of the layer to make the transition seamless between it and the original door. Figure 82 shows the final edge of the door with the reflection removed. Figure 83 shows the final image.

80 The reflection of the floor is too overpowering.

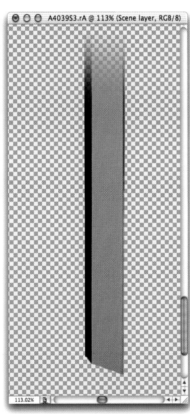

81 In a layer the upper portion of the door is cloned to cover the dark lower portion.

82 The door repaired.

83 The final image.

Another New Look

Figure 84 shows another shot where the client basically wanted a new image. "No chance of a reshoot, just Photoshop it." Yes, Photoshop has become a verb in the industry.

"Get rid of those stupid flowers!" I definitely agreed with that one. The flowers were so out of focus, they made no sense in the overall image. Very distracting! With the Clone Tool, I cloned various parts of the background over the flowers to eliminate them. Figure 85 shows the result.

"Change the color of the chair, make the rug look richer, change the walls..."; the requests went on and on. Figure 86 shows the chair. Figure 87 shows the alpha channel for the chair through which it was selected for color adjustments. First, I isolated the

chair using the Pen Tool, and then saved the selection into an alpha channel in the same way as shown in previous exercises. Figure 88 shows the chair with its new color, courtesy of the Hue/Saturation command.

I personally felt some additional changes were necessary. The wine glass sitting on the table (Figure 89) was too bland. I decided to add a few highlights to give it some presence (Figure 90). With the Paintbrush Tool and the Gradient Tool, I added the highlights.

I created shapes for the highlights with the Pen Tool. The shapes were made into selections and, with the Gradient Tool set to Foreground to Transparent, I applied a white gradient to the selected areas.

Figure 91 shows the completed image after all the alterations. If you compare it to the original in Figure 84, you can see the amount of work that went into it to make the shot more dramatic and pleasing to the eye.

84 The original shot waiting to be altered.

85 With the Clone Tool, the flowers were removed.

86 The chair needs to have the color changed.

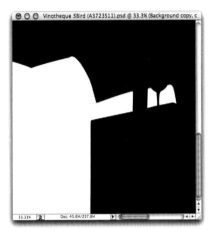

87 An alpha channel was created for the chair.

88 The chair with its new look.

89 The wine glass needs to pop.

90 Highlights bring the glass to life.

91 The final, retouched image.

Adding a Little Color

Figure 92 has a shot that could use a little help—adding a little green to those faded bushes in the background, adding some lawn to brighten the ground, filling the orange tree with fruit. And yes, as in an earlier exercise, someone forgot to open the wine!

92 The original shot needs a little retouching to make it livelier.

The greening of the scene was easy. The Paintbrush Tool in Color mode was used to paint over the bushes and gravel with a different green tint for each (Figure 93). Color mode allows the tool to change the hue of the image without affecting the luminosity so that the details remain, but their color changes. I used a slightly lighter shade of green where the lawn is visible through the wine glass on the table. This was necessary because glass would have the affect of refracting the light and lightening the color seen through it.

NOTE
The modes for all of the tools are chosen in the Options bar.

I used the Clone Tool to add a couple of oranges. The only fruit was on the lower branches and made the tree look bare (Figure 94). Figure 95 shows the additional fruit, which gives the tree a more symmetrical and abundant look.

Finally, Figures 96 and 97 show the top of the bottle before and after opening. The technique used here was similar to the one discussed earlier in this chapter as seen in Figures 51 and 52. The final shot was far more pleasing (Figure 98).

93 The Paintbrush Tool in Color mode was used to add color to the faded bushes in back and to add a lawn.

94 The orange tree does not have enough fruit on it.

95 Oranges from elsewhere on the tree were cloned to make the tree appear more symmetrical and abundant.

96 The top of the bottle is unopened.

97 The bottle is retouched to make it look opened.

98 The final image.

Adding Motion

After so many complicated exercises, let's take a breather and look at a simple retouching job. Figure 99 shows a corkscrew device that was to be shown in a mail-order catalog. The client wanted to demonstrate the movement involved in the operation of the device.

The first thing to do was to isolate the lever that would be in motion. I used the Pen Tool to create a path to select it (Figure 100). I copied the selected lever twice into two new and separate layers.

Each layer was rotated (Edit > Transform > Rotate) and lowered in opacity to get the effect visible in Figure 101.

99 This image of a corkscrew needs to show movement.

100 The lever was selected with the Pen Tool.

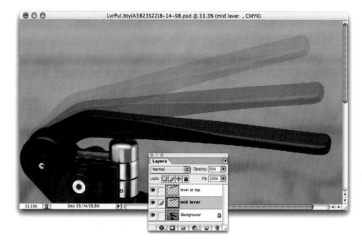

101 Copies of the lever were rotated and the opacity was lowered to simulate movement.

102 The original image.

Fine-tuning

In the final example of retouching and image enhancement, I want to show you the steps that were taken to change the image in Figure 102 to make it more what the client wanted. The clients, in this case, were friends and were architects of the house where this bathroom exists.

An architectural magazine was going to run a story on this award-winning house design. My friend shot the interior photos himself. No art director or stylist was present to prepare the scene, so the job fell on me to make the shots perfect.

The client wanted the towel rack removed. There is an empty space below the sink on the right. They wanted a similar set of wooden doors, as on the lower left, over the empty space. Finally, for mood purposes, they wanted the candle at left to be lit.

The cloning in several of the other examples in this chapter was fairly easy because the background was almost a flat color. I didn't have that advantage here. Eliminating the towel rack was a challenge because the wall and floor behind are each textured, plus there is a distinct pattern of tiling where the two meet (Figure 103).

I copied and pasted over sections of the tile area over the towel rack, making sure to match the existing pattern. I paid close attention to repeating the pattern correctly (Figure 104). The plain area of the wall behind the rack was done with the Clone Tool. Figure 105 shows the wall with the rack eliminated.

103 There is an intricate tile pattern on the floor and wall that had to be maintained when removing the towel rack.

104 Sections from other parts of the tile pattern were copied and pasted into position to rebuild the area where the towel rack once stood.

105 The final wall without the towel rack.

106 The wooden door on the left is copied to a new layer.

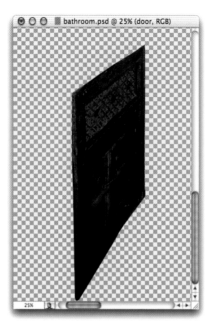

107 The door is flipped and distorted to cover the hole on the right side of the room.

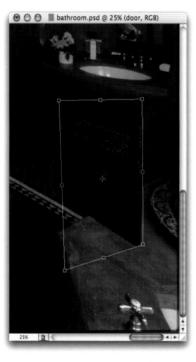

The wooden doors on the left of the image were selected and copied into a new layer (Figure 106). The layer was flipped (Edit > Transform > Flip Horizontal) and then distorted to fill the shape on the right (Edit > Transform > Distort) as seen in Figure 107. The overlap of the new door over the counter was later removed.

For the finishing touch, the candle in Figure 108 had to be lit. I lit the candle by adding a tiny wick (Figure 109) and a wisp of light with the Paintbrush Tool to the end of the wick (Figure 110). The flame was actually three paint strokes. The first stroke, the largest, was done in a red color. The middle stroke was colored orange. The smallest was done in white. The strokes for the wick and flame were created using the Paintbrush Tool with Fade applied. Figure 23 in Chapter 6 explains this feature.

Because the candle is now producing light, it had to light up the wall behind it. I made a small heavily feathered selection in the area of the wall behind the flame (Figure 111) and lightened it with the Levels command (Image > Adjustments > Levels). Figure 112 shows the final image.

The bottom line is that there are no reasons why you can't have that perfect shot. A little skill and a lot of imagination is all you need to get it right. A nice budget doesn't hurt either.

108 The unlit candle.

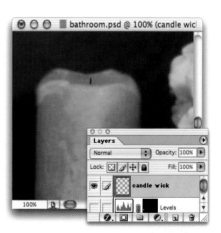

109 A tiny black stroke is painted to represent the wick.

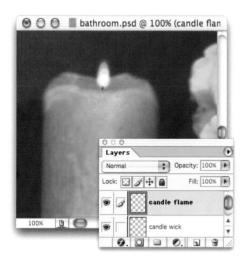

110 The flame was created with three strokes of different colors.

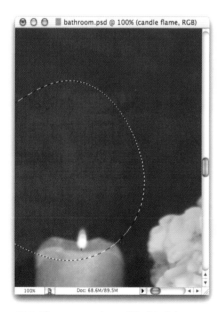

111 The area on the wall behind the candle was selected and lightened to simulate the glow of a lit candle.

112 The final image.

Compositing

Photoshop. The very name implies the use of photography and, not surprisingly, a large number of Photoshop users are photographers. Many use it just to enhance their photographs or fix some flaw, others composite various elements from different pictures to form a single image. Some do it masterfully, and some do it just for fun. One of the reasons that Adobe has used such venues as the PMA (Photo Marketing Association) conference to introduce new versions of the program is that both professional and amateur photographers are such a large segment of their customer base.

I remember sitting with a photographer friend of mine waiting for that cloud formation to come into view over the landscape for that perfect shot. "If it could only hold that shape for another 20 minutes!" Today, he can shoot the landscape and the sky separately and seamlessly composite them into that perfect image. Sure, compositing is nothing new, but compare the cost and time of the traditional methods to those available the Photoshop way.

I am not a photographer—I am an illustrator. In the process of creating my illustrations, I often work with various photographs to achieve the effect the client is looking for. In some cases, the client provides a series of their own images that must be integrated into the final image. In others, the entire illustration is based on an existing photograph.

Using Photography in Your Illustrations

This chapter deals with how I use photography as part of the overall image. The advent of digital photography made it easier and far more effective to incorporate photography in my commercial illustrations. Instant access to the photograph makes it an immensely useful tool in the production process. I used to find it easier and faster to illustrate an entire image. To use photography meant taking the shot and wasting time and money to get the film developed. What if the shot didn't come out the way I wanted? Not being a photographer, this was often the case. Wasted time.

Today I look at the shot immediately after it has been taken, and if it works, I'm set. After I import it into the computer, I am ready to continue with the illustration.

One of the biggest boons for those who do the type of commercial illustrations that I do has been the development of CDs or even whole libraries of digital stock photography. These are generally royalty free, meaning that after we buy them, we can use them in almost any commercial way without further permission or additional fees.

Personally, I have an extensive collection of such images from Photodisc, one of the leading names in the field. Throughout this chapter, you'll see that occasionally I need to find images of fairly unusual things: a slice of pineapple, a fish, a pair of blue jeans, and on and on. I'm almost sure to be able to find elements such as these somewhere in my Photodisc library. It's a real timesaver.

Let's start this chapter with an example where the stock images became the source material for a finished illustration.

Composite Illustration Example 1: Chevron Promotional Brochure Cover

Figure 1 shows the comp that was given to me by the art director at an ad agency. The finished piece was to be a printed folder that contained information on a promotion that the client was having. I was given very specific instructions as to the equipment to be shown and the placement of each individual element in the illustration.

1 This is the illustration comp that was provided by the client for look and positioning of elements.

The Heavy Equipment

The client supplied me with brochures that contained pictures of the heavy equipment they wanted to appear in the illustration. Unfortunately, none of the pictures matched the angle that was required for the layout. This meant that I would have to illustrate the machines from scratch. Figure 2 shows the Pen Tool paths that I created for the machine in the foreground. I separated the individual paths to select areas for rendering.

NOTE

The production process mentioned above is covered in Chapters 2 and 6 using other examples.

Other elements in the illustration, such as the shovel and steel drums, I also created from scratch. The majority of the remaining elements were stock image files that I modified to create the composite.

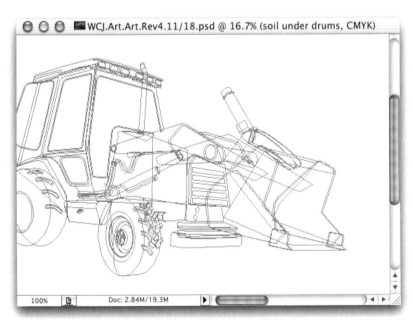

2 The entire tractor was created with the Pen Tool. Here we see the paths that would later be used to make selections for rendering.

Creation of Man

Figure 3 shows a close-up of the man in the illustration. I nicknamed him Frankenstein because, very much like his namesake, he is made up of many separate body parts from a variety of photos.

The jacket he is wearing was very important because it was a give-away in the promotion. I was given a sample jacket because, not only was it part of the main illustration, but also I would have to do a separate illustration of the jacket itself for another part of the folder.

3 Although this man looks like a single image, he is actually composed of pieces from many different photographs.

Changing Fashion Styles

I searched through my stock photo collection to find a person wearing a similar jacket that would have all the necessary folds and shading. The doctor image of Figure 4 met my needs. It was longer than the client's jacket, so I had plenty of room to work with. Using the Photoshop Pen Tool, I surrounded the lab coat, except that I deliberately created a smooth rounded corner at the bottom right and left where I wanted the coat to end. I made the path into a selection from the Paths palette and copied and pasted its contents into a separate layer (Figure 5).

The lab coat had most of the basic elements but required some modifications to make it look like the actual promo jacket.

The angle of the photo was opposite of what I needed, so I applied a simple Flip Horizontal (Edit > Transform > Flip Horizontal) to correct it (Figure 6).

The book and hands would have to be replaced to match the clipboard and hands in the layout. Using the Clone Tool, I removed them by cloning areas of the lab coat over the book and hands (Figure 7).

NOTE

This process is outlined in detail in Chapter 3 (in the first exercise, in which a leather case is removed).

The pockets in the promotion jacket had flaps. This was an easy addition to make. With the Pen Tool, I created a path that formed the shape of the flap (Figure 8). The path was made into a selection. I then created a new layer by copying the pocket section (Layer > New > Layer via Copy). This added the flap over the pockets in the photo. The addition of a simple drop shadow to this layer (Layer > Layer Style > Drop Shadow) gave the flaps a realistic, three-dimensional effect (Figure 9).

4 This is the image from which the coat was assembled.

5 The entire shape of the coat was outlined with the Pen Tool.

6 The image was flipped to match the direction of the standing man in the layout.

7 I used the Clone Tool to cover the hands with material of the coat cloned from elsewhere in the image.

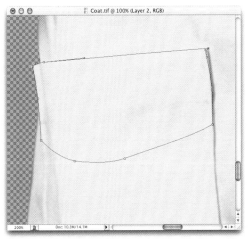

8 With the Pen Tool a path was created to represent the flap that was needed for the jacket.

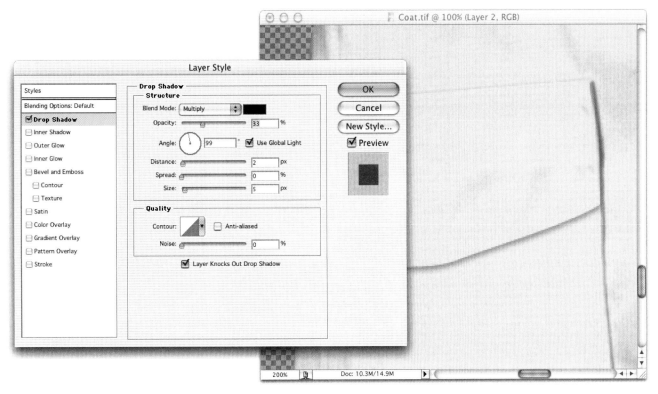

9 With a Layer Style of Drop Shadow, a three-dimensional realistic effect was added to the pocket flap.

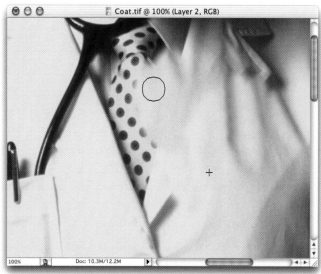

The open collar and tie were cloned out to match the closed collar look of the promo jacket (Figure 10).

The doctor's coat had standard buttons, but the promotional jacket I was copying had snap buttons. To make this change, I started by removing the shadow over the existing button by cloning the lab coat texture over it (Figure 11). I then selected the button with the Elliptical Marquee Tool. Holding down the Shift key constrained the selection to a perfect circle. To create the snap look, the circles were then filled with the basic color of the lab coat and copied to a separate layer followed by the applications of Layer Styles > Drop Shadow and Bevel and Emboss (Figure 12).

10 Like the hands, the open collar and tie were removed with the Clone Tool.

11 This is the button that was in the original image.

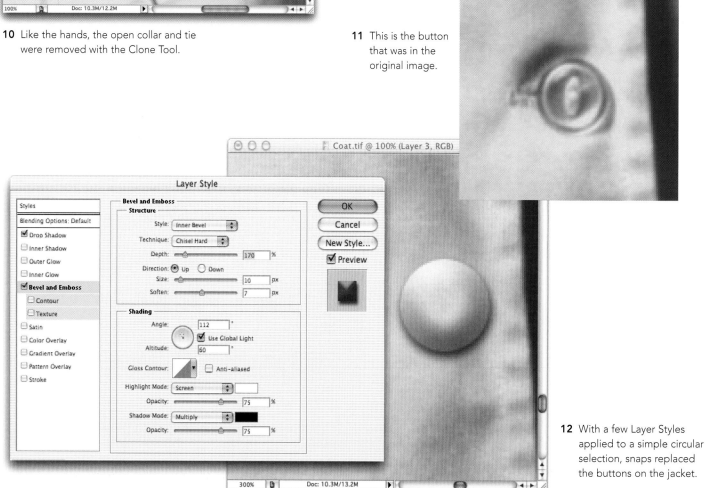

12 With a few Layer Styles applied to a simple circular selection, snaps replaced the buttons on the jacket.

To construct the drawstrings on the promo jacket, I moved into Illustrator to create vectors with the Pen Tool (Figure 13). I then imported them into the corner edges of the jacket. If uncertain of how to do this, look back at Chapter 2, which has several examples of how to make such cylindrical objects in Illustrator.

The color was the easiest thing to fix. I selected a blue color that matched the color of the promo jacket as the foreground color. The transparency was locked for the layer containing the lab coat. The layer was then filled with the blue color using Multiply as the mode (Edit > Fill > Fade > Multiply) (Figure 14).

The company logo was next to set up. The logo was reproduced in Illustrator as seen in Figure 15. The client supplied me with a scan of the logo. The scan was not clean enough for my needs, so I imported it into Illustrator, and traced it to create a new clean logo. I then imported it into a Photoshop file via Copy and Paste and put it into place over the breast of the jacket (Figure 16).

To guarantee that the sizes would be as close as needed, I turned the rulers on in Photoshop (View > Rulers). I measured the size of the area where the logo was to go. I resized the logo in Illustrator to match the size needed. When in Photoshop, I did any additional resizing with Scale (Edit > Transform > Scale) but, at this point, it would be minimal, thus avoiding any degradation of the image.

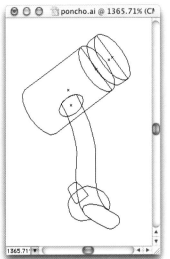

13 The drawstrings for the jacket started out as simple vectors created with the Pen Tool.

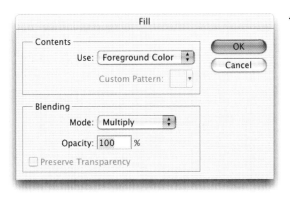

14 The white lab coat is converted to the deep blue of the promo jacket.

15 The logo was re-created as vectors in Illustrator.

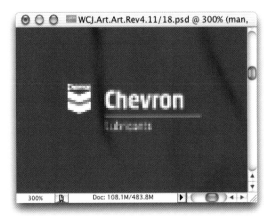

16 The logo is imported into the Photoshop image and placed in position over the breast of the jacket.

Putting on a New Face

The man's head had to be looking down at the clipboard, and he had to be wearing a hard hat. Again I searched for a stock image and found one containing the necessary elements (Figure 17). The man in the upper half was selected with the Pen Tool and imported into the image of the jacket. The head was flipped and resized to fit the body (Figure 18).

The hard hat in the layout was white and had a logo on the front of it. The red hard hat was selected using the Pen Tool. It was desaturated and lightened using the Hue/Saturation command (Figure 19). To give it that sparkling, white appearance, I applied a slight Levels adjustment.

I added color to the Illustrator file that I'd previously made for the Chevron logo and then copied and pasted it into the front panel of the hat. I then distorted the logo using the Distort function (Edit > Transform > Distort) to follow the correct angle (Figure 20).

To create the hood, I made a new layer above the one containing the head and hard hat. With the Clone Tool set to Use All Layers, I cloned sections of the blue jacket into place to form a hood over the man's head. I chose an area that had a fold in it so that a fold would appear at the top of the hood. In a separate layer, a shadow was added with the Paintbrush Tool to simulate the shadow being cast by the hood on the hard hat (Figure 21). The same little pull string used for the bottom of the jacket was duplicated and placed at the bottom of the hood.

17 The head for the man in the final art was taken from this image.

18 The head was imported into the final art file, flipped, and resized to match the direction and size needed.

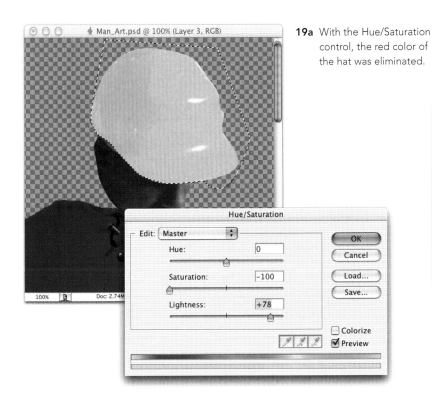

19a With the Hue/Saturation control, the red color of the hat was eliminated.

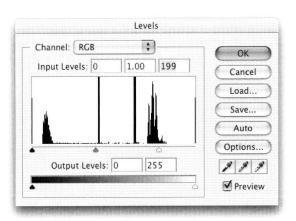

19b With the Levels command, the hat was further brightened.

20 The logo was imported from Illustrator and placed in position on the hard hat.

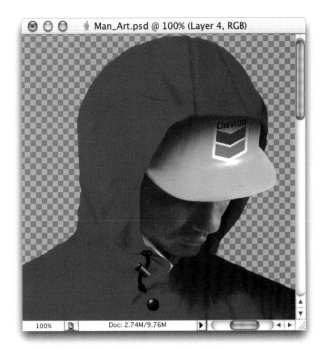

21 The hood was added to the jacket and a shadow was placed over the hard hat.

Slight of Hand

The hands came from yet another stock image (Figure 22). Using the Pen Tool, I selected the hands and copied them over to the image with my Frankenstein creation. Each hand was placed on its own layer (Figure 23). However, I needed the pencil to be in action. My Frankenstein is in the act of writing—not merely holding the pencil in his fingers as the man is doing in Figure 22. I therefore erased the original pencil with the Clone Tool. I placed a new pencil in position by making a simple line with the Line Tool (Figure 24). The pencil was given a shadow in the same manner as was the straw in Figure 6 of Chapter 2.

Frankenstein's clipboard, being a rectangle, was so easy to make that I stayed in Photoshop, making a rectangular shape with the Pen Tool and filling it with a gradient (Figure 25). The layer of the clipboard was placed below the layer with the lower hand to make it seem as if that hand is holding it. It was above the layer with the hand and pencil. This made it hide a portion of the hand so that it looked as if the hand is writing on the clipboard.

22 The hands were taken from this image.

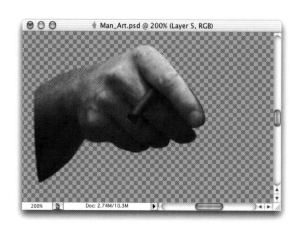

23 Each hand was selected and imported into the final art image.

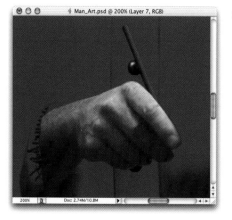

24 The position of the pencil the man is holding was changed to make it look as if he is writing with it.

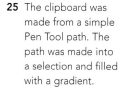

25 The clipboard was made from a simple Pen Tool path. The path was made into a selection and filled with a gradient.

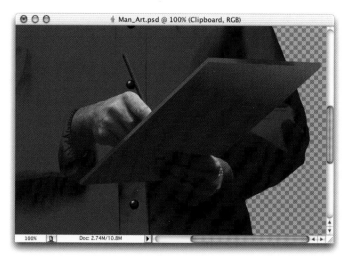

26 The man's legs were copied from this image.

27 The legs were selected and copied over to the working file.

A Little Legwork

The legs were clad in jeans and had to conform to a specific stance. I found an image (Figure 26) that came close to what was required. I selected the legs of the man and copied them over to the working file (Figure 27). Again, a few modifications were needed. First the hands that overlapped the leg on the left (Figure 28) were eliminated with the Clone Tool (Figure 29). Also the angle of the leg on the right was slightly off. So finally, using the Lasso Selection Tool, I surrounded the leg and cut it into its own layer (Layer > New > Layer via Cut). The leg was then rotated (Edit > Transform > Rotate) to match the angle in the layout (Figure 30).

Using the Clone Tool, I filled in the area where the leg was attached (Figure 31).

28 The clenched hands had to be removed.

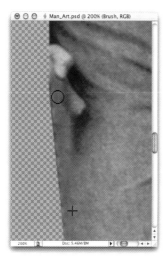

29 The Clone Tool was used to remove the hands.

30 The position of the raised leg had to be modified. The leg was selected and rotated to match the position in the layout.

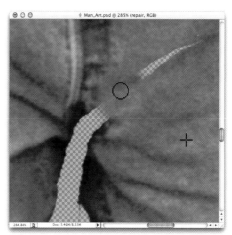

31 With the Clone Tool the gap created by the repositioning of the leg was filled in.

Getting Down and Dirty

To create the various areas of dirt in the composite image, I found I needed no less than four additional stock photos, making a total of eight stock photos used in creating this unified image. Figure 32 shows the sources of the various areas of soil.

32 The soil in the final art was made from a composite of multiple images.

Composite Illustration Example 2: A Poster for International Events

Another illustration that involved the compositing of multiple images was a poster that was created for International Events. The client asked for very specific imagery that included volcanoes, golf courses, scuba divers, and a lot more visuals, as seen in Figure 33. My Photodisc collection came to the rescue once again for the majority of the imagery.

I created the main element from scratch (as well as certain elements inside it). You may recall this particular example from Chapter 2. The rest was a composite of multiple images that involved some alteration to fit the overall theme that was needed.

This particular client elected not to provide me with an elaborate, detailed layout. They gave me a set of verbal instructions and left it up to me to come up with a solution.

Extracting an Image

The golf course scene in the foreground (Figure 34) was made up of two different images. The golf course and the two players came from the image in Figure 35. As visible in Figure 34, some distance separates the two figures. The first thing I did was to make two duplicates of the image, one for the man and the second for the woman. Then I used the Extract filter (Figure 36) to extract the woman from one duplicate and the man from the other.

34 Here we see the detail of the golf course in the foreground of the poster.

33 This is a poster that was composited of many images that were combined to form a single entity.

35 The two golfers were taken from this image.

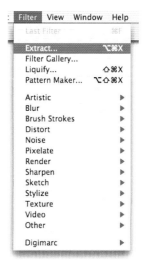

36 This is the Extract filter.

The Extract filter is not an easy tool to work with. The actual procedure might be easy, but the results usually need a little fixing (as discussed a little later in this chapter).

Another good reason to create a duplicate, as I just mentioned, is the fact that the Extract filter does not always work as perfectly as you might want. There usually is a need for some retouching after using the Extract filter. That is easy to do if you still have the original to clone from.

NOTE

The method of separating an element from an image to be exported into another image works best if there is a good amount of contrast between the element and its background.

The Edge Highlighter Tool is used to outline the edge of the element in the image you want to separate. A brush size is used that will encompass enough of the element plus its surrounding background. Figure 37 illustrates this concept. To separate the circle from its background, brush size A is too big, brush B is too small, but brush C has just enough space for the filter to do its work. Figure 38 shows the male figure outlined.

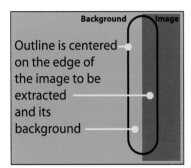

37 The box on the left illustrates the concept of outlining the image edge. The box on the bottom shows the proper brush size selection. Brush C is the proper size to cover enough of the image and background for the filter to make a distinction between the two.

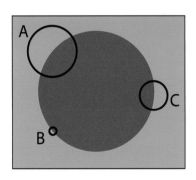

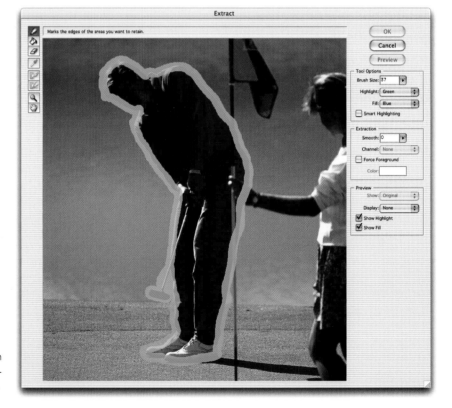

38 The male figure is outlined with the Edge Highlighter Tool within the Extract Filter dialog box.

· ·

NOTE

You can change the size brush many times along the outline. Larger brushes are good in areas such as flowing hair.

The Fill Tool (Bucket) is then used to tell the filter which side of the outline you want to keep. Figure 39 shows the male player filled to indicate he is to be the element extracted from the image.

Pressing the Preview button shows the extraction (Figure 40). Pressing OK performs the extraction.

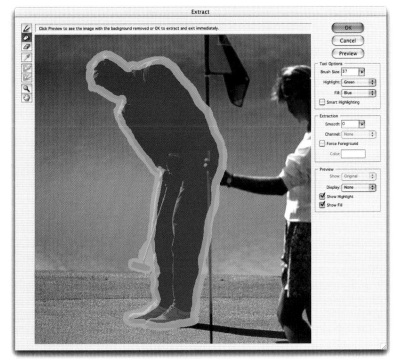

39 Once the outlining is complete, the Bucket Tool is used to fill the area you want to extract.

40 The Preview button displays the extraction of the image from its background.

As mentioned earlier, the final results are not always what you might want. Because of the rough edges and similarity of tonality in some spots, the extraction was less than perfect in this example. Figure 41 shows a close-up of the shoes, and some obvious blemishes are visible. This is where having the original intact comes in handy.

I normally use the Clone Tool to fix these problems. Here is a little trick that saves time and works well. This should be done immediately after the extraction. Make sure you have not changed the size or resolution or moved the elements from where the Extract filter placed them.

Make sure that Aligned is selected in the options bar for the Clone Tool (Figure 42). Zoom in very closely to a specific part of the extracted image. Zoom in to the identical spot in the original image. Figure 43 shows a 1200% zoom into the upper part of the shoe in both files. With the extracted (to be retouched) image selected as the active file, Option-click (Alt-click on a PC) with the Clone Tool on a particular pixel in the original image. Because the Clone Tool can clone from one image to another, you have just told it where to clone from. Now click the exact same pixel in the extracted file. You have now established a connection. You can zoom back out and begin cloning. Start cloning in the blemishes and the tool will pick up the information from the unblemished original. Figure 44 shows the extracted file on the right cloning information from the original on the left.

The same extracting and cloning processes were applied to the female golfer. The two golfers were then placed in position on the golf course and shadows were added.

41 The extraction is not always perfect. Here we see some areas that are not acceptable.

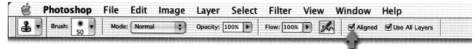

42 The Alignment control in the options bar for the Clone Tool.

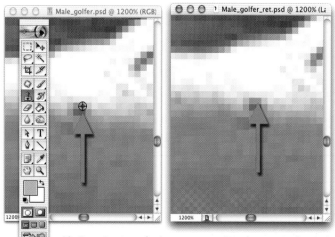

43 Zooming into the image to a point where a single pixel can be seen makes it easy to pinpoint the position for cloning from one image to another. The image on the right is the active file being retouched. The image on the left is the original image from where the Clone Tool is establishing alignment.

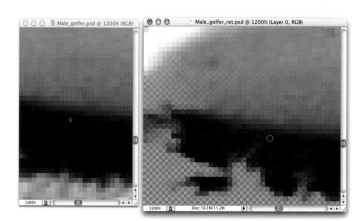

44 The extracted image on the right is being repaired by cloning from the original image on the left.

45 This is the detail of the contents in the goblet, the central element of the poster.

Going Underwater

Figure 45 shows the detail of the contents in the goblet. Figure 46 shows the diver.

The client was not happy with the monochromatic nature of the image and requested that some color be added and detail brought out in the diver. In studying Figure 47, you can see that the concerns were justified.

46 The diver was imported from this original image.

47 The original image is very monochromatic. The client requested that some additional color be added to give it more separation and excitement.

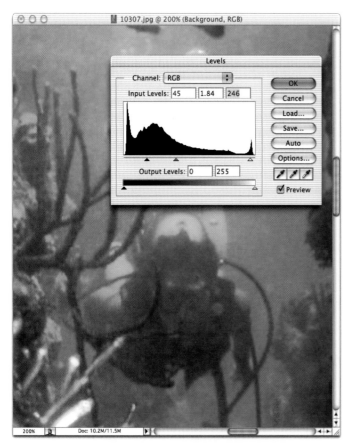

48 Using the Levels command, a little contrast was given to the original image.

I started by adding a little more contrast to the image. I used Levels (Image > Adjustments > Levels) to make the highlights a bit brighter. I pushed the shadows a little darker. Finally, I adjusted the midtones to get a little more detail to show through (Figure 48). There was a definite need for additional color in the scene. I started by selecting the fins with the Pen Tool. In a separate layer, I filled the selection with a bright orange color (Figure 49a). I put the layer in Hard Light mode (Figure 49b).

I chose to put this layer in Hard Light mode because Hard Light, like its close relatives Soft Light and Overlay, lightens any part of the underlying image where the Hard Light layer is light, and darkens those parts where the Hard Light layer is dark. It works channel by channel, and the channels in this orange color are very different: The red is light, the green medium, and the blue dark. In the underlying image, the color scheme is the exact opposite: red dark, green medium, blue light. The Hard Light layer basically destroys the underlying red and maxes out the underlying blue, but it retains detail in the green, which is what I needed.

This added the color to the fins while allowing their details and shadows to show through. Yeah, I know, what detail? There is a tiny bit though, and every little bit helps. Finally, I softened some of the edges with the Blur Tool to conform to the softness of the image.

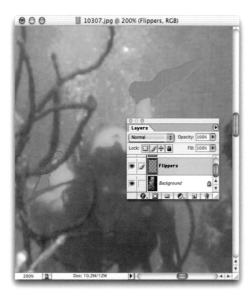

49a The fins were selected with the Pen Tool and color was added.

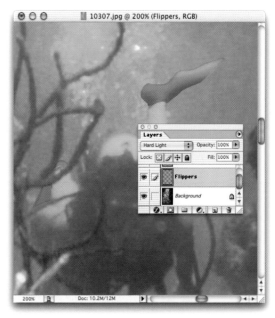

49b The layer was put in Hard Light mode to let the details of the fin show through.

50 Skin tones were added to differentiate the diver from the background.

In another layer, I added some skin tones by using the Paintbrush Tool, as seen in Figure 50. Using a flesh-toned color, I painted right over the diver's limbs and face. The opacity for the skin layer was lowered to 80% to lessen the intensity of the color and allow some shadow areas to come through.

To add an impression of sharpness, I created a small path with the Pen Tool to represent the goggles and, in a new layer, stroked it with a thin black Paintbrush Tool (Figure 51). To make the goggles look three-dimensional, I gave them a Bevel and Emboss Layer Style (Figure 52).

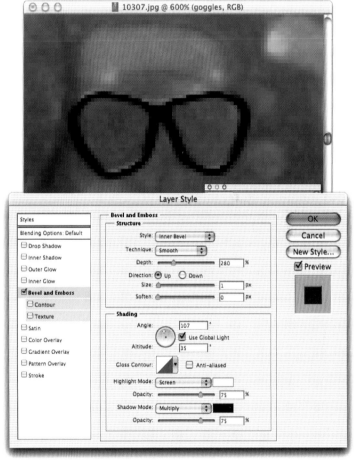

51 In a separate layer, using the Pen Tool, a shape was generated and stroked to simulate the goggles worn by the diver.

52 Adding a Layer Style to the layer with the goggles gave them a three-dimensional look.

I added a little more color here and there, but the client did not like the big, dark rock formations on the right side. The solution was to hide them with elements—namely, fish—from a stock photo of another underwater scene (Figure 53). With the Pen Tool, I selected a small group of fish on the upper left of the image (Figure 54). They were then copied over to the working file with the diver. Their angle was already perfect, so I needed no further transformation. The underwater scene was complete (Figure 55).

53 This second underwater scene provided the additional fish that were copied to the working file with the diver.

54 This small group of fish was selected with the Pen Tool and copied over to the image with the diver.

55 The new fish are seamlessly composited into the underwater scene.

56 The underwater scene of the diver was positioned under the layer of the surfer.

The diver image was then copied over to a file that had been set up to assemble all the composite elements within the goblet. The file already contained the image of the surfer. The diver layer was positioned above the surfer layer (Figure 56).

To make the two scenes blend into each other, I applied a Layer Mask (Layer > Add Layer Mask) with a small gradient from white to black to the layer with the diver scene (Figure 57). If you don't remember the function of a Layer Mask, refer back to the explanation of it in Chapter 1. Figure 58 shows the Layer Mask itself, which can be displayed by setting the Channels palette as shown.

57 A Layer Mask was applied to the diver layer to soften the transition between it and the layer of the surfer.

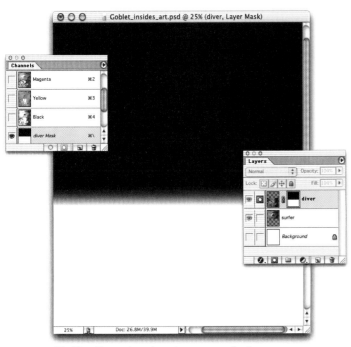

58 The Channels palette is set up to display the Layer Mask.

In a separate file, I created the basic shape of the goblet (Figure 59).

The completed surfer, diver, and volcano layers were imported into the file with the goblet and turned into a Clipping Group with the goblet shape (Figure 60).

The final poster had to be a vertical piece of art. This posed no problem for the goblet, of course, but the background image I wanted to use (Figure 61) was horizontal. Its sky didn't extend upward nearly as much as was needed to fill the poster.

59 Here is the file of the basic shape for the goblet.

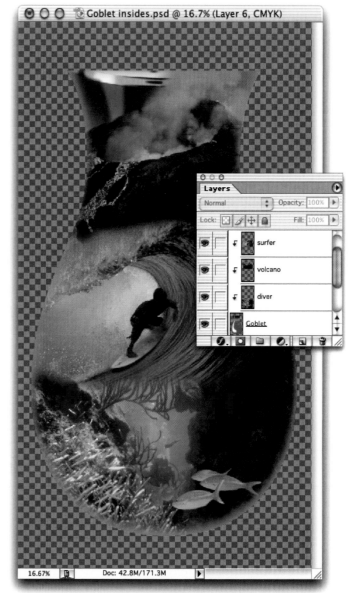

60 Here is the goblet with all the images that make up its contents being clipped by the shape of the goblet interior.

Therefore, I applied the Image > Canvas Size command (Figure 62) to expand the height of the image but not its width. By default, unless we specify a different background color in the Color Picker, the additional image space comes in as white, which was fine. But by default, that extra white space would be divided equally above and below the image.

Instead, I set the positioning guide at the bottom of the dialog box to force the existing image to the bottom, meaning that all the extra space would come in at the top.

I separated the area of the scene into its own layer by selecting it with the Rectangular Marquee Tool and choosing New Layer via Cut from the Layer menu.

61 This is the image that served as the backdrop for the poster.

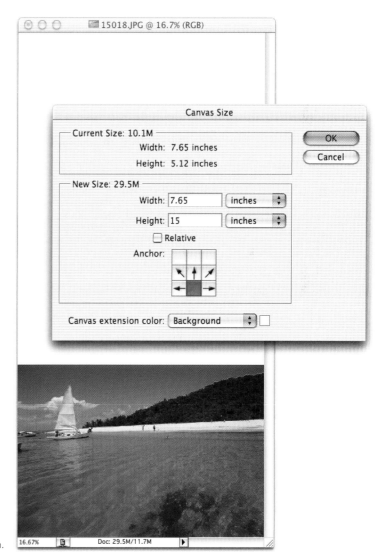

62 A blank area to accommodate more sky was added with the Canvas Size function.

Using the Eyedropper Tool, I selected the color right at the top edge of the sky for the foreground color (Figure 63). I chose a second, darker blue for the background color. I made the Background layer active by clicking it in the layer palette. This made sure that the additional sky would be added to the Background layer. I applied a gradient with the Gradient Tool in the Background layer, filling up the sky (Figure 64). There was an obvious seam showing where the new sky met the original, because the new sky was absolutely consistent in color as it moved across the page, and the original sky wasn't. Also, as visible in Figure 65, there is a grain to the original image that is lacking in the extended sky.

63 With the Eyedropper Tool, the color at the top edge of the sky is selected as the foreground color.

64 A gradient was applied to the Background layer and that became with sky for the poster.

65 The new sky area lacks the film grain of the original, which is why there's such an obvious line where the two skies abut.

To add the grain, first the Add Noise filter (Filter > Noise > Add Noise) was applied to the new sky at an amount that closely matched the existing grain in the old sky (Figure 66). Then I blurred the Background layer slightly (Filter > Blur > Gaussian Blur).

Using a large, soft-edged Eraser Tool, I erased the edge where the old sky met the new sky from the layer with the beach scene. Because the eraser edge was soft, the resulting blend between the two layers is smooth (Figure 67). I also lowered the opacity for the eraser so that it left behind a ghost, adding to the effectiveness of the blend.

NOTE
The Eraser Tool is being used in a layer, so it is erasing to transparent. If the transparency for the layer is locked, the tool will erase to the color currently selected for the background color, which in this case is a blue.

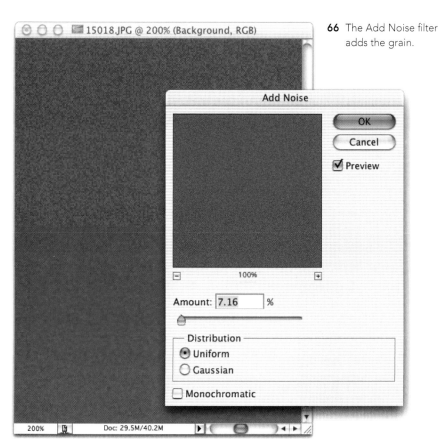

66 The Add Noise filter adds the grain.

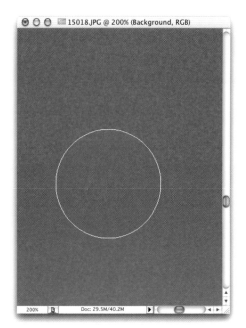

67 After a light application of the Eraser Tool, the edge where the two halves meet has vanished.

Let's go back in the file with the goblet. It was time to complete all the elements for it so that it could be imported into the final art file. In Chapter 2, you may recall that we constructed an elaborate paper umbrella of the kind that grace many tropical drinks. It was now time to bring this umbrella into the picture and place it on top of the goblet (Figure 68).

The umbrella file was duplicated and, after modifications, served as a reflection of the original umbrella on the face of the goblet. Note in Figure 69 how the spokes have been filled with black and the

body of the umbrella has been lightened. This was done because the reflection should be looking at the back of the umbrella with the light shining through it.

I imported the reflection umbrella file into the goblet file and placed it behind the layer with the original umbrella. The layer was named "umbrella reflection." It was scaled down in size (Edit > Transform > Scale) to appear further from view (Figure 70). The opacity was lowered to allow the goblet details to show through, and it was clipped with the layer of the goblet so that it would only be seen within the goblet shape (Figure 71).

68 The umbrella is added to the top of the goblet.

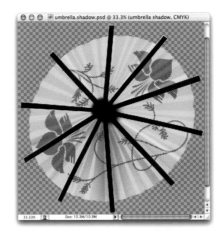

69 This is a second version of the umbrella with modifications made to make it look like a reflection of the original umbrella.

70 The layer with the reflection of the umbrella was scaled down slightly.

71 The opacity for the umbrella reflection layer was lowered to allow the details of the goblet to show through. It was then made into a Clipping Group with the layer of the goblet.

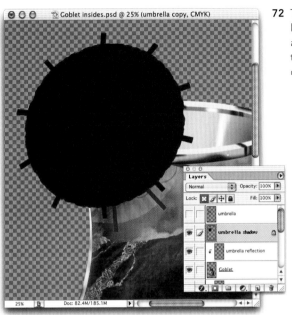

72 The original umbrella layer is duplicated and filled with black to serve as the shadow of the umbrella.

I duplicated the layer of the original umbrella. It was automatically named "umbrella copy" in the Layers palette. I renamed it "umbrella shadow." Its transparency was locked to ensure that only the active pixels would be filled, and it was filled with black (Edit > Fill) as seen in Figure 72. Then the transparency was unlocked so that the layer could be blurred. I applied the Gaussian Blur filter (Filter > Blur > Gaussian Blur) to soften what was about to become the shadow of the umbrella (Figure 73). The blurred layer was duplicated and named "umbrella shadow 2." This second duplicate would be used for a shadow in a later step.

I moved the shadow layer into position under the umbrella. Its opacity was lowered and clipped with the layer of the goblet as demonstrated in Figure 74.

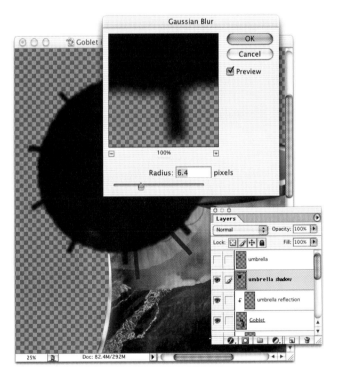

73 The layer for the umbrella shadow is blurred to soften the edges.

74 The opacity for the shadow layer was lowered and the layer was clipped with the layer of the goblet.

Figure 75 is a Photodisc image. I borrowed one of the pineapple slices and placed it in position at the top and behind the umbrella. The layer that was previously created and named "umbrella shadow 2" was placed over the pineapple slice and clipped with the pineapple layer to represent the shadow being cast by the umbrella onto the pineapple (Figure 76). This helps to establish the relationship between the various elements within the three-dimensional environment being created.

The file of the straw, also discussed in Chapter 2, is imported into the goblet file (Figure 77). The shadow for the straw is made in the same way as was the shadow for the umbrella (Figure 78). A Layer Mask is applied to the layer of the straw so that it fades into the glass (Figure 79).

Finally, I copied the lip of the goblet into a layer of its own and placed that layer in the forefront to create the illusion that the straw and pineapple are inside the goblet (Figure 80).

75 This image provided the pineapple slice needed for the top of the goblet.

76 The pineapple slice is in position at the top of the goblet. The layer of the umbrella shadow is duplicated and clipped with the layer of the pineapple slice.

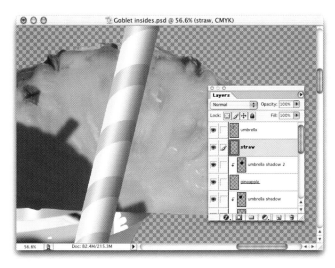

77 The straw was added to the mix.

78 A shadow for the straw was created and clipped with the pineapple slice.

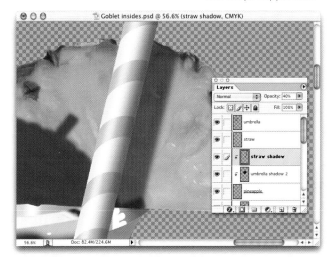

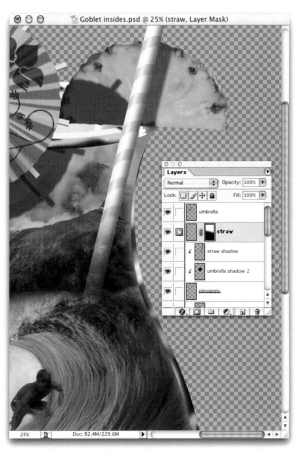

79 A Layer Mask was applied to the straw layer to make it fade into the drink.

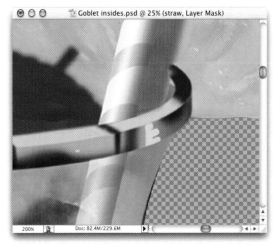

80 The top rim of the goblet was copied and placed in the front to create the effect that the contents are indeed inside the goblet

The 3D Connection

The beauty of 3D applications is that they enable you to create entire scenes and to view them from different angles. These scenes can be elaborately lit and have shadows and reflections automatically generated precisely where they should be, based on the objects in the scene and the materials from which they are made. The materials can be solids such as wood or metal, or transparent such as glass. The program will even generate the distortions created by the refraction of light through a translucent material such as water.

This book, however, is not about 3D software but rather the creation of images using Photoshop. However, a little introduction of how these 3D applications work is necessary to open your eyes to the possibilities available through this medium. Sometimes turning to a 3D program can be of tremendous help in solving problems or eliminating the need for extensive experimentation to determine how something should look.

A 3D Primer

To better understand how these 3D applications work, let's get acquainted with some of the functions available in the 3D world.

Like Photoshop and Illustrator, 3D software has primitives such as spheres and cubes that can be created with a simple click of the mouse button. More complex elements are created using tools that vary between the various applications on the market. In this introduction, I use simple objects as examples.

After an object is created, it is placed into a three-dimensional space within the computer. To easily place the object within that space, 3D programs give you multiple views of the space. Figure 1 shows three objects placed on a surface in a 3D program. Notice that the four views are named for the particular view that they represent.

The Camera view is the main view that will display the composition. The Top, Front, and Right views give you a visual relationship of the position of the objects within the space. The blue object shown in these views is the camera. Bottom, Back, and Left are also available by opening those views from a menu. If you have the screen real estate available, you can have all the views opened simultaneously.

When an object is created, it comes in as a simple, wireframe representation of the object (see the three objects in Figure 1).

1 Navigating within the 3D space is done by viewing the scene from different angles. Each angle has its own window.

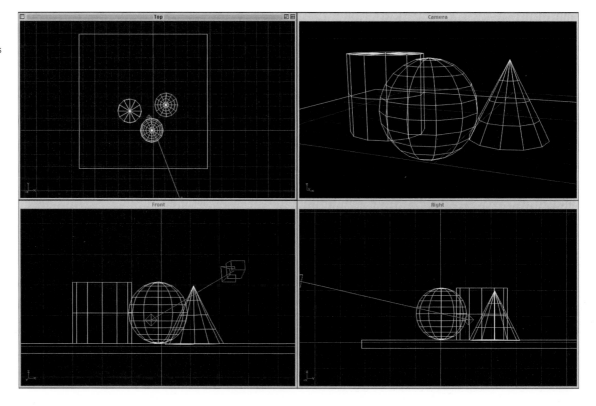

When you render a 3D scene, the computer adds skin to the objects, making them appear to be solid shapes (Figure 2). You can assign attributes to the objects such as color, but it doesn't stop there. The material that an object is made of can be very complex. Most 3D programs come with a variety of materials that you can assign to an object such as wood or plastic. These preconfigured materials can be edited to create your own materials library. Later in this chapter, you will see one of the material editing windows where attributes such as transparency or reflectivity can be added to an object.

Step into a windowless room with no light on and what do you see? Nothing. We require light to see our surroundings. Likewise, in the 3D world in the computer, light is needed to view the scene. Light sources can be added to the scene as spotlights, ambient lighting, or distant lights. These lights can also be given colors and varying intensities.

As with the objects, the light sources can be repositioned anywhere within the space. The direction of the flow of light can be controlled. Figure 3 shows two views of our scene where a spotlight has been added that points toward the sphere. The little yellow object that looks like a spotlight represents the light source. The blue cone emanating from it represents the direction of the light beam.

All the attributes assigned to the objects and the light sources become visible as a true scene when the image is rendered. At this point, the program generates the scene so that all the elements can take on a realistic look rather than the wireframe visible while you are composing the scene. The method used for rendering will make a difference in the final result.

2 Objects are solid when rendered.

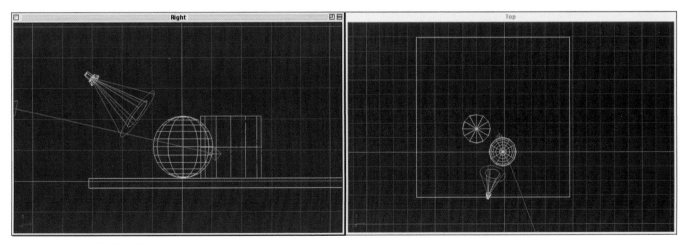

3 A spotlight is added to the scene.

In our scene of three objects with one light source, each object has been given a material. The cylinder is made of chrome. The cone is made of polished wood. The sphere is made of glass that has a slight blue tint. A simple flat rendering will produce an image such as the one in Figure 4. This method is fast but lacks all the visual data that you would expect from the materials assigned and the effect of the spotlight. To see the shadows and the actual materials, such as the glass of the sphere, you need to render the scene with raytracing. This method will obviously take longer, but the result will be more what you would expect from a 3D rendered image. Figure 5 shows the scene rendered using raytracing.

The scene comes to life! The objects are made of what they were meant to be.

4 A basic render will show the colors but not lighting effects and the materials the objects are made of.

5 Raytracing will render an image with a realistic look.

In Figure 6, additional red and blue light sources have been added. You can see the effect they have on the scene when compared to the same scene in Figure 5.

Finally, as with all the elements in the scene, the camera can be repositioned anywhere within the 3D space. In Figure 7, the camera has been moved to show the side of our scene. Unlike the 2D world of Photoshop and Illustrator, this is a truly three-dimensional world where you can travel around and through the space and view your objects from any angle.

Now, let's look at the connection between Photoshop and this exotic 3D realm.

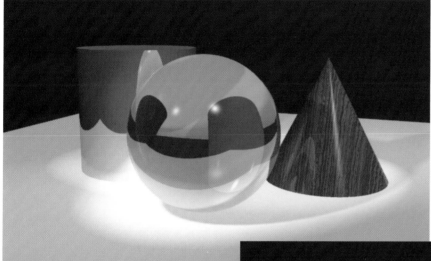

6 Additional colored light sources are added to the scene.

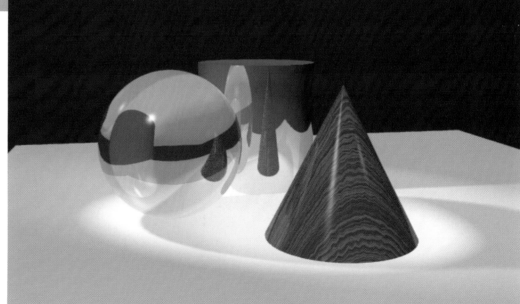

7 The angle of the camera has been changed to view the scene from the side.

Texture Mapping

Texture mapping is a specific area where Photoshop proves extremely useful to the 3D artist. 3D applications do have a feature called Texture Mapping, a process in computer-generated images where the skin of an object, or its texture, is derived from another image file. To create the texture maps, Photoshop is widely used in the 3D graphics industry. During my stint at Industrial Light and Magic, creating skins that would be applied to a 3D geometry was one of my duties. Most applications come bundled with a wide range of preconfigured textures that can be applied to an object, such as wood grains, marble swirls, and so on. In most cases, the programs also enable you to completely alter the presets and create new textures.

Facades that have a bit more detail require a texture map. Figures 8 through 10 have three views of an example of a 3D geometry with the texture maps applied. These were created by Illustrator and Media Designer, and an old friend of mine, Nathan Moody. Figure 11 shows the basic art for the texture map that he created in Photoshop. Figure 12 shows the details added in various layers to the Photoshop file.

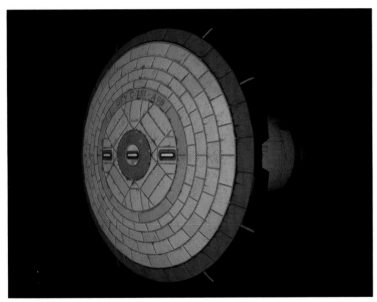

8 This is a three-quarter view of a spacecraft generated in a 3D application.

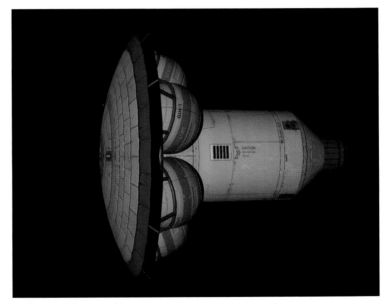

9 This is a side view of the same spacecraft.

10 This is a three-quarter, rear view of the spacecraft.

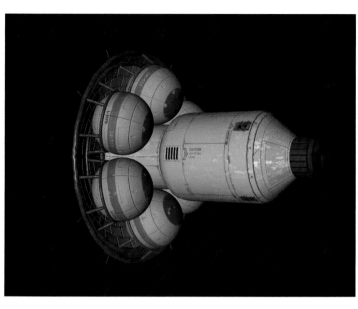

11 This is the basic art that Nathan created to serve as the texture map or skin that covered the surface of the shield of the spacecraft.

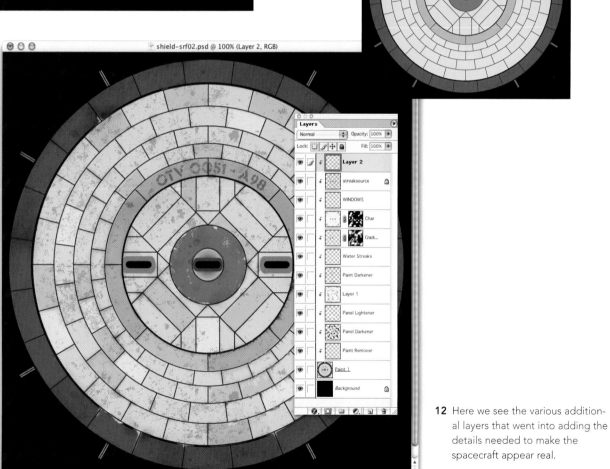

12 Here we see the various additional layers that went into adding the details needed to make the spacecraft appear real.

Bump Maps

There are several additional "maps" that go into a 3D object. Bump maps are used to give the surface of an object roughness or bumpiness. The 3D programs use the luminosity values (lights and darks) of an image to determine the height of the bumps on a surface. A 50% gray represents the ground plane and has no effect on the object. Lighter tones create bumps on the surface, whereas darker tones create dents.

Figure 13 shows the bump map Nathan created to add a three-dimensional texture to the shield surface on the spacecraft. This surface texture reacts to the light source being directed toward it. The brick-like pattern is almost white, which will make the plates on the shield raise off the surface. The gray tones on the plate shapes will act as dents on the surface of the plates. The black lines in between the plates will be deep insets.

Figure 14 shows a close-up of the fuel tanks. Here a texture map was used for the surface material and a bump map was used to create the indented areas and the separations between plates. Figure 15 shows the texture map of the fuel tanks, and Figure 16 shows the bump map. Notice that the gray rectangles and circles are making indented areas on the surface of the tanks. The black lines are creating a separation on the surface as if there are individual plates fitted together to form the spheres.

NOTE
Compare the usage of tones in the bump map (Figure 16) to the final rendering (Figure 14).

13 This is the image that was used as the bump map by the 3D application to roughen the surface of the shield. This gives a textured surface that simulates the dents from wear and tear on the spacecraft.

Reflection Maps

The 3D world has many more kinds of maps. Reflection maps are images mapped onto the 3D surface to create the illusion of a reflection of the surrounding environment. All of these maps are created in Photoshop, but how they are applied depends on the 3D application.

14 The actual surfaces of the fuel tanks have indented areas as well as separations between the plates.

15 Here we see the texture map or skin of the fuel tanks. This is like the paint on the tank.

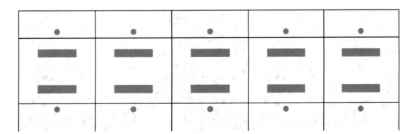

16 This is the bump map that created the indents and separations between the plates on the fuel tanks.

Creating the Various Types of Maps Used in 3D Software

Figure 17 is one of my early experiments, involving some stock textures and others that were created in Photoshop.

The table in the center of the room is an example of a wood grain that was generated within a 3D program. It appears fairly believable but can't compare with the materials for the other objects in the room that were imported textures from Photoshop.

The floor is an elaborate work of inlaid marble sections. I started by opening a series of stock photo marble texture images in Photoshop (Figure 18). Then, in Illustrator, I created a path for every section of the floor that had a different kind of marble (Figure 19). I then imported these into Photoshop via Copy and Paste. In Photoshop the paths were separated into the individual segments of the floor (Figure 20) so that they could be filled with a solid color to act as a mask for clipping the marble textures.

Figure 21 shows the assembled floor in Photoshop. This image was then imported into the 3D program—which, for reasons I'll discuss momentarily, I will not name—and wrapped onto the plane that served as the room floor.

Making the floor highly reflective, within the 3D program, makes it look as if it is made of polished marble. The same original marble images were used for the columns that surround the room.

The urn sitting atop the table also has a texture map that is shown in Figure 22. This image for a texture map was made by creating a simple border design in Illustrator and, in Photoshop, adding some gold and white stripes that surround an imported stock image of Venice.

17 This is an experimental scene generated in a 3D application.

17a The wood texture of the table was generated using the material editor that comes with the 3D software. It lacks the realism of the rest of the scene, which used textures created in Photoshop

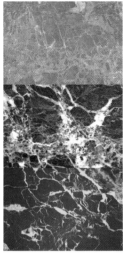

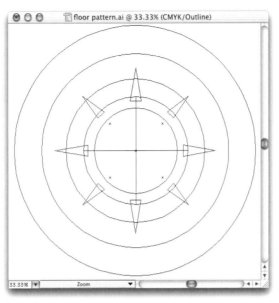

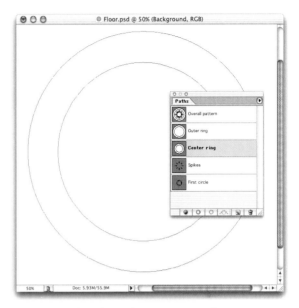

18 Various stock photo marble textures were used to make the texture map for the floor.

19 The paths to form the pattern on the floor were created in Illustrator.

20 In Photoshop the paths were separated into individual paths for each segment of the floor.

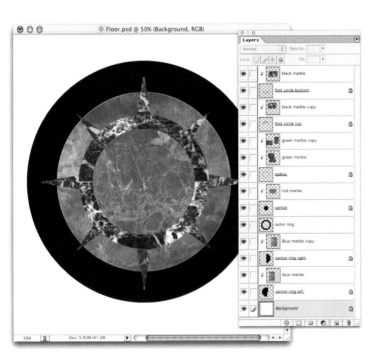

21 The Illustrator paths were turned into selections in Photoshop to clip the marble textures to form the design.

22 This is the texture map used to cover the vase on the table.

Designing in 3D

Photoshop and the 3D programs work hand in hand for mutual benefit, just as Illustrator and Photoshop do. You've just seen how small elements created in Photoshop can improve the quality of jobs that seem to cry out to be done exclusively in a 3D program. And, even when a large job is to be executed primarily in Photoshop, small elements created in a 3D application can often result in faster and more accurate compositing.

So let's take a look at some interesting uses of 3D elements within Photoshop images.

I will not name any 3D package in this chapter so as not to bias you toward any particular product. Some of you will undoubtedly recognize the interface of the programs used. Keep in mind that it is the concepts behind the examples rather than the actual working application that is important here.

The world of 3D software is filled with many players. Some products are very complex with price tags to match. Others are intended for the novice or amateur user who does not need all the bells and whistles of the higher-end programs.

A good friend commissioned me to come up with an image for a dark, dirty street scene. The project was for a game web site for the late Lisa (Left-Eye) Lopes. In the web site there were many worlds of different colors and atmospheres that the player would travel through to get information and samples of Ms. Lopes's latest album. I was asked to create a scene for the dark red world where the viewer is looking down a big city street. Figure 23 shows the final image.

All the many buildings and details had to be rendered and all had to conform to proper perspective to make the scene believable. A building originally created for the foreground would not appear in proper perspective if it were suddenly moved back a few blocks and across the street.

23 This image was part of a web site game.

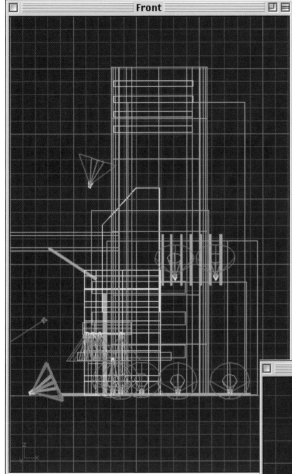

24 The 3D geometry for one of the buildings in the scene.

I decided to make the shapes within a 3D environment because I wanted to have the freedom to arrange and rearrange the various shapes to compose entire city blocks. It also gave me the flexibility to play with different shapes for the buildings before committing them to the scene. Creating the proper 3D perspective within the 2D environments of Photoshop and Illustrator would have greatly limited my ability to reposition buildings and other objects.

Figure 24 shows one of the basic building shapes that I created in my 3D application. The blue cones scattered throughout represent light sources. They are used to illuminate certain areas and cast shadows on others.

Figure 25 shows the right-side view of the same building in Figure 24 along with three of its neighbors that were constructed similarly.

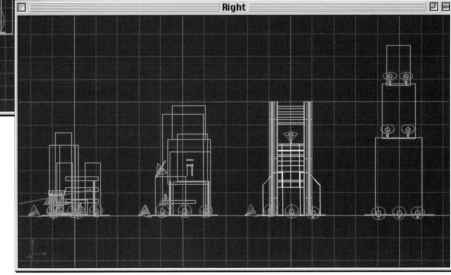

25 Buildings were placed side by side along a city avenue.

Figure 26 shows the Camera view. Remembering that 3D applications enable us to render the same scene from different points of view, this, for the time being at least, is the view that will be rendered after all the elements have been put in place. Once again, the blue cones are light sources that have been placed at strategic places throughout the scene.

Another great advantage of working in a 3D application is the reusability of elements. The individual parts of each building can easily be copied and used on other buildings. The columns in Figure 27, for example, were copied and rotated to form the details of some of the other buildings indicated by the arrows.

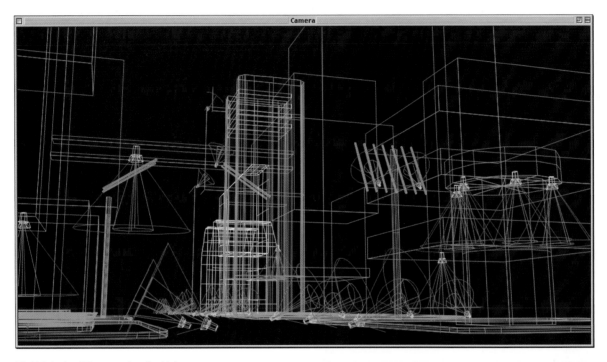

26 This is the "Camera view," which establishes the viewer's position for the scene

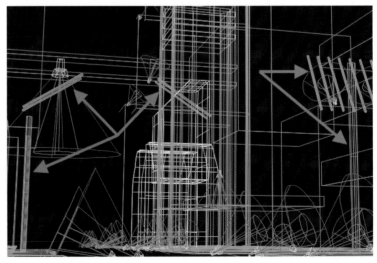

27 Objects created in a 3D space can be cloned and modified to fit in other situations.

Adding the Textures in Photoshop

After all the various buildings were completed, they were placed onto a grid of city blocks. Figure 28 has the Top view that shows the buildings as they have been placed into the actual city blocks. Many of the blocks are still empty. As mentioned before, some lighting was set in the 3D program to lighten certain facades and create the necessary shadows. Texture mapping was not used in this image because I was planning on doing that directly in Photoshop. I also did not want to have to set up all the lighting within the buildings necessary for the look and feel of windows. This would all add to the rendering time that it would take for the 3D program to produce the final image.

Now it was time to start the final, time-consuming rendering of the buildings. The more detail the 3D models contain, the longer they will take to render. The computer must figure out what the light sources are doing to the scene, how the shadows will fall, and so on. Each individual city block was rendered separately (Figure 29). Each element could then be placed in a separate layer within Photoshop. Figure 30, a Photoshop file, shows all the buildings in place, before details were added.

29 This is the render of the building in the foreground across the street from the viewer.

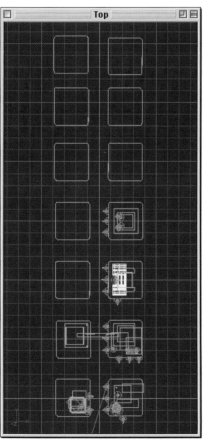

28 The buildings are arranged into city blocks on a grid.

30 This is the composite within Photoshop of all the buildings in position.

Dark red city.psd @ 63.4% (Background, RGB)

100%   Doc: 8.79M/8.72M

31 A close-up of the doorway visible on the lower right of the final scene in Figure 23.

To add credibility to the final composite, I turned to some stock photos. Figure 31, taken from the area at the lower right of the final image, shows the details of the door and surrounding area. Figure 32 shows the stock image from which the door and steel drum were taken. Figure 33 shows the image from where all the window details of the taller buildings were taken.

NOTE

The methodology used to add the details to the buildings is discussed in detail in Chapter 4. Although I use other examples, the concepts are the same.

32 This is the stock image that was used to provide some of the details for the doorway in Figure 31.

33 This is one of the images that provided the windows for the buildings.

Incorporating 3D Elements into Photoshop Images

I relied on a 3D program to create part of the art for Private File, a software package for Aladdin Systems. The idea was to show a secure package. An oversized lock system over a simple mailing envelope was what the ad agency asked me to create. Figure 34 shows the final art. I turned to a 3D application to help establish the look and impact of the image. Being able to view the object from different angles enabled me to experiment with different views to get the most dramatic angle needed for the final art.

Figure 35 shows four different views of the model in progress. This is typical of 3D programs, which allow many different views of the objects to help us make the right decision as to where they should be placed. The Camera view (upper right in Figure 35) is the scene as from the camera. Some 3D applications give you multiple lens settings for the camera just like in a photography studio. Different lenses on a camera will give you different distortions or expand the viewing area as with a "wide-angle lens." Lens settings in the 3D application will simulate the real-world camera lenses and re-create the effects.

34 The final art for Private File, a software product by Aladdin Systems.

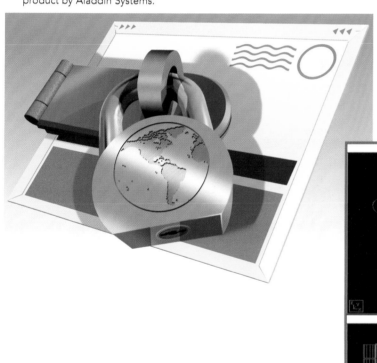

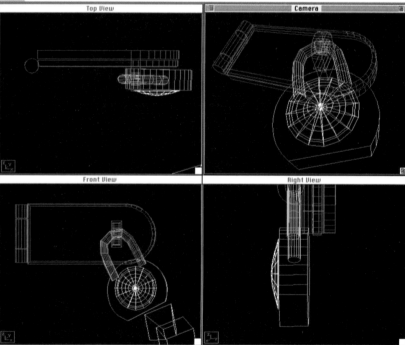

35 3D programs give you multiple views to facilitate navigation in a 3D environment. Here we see four views of the geometry for the lock mechanism in the image.

In this case the surface materials available in the 3D program were used to create the properties. Figure 36 shows the dialog box where surface materials can be modified.

Note that there are red lines within the art that indicate that the bolt section of the lock is currently selected. The Surface Info window reflects the material for the currently selected object. Because the bolt is made of shiny metal, the Reflectiveness attribute is

boosted while Transparency is set to 0. In this particular program, a preview of the material is available on the upper right of the dialog box.

Setting this reflectivity higher guaranteed that the other portions of the lock mechanism would be properly reflected in the bolt, eliminating the need for me to illustrate them. Because the envelope was not part of the 3D elements, I created the reflection of the envelope, visible at the bottom of the lock, in Photoshop (Figure 37).

36 This is a surface generator from one of the many 3D applications available on the market.

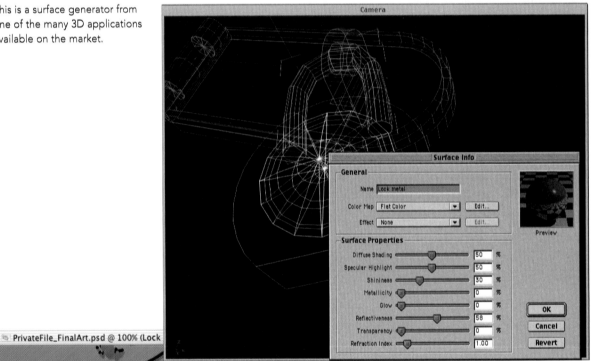

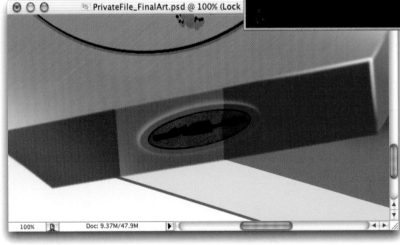

37 The reflection of the envelope is visible on the bottom of the lock. This effect was added in Photoshop following the rendering of the lock in a 3D program.

Figure 38 has the bottom of the lock without the reflection. The shape for the bottom of the lock was selected and copied into its own layer. It was then filled with a simple gradient. Figure 39 shows that the layer of the envelope has been duplicated and rotated to mimic the way the reflection would appear. That layer is clipped by the layer of the bottom of the lock and lowered in opacity.

The keyhole visible at the bottom of the lock (Figure 37) was originally created as a set of paths in Illustrator as seen in Figure 40. The paths were used in Photoshop to fill areas with appropriate colors. The actual keyhole was filled with black.

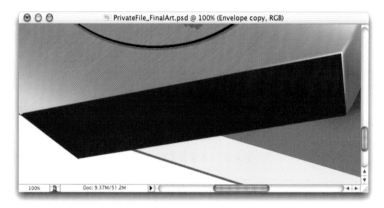

38 The bottom of the lock was copied into a separate layer and the shape filled with a simple gradient.

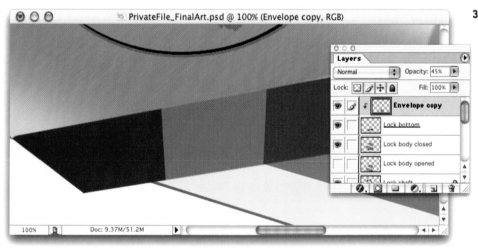

39 The layer with the bottom of the lock was used to clip the layer containing the rotated duplicate of the envelope.

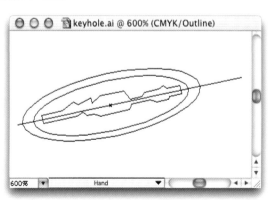

40 The shape for the keyhole was generated in Illustrator.

Using 3D to Study Shadow Effects

Complex elements often need to be added to make the final art believable.

The image "Verbum Be-In 8" was commissioned for a poster announcing a Digital Be-In event (Figure 41). The client wanted a Moübius strip in a circus-like setting with colored spotlights hitting it from all sides. The shadows cast from these light sources would take the shape of a figure 8.

Due to the abstract nature of the image itself, I could not create the image in a 3D program, but I turned to a 3D program to create the needed study.

When an object is lit from multiple sides, the resulting shadows affect each other.

In this situation, there are not only multiple light sources, but also multiple colors for the lights. The shadow shapes were actual font type number 8s that were blurred and distorted so as to seem to fall onto the background as shadows would.

Determining what color the shadows would have been required some research. Before the computer, I usually had to construct elaborate sets, lit with colored gel covered lights to study the effects. Computer-generated 3D renderings have simplified this process.

I created some simple colored objects within the 3D program. I added light sources that were colored the way I needed and positioned them to hit the objects from the same directions as were required for the poster scene. The program computed the results and gave me a reference from which to choose the colors I needed (Figure 42).

3D programs export their final art in a variety of formats that Photoshop can read. I therefore opened Figure 41 in Photoshop and used the Eyedropper Tool to sample each critical color area. Then, I filled the corresponding area in my Moübius strip image with that color.

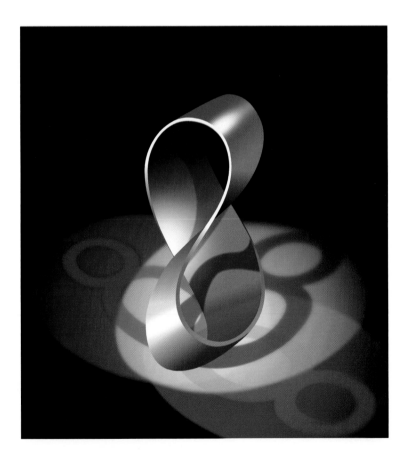

41 In the image "Verbum Be-In 8," the client wanted a Moübius strip in a circus-like setting with colored spotlights hitting it from all sides. The shadows cast from these light sources would take the shape of a figure 8.

The five images that we've worked on in this chapter were in a progression that showed how Photoshop and the 3D applications interrelate in a sensible workflow. We started with Nathan's spacecraft, which would have been, in my opinion, impossible to execute without a 3D program, although Photoshop offered some assistance. Then we studied the room with a marble floor and the artificial city. I suppose that either could have been done totally in Photoshop and Illustrator, but they would have been fiendishly difficult, beyond the capability of all but the most expert Photoshop artists. If done totally in a 3D program without the aid of

Photoshop, however, neither image would have reached the same quality level. Finally, the lock and envelope image, followed by the Moübius strip. To be honest, I could have executed either with the Photoshop/Illustrator combination alone, but it would have taken several times as long.

Through the years, these 3D applications have become very sophisticated. There are no areas of visual communication where they have not been included in one form or another. The beauty of it all is that as a Photoshop artist, these programs have opened up new avenues for income and just plain fun.

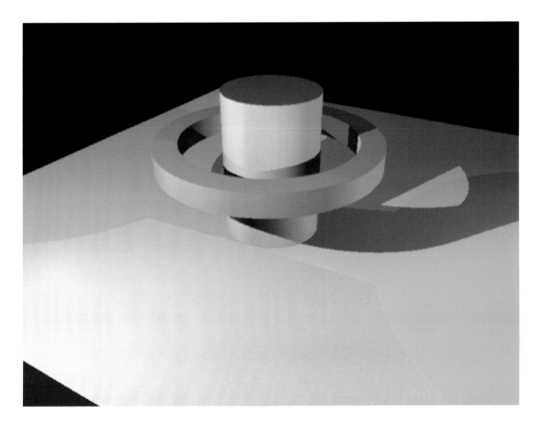

42 In a 3D program, I created some simple objects as reference. I added light sources that were colored the way I needed and positioned them to hit the objects from the same directions as were required for the poster scene. The program computed the results and gave me a reference for lights and shadows to use for the colors I needed.

A Magazine for Realtors

The chapters in this second part of the book put it all together. Here, through a series of case studies, we examine in a step-by-step fashion the process I go through to create a completed image. What I cover here is what happens after the client has approved the layout and given me the go ahead to complete the art.

Many different techniques are demonstrated and should be studied for the process and not necessarily the context in which they are used. You may never have to create a moldy bathroom tile, but the steps used to create it might apply to some particular challenge you have before you.

You may just need a change in color or use a different setting in a filter to completely change the mood. Consider this chapter a "mix-and-match" game, in which the goal is to find the solution to an imaging problem you might have on your screen right now. Same steps, different content, different end result.

I have divided the chapters in the second part into sections that pertain to specific jobs. I will first present the final art and then take you through all the steps I went through to create it. Some photographs are involved, but they are very easy to replace. By following the steps, you should be able to reproduce a similar end result yourself.

The main thing is to learn and have fun in the process.

The Assignment: Make It Look Bad

I was commissioned by a magazine to create a series of illustrations of things to look for when purchasing a house. This was particularly interesting to me because it was a departure from the usual work that comes my way. Most often I am asked to make things look good. "Make it look pretty!"

This assignment was to make things look bad, really bad. I was given four illustrations to create. I cover three of these in this chapter: a moldy bathroom tub and wall, lead paint pealing off a window sill, and a hazardous walkway. This project presented a great challenge for my skills and a taxing situation that would require the use of just about every Photoshop feature.

All the comps submitted to the client were created in Illustrator as shapes that were stroked with thin, black lines. These Illustrator files were imported into Photoshop as pixels and saved as JPEGs for easy transmission through email.

Moldy Bathtub

Figure 1 shows the final art I created to represent a moldy bathroom tub. It seems the seller of this house never heard of cleansers. Nevertheless, this is what I had to create.

1 This is the final art for an illustration that depicts a moldy bathroom tub.

The client had a good visual sense, so the comp that I sent her was just to show layout. Color was not necessary. Figure 2 shows the comp that was sent to her via email for approval. I prepared the comp in Illustrator by creating the various paths for the shapes and stroking them in black.

I decided to re-create a view that a person would have if inspecting such a scene—looking from the outside, down into the tub. The perspective lines that I gave the wall tiles direct the viewer's eyes into the scene, drawing attention to the mold.

The client liked what she saw and gave me the go-ahead to start the final art. To make the comp, I had to create a basic set of paths. These were now imported, via Copy and Paste, into Photoshop as paths (Figure 3).

When you import paths in this fashion, Photoshop gives you options on how the paths will be read. Figure 3 shows the dialog box that pops up when the Paste command is chosen. The first choice is Pixels. This method converts any attributes you may have assigned to the paths in Illustrator, such as stroke weight and fill colors, into pixels that display those attributes.

The second choice is Paths. This is the one I used in this case because I hadn't used Illustrator to assign the complicated fills and strokes I would eventually want, thinking that this could be better accomplished in Photoshop.

The third choice is Shape Layer. This creates a regular Vector layer that will be filled with the currently selected foreground color with the path as the mask. The shape of the path created in this type of layer is filled with the color of the layer. Figure 3a shows a Shape, or Vector layer. The Foreground color, in the Tool palette, is set to blue, so the color of the layer is blue. The Layer palette shows the path next to the color thumbnail.

Because this is a path, it can be modified at any time. Because it is a layer, the color can also be modified at any time. Your manual has a good description of this feature if you still do not fully understand it.

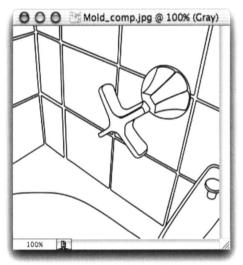

2 This is the comp supplied to the client.

3 When importing elements from Illustrator into Photoshop, you are given a choice of how the data will be read.

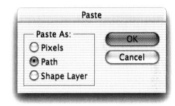

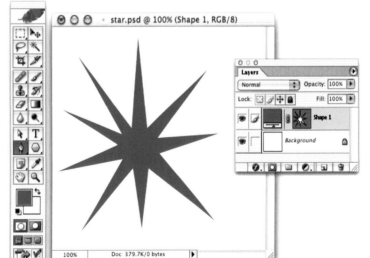

3a A Vector layer is filled with the currently selected foreground color and uses the vector, or path, for that layer as a mask for where the blue will be seen.

Back to our project. With the Pen Tool, I refined the paths and added a few more for the details as seen in Figure 4.

I separated the paths for each of the elements (spigot, walls, and so on). This was done by duplicating the path and then eliminating the unwanted paths, leaving behind only the paths necessary for each element. Figure 5 shows the Path palette with the individual sets of paths.

Creating Wall Tiles

First to be tackled were the walls. The paths for the walls were turned into an unfeathered selection (Figure 6). A new layer was created to house the walls. This was done by clicking the Make New Layer icon at the bottom of the Layer's palette.

A light yellow was selected for the foreground color with a slightly darker version of the same yellow selected for the background color. Using the Gradient Tool on the new layer I just made, I applied a gradient to the selection (Figure 7).

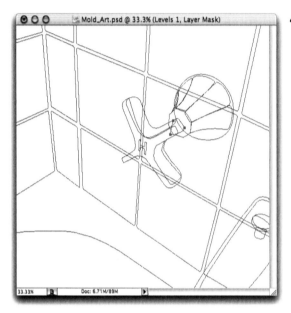

4 These are the paths in the Photoshop document.

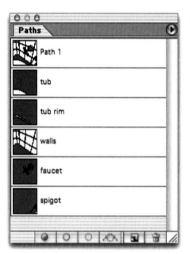

5 The paths were separated into the individual paths for each of the elements.

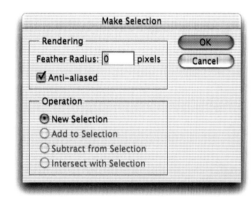

6 The Make Selection dialog box, accessed through the Path's palette.

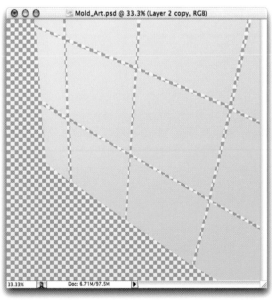

7 The paths for the wall tiles were loaded as a selection and filled with a gradient.

A little texture was needed to make the tiles look real. The Add Noise filter was applied (Filter > Noise > Add Noise) as seen in Figure 8. The Facet filter was applied (Filter > Pixelate > Facet). This filter has no dialog box. It just expands the noise into small, faceted shapes that look more like the texture of ceramic wall tiles. The noise added the randomization that Facet used to texturize the entire area of the tiles.

I next added dimension to make the tiles look as if they were protruding from the wall's surface rather than just painted onto it. Layer Styles did the trick. Double-clicking on the wall layer in the Layers palette brought up the Layer Style dialog box. First, a slight drop shadow was added (Figure 9). This automatically separated the tiles from the wall and made them look three-dimensional.

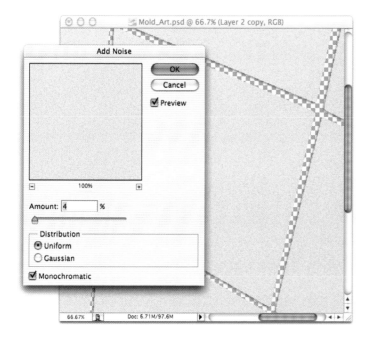

8 The Add Noise filter was applied to the wall tiles.

9 The tiles are given a Layer Style of Drop Shadow.

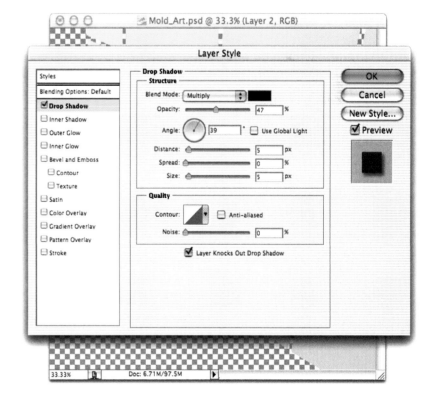

The next task was to make the tiles appear as if the edges were rounded rather that sharp. The Layer Styles of Inner Shadow (Figure 10) and Inner Glow (Figure 11) accomplished this effect. The tiles now had the look of real wall tiles as shown in Figure 12.

A new layer was created behind the layer with the tiles for the grout between the tiles. I filled this layer with light gray. The Add Noise filter gave it the necessary grain to appear realistic (Figure 13).

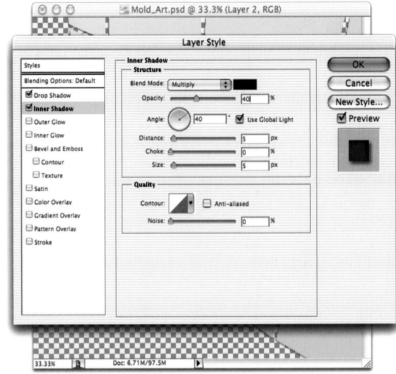

10 The tiles are given a Layer Style of Inner Shadow.

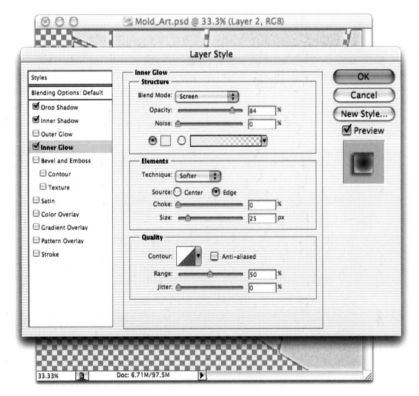

11 The tiles are given a Layer Style of Inner Glow.

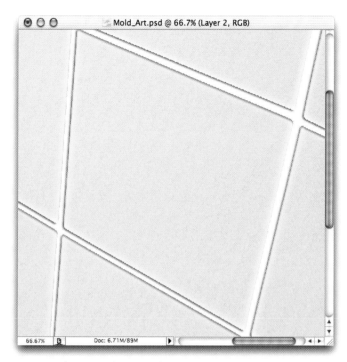

12 A combination of Layer Styles gives the tiles dimension.

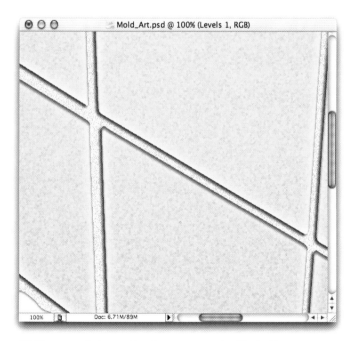

13 The space between the tiles appears to be filled with grout.

Creating a Chrome Spigot

The hardware visible in the image was a bit more involved. For one thing, it was made of polished metal, so I had to create reflections. In a new layer, the path for the spigot was filled with a basic gray tone (Figure 14). Most of the area would be covered with other tones and reflections, so the particular gray chosen was not critical.

Transparency was locked for the layer to ensure that any tones painted on the spigot would stay within that shape. With a soft-edged Paintbrush Tool, I added some tones to the edges of the spigot as seen in Figure 15. These tones added sheen and the hint of reflections to the edge of the spigot.

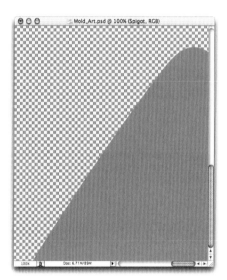

14 In a new layer, a shape is created and filled with gray to represent the spigot.

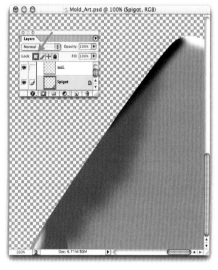

15 The Transparency for the layer is locked. With the Paintbrush Tool, some tones are added to the edges to serve as reflections.

In a new layer, a small white patch was created at the lower right of the image (Figure 16). This layer was to be the right side of the spigot. Neither the shape nor the color used was crucial. It merely served as a shape to clip another layer that would have a reflection in it.

To make the reflection, I needed a layer that had all the wall tiles in it merged. However, I also wanted to keep all the original layers of the wall intact. To do that, I made all the layers that made up the wall visible and turned off the Eye icon for all the other layers to make them invisible. I then created another layer. With that new, blank layer selected as the active layer, I chose Merge Visible (Figure 17) from the Layer palette submenu with the Option (Alt on a PC) button pressed. All the layers that made up the wall were merged into the new layer while leaving all the original layers untouched.

NOTE

Merge Visible merges all layers currently visible (Eye icon is on) into the currently selected layer. It overwrites the layer that is selected. This is why I created a new layer to house the merged elements.

The layer that contained the merged wall was then distorted to appear like a reflection on the metal spigot. I selected that layer and went into the Liquify filter (Filter > Liquify). Using the Warp Tool in Liquify, I distorted the wall as seen in Figure 18.

The distorted layer was then darkened using the Hue/Saturation command (Image > Adjustments > Hue/Saturation) and placed in position over the edge of the spigot (Figure 19).

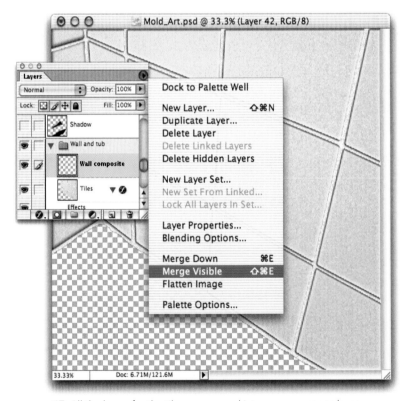

16 A small white shape is painted to serve as the basic shape for the side of the spigot.

17 All the layers for the tiles are merged into a new separate layer.

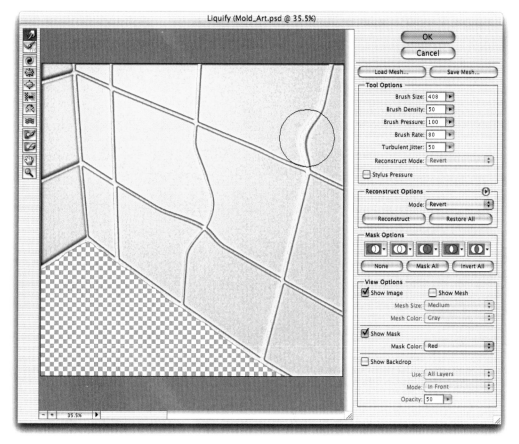

18 The layer with the merged tile layers is distorted with the Liquify command.

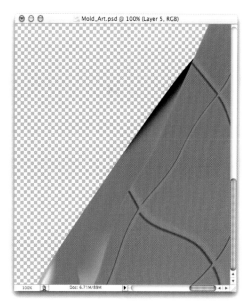

19 The distorted layer is darkened and placed in position over the edge of the spigot.

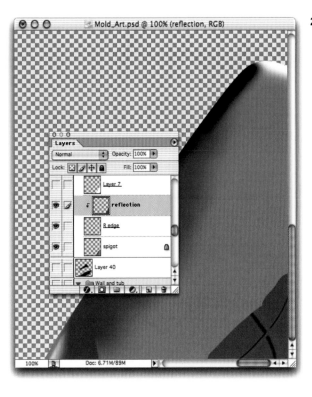

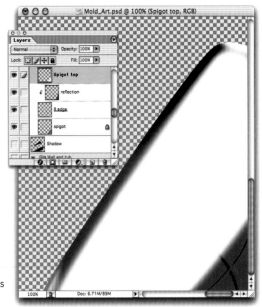

20 The distorted layer of the tiles is clipped by the layer with the white shape for the side of the spigot.

21 A shape to represent the top of the spigot is created in a layer.

I then used the white shape that I had painted in Figure 16 to clip the distorted tiles by establishing a layer Clipping Group (Figure 20). For an explanation of how a Clipping Group works, see Chapter 1.

A similar procedure was used for the top of the spigot. The main difference is that in this case, the shape is important. Using the Pen Tool, the shape was carefully drawn and filled with white on a separate layer (Figure 21).

The layer with the distorted wall was duplicated and clipped with the layer containing the top of the spigot as seen in Figure 22. I also lightened this second layer of reflection to conform to the overall lighting of the scene. In most bathrooms, the lighting comes from the ceiling, and this was the effect I was trying to achieve. Because the top of the spigot is closer to this theoretical light source than the right edge is, it stands to reason it should appear slightly lighter.

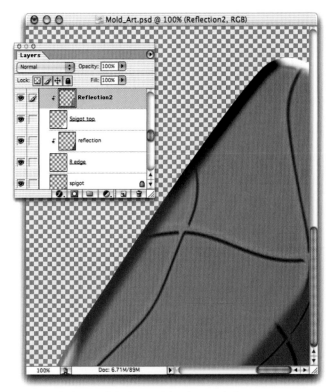

22 A duplicate of the layer of the distorted tiles is clipped by the layer of the spigot top.

A few additional highlights were needed to make the chrome look shiny. I chose the Paintbrush Tool with a round brush tip and manipulated the Fade option (Figure 23). This sets a point at which the Paintbrush seems to run out of paint. I set the Foreground color to white and clicked where I wanted the streak of light to begin. I then Shift-clicked where I wanted the streak of light to end (Figure 24).

NOTE

Shift-clicking with any of the tools that can be used to stroke (Paintbrush, Eraser, Clone, and so on) connects the first click to the second click, thus creating a straight line between them.

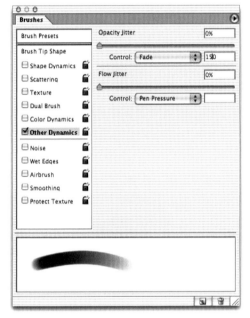

23 The Paintbrush Tool is assigned a Fade amount.

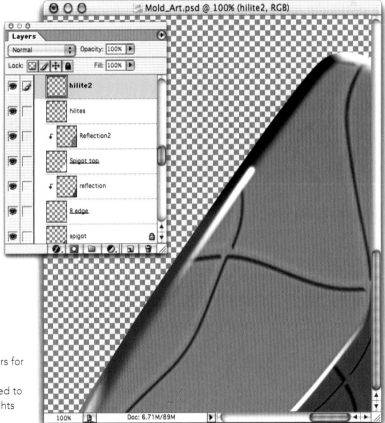

24 In separate layers for each highlight, streaks are added to simulate highlights on the chrome.

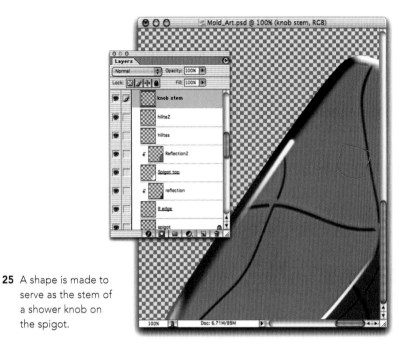

25 A shape is made to serve as the stem of a shower knob on the spigot.

Creating the Shower Pull Knob

Next came the shower pull knob on top of the spigot. I created a new layer that I named "Knob stem" to start forming the knob. A small path was outlined with the Pen Tool to serve as the shape for the stem of the knob (Figure 25). The path was made into a selection and filled with a gray tone. Using various paintbrush sizes and different tones of gray, I painted some highlights and reflections onto the stem (Figure 26).

A new layer was created and called "Knob edge." This was to be the edge visible along the side of the knob. As with the stem, a path was created, filled, and stroked with various tones to simulate reflections and highlights (Figure 27).

26 The shape is filled with gray. Reflections and shadows are added with the Paintbrush Tool.

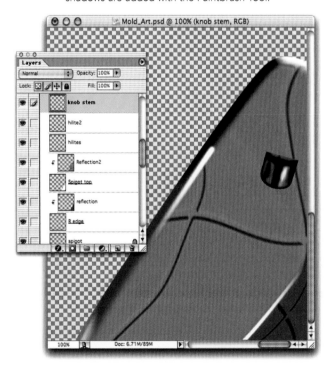

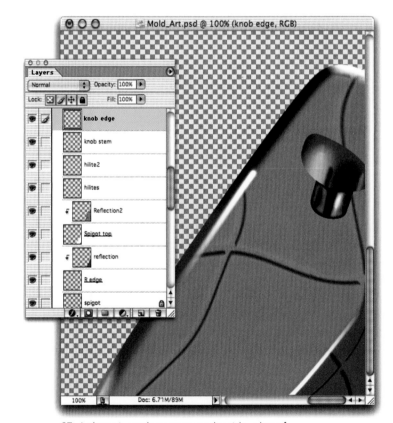

27 A shape is made to serve as the side edge of the knob.

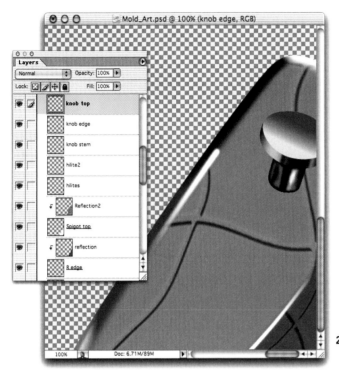

In Figure 28, we see a new layer called "Knob top." A disc shape was made with the Pen Tool and filled with a gradient.

I wanted a bright edge along the top. The Layer Style Inner Glow simulates this effect, but it applies it to the entire edge. I wanted the highlight only along the top. The Layer Style Inner Shadow works along one edge, so I chose that style. Because it was a highlight I was after, I changed the color from black to white and the Blend mode from Multiply to Screen (Figure 29). Figure 30 shows the result of the layer style giving the top edge of the knob a highlight.

28 The top of the knob is added.

29 The top of the knob is given a Layer Style of Inner Shadow. The color and mode are changed so the style acts as a glow rather than a shadow.

30 Here we see the result of the Layer Style.

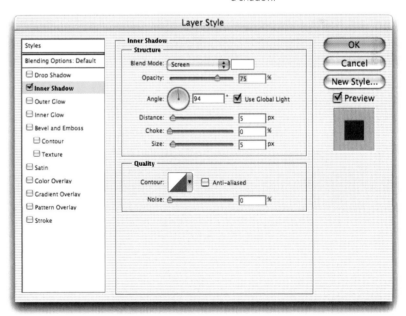

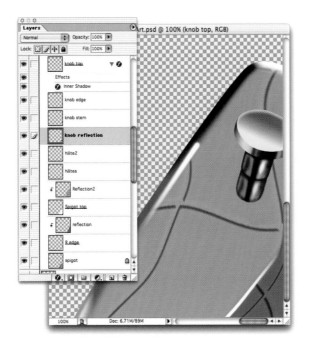

31 The stem is duplicated and repositioned to serve as part of the reflection of the knob on the spigot.

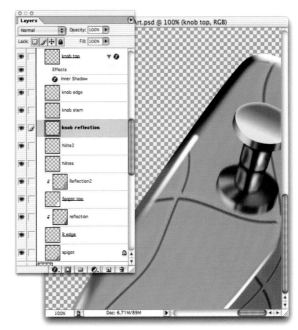

32 The top of the knob is duplicated and altered to serve as the reflection and blurred slightly with the Motion Blur filter.

The layer that contained the Knob stem was duplicated. It was renamed "Knob reflection" and repositioned to appear below the original stem (Figure 31).

The layer with the knob top was also duplicated, repositioned, and placed below the reflection of the stem. Some alterations were made to the shadows and highlights. I then merged it into the layer of Knob reflection and gave it a slight Motion Blur filter to soften the look (Filter > Blur > Motion Blur). Figure 32 shows a convincing reflection of the knob.

As with the other flat surfaces of the spigot, a duplicate of the layer of the distorted wall reflection was clipped into the top of the knob (Figure 33).

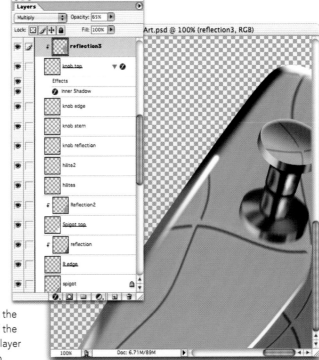

33 A duplicate layer with the distorted reflection of the wall is clipped by the layer of the top of the knob.

Creating Water Drops

Moisture was next. It was necessary to show drops of water sitting atop the spigot. In a new layer called "drops," I used a hard-edged paintbrush to create a bunch of shapes that would eventually be turned into drops of water (Figure 34). The color was inconsequential because it would never be seen in the final image. The entire effect would be created in the Layer Style window.

34 In a layer, a bunch of spots are created to serve as droplets of water sitting on the spigot.

35 The drops are given a Layer Style of Drop Shadow.

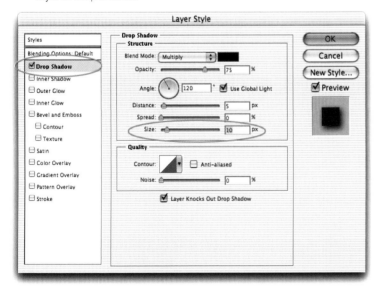

Sometimes an ounce of real-world experimentation is worth a pound of Photoshop adventuring. I sprinkled a few drops of water on a flat piece of plastic and studied the way light reacted with the water so that I could re-create it in Photoshop. The first thing I noticed is that even though water is transparent, it does have mass, which will cast a shadow. I therefore double-clicked the drops layer to bring up the Layer Style window for it. The first choice was Drop Shadow (Figure 35). I increased the size slightly.

It is important to note here that none of these effects will be noticeable until the very last Layer Style. The best way to get an idea of what is happening in the figures that correspond to this exercise is to look at the small preview icon on the right side of the dialog box.

Next came the effect of adding a slight shadow inside the drops. I chose Inner Shadow (Figure 36). I set the Blend mode to Overlay to darken some of the tones in the layers below the make up the spigot.

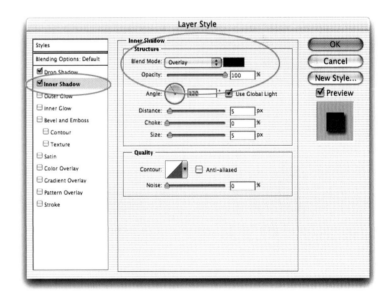

36 The drops are given a Layer Style of Inner Shadow with the Blend mode set to Overlay.

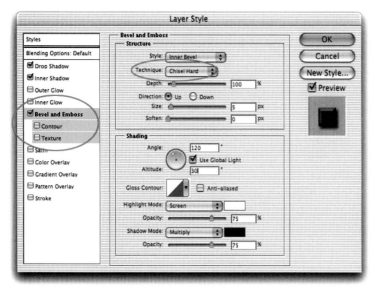

37 The Layer Style of Bevel and Emboss is modified.

Next came Bevel and Emboss (Figure 37). This is where the main action was to take place. To create the effect that the water drops were rounded, I chose Chisel Hard. Sounds like the opposite, but with a few modifications ... well, you'll see.

I pushed the Depth up to a high amount. This would intensify the lights and darks produced to form the chisel. I then pushed up the Soften amount to blur out the chisel effect (Figure 38).

I then played with the lighting for the bevel. I set the Angle to 90 degrees so that the light source was from above and the Altitude to 20 degrees for a slight angle to the light (Figure 39). Because the Use Global Light was checked, this automatically set those parameters to all the other Layer Styles.

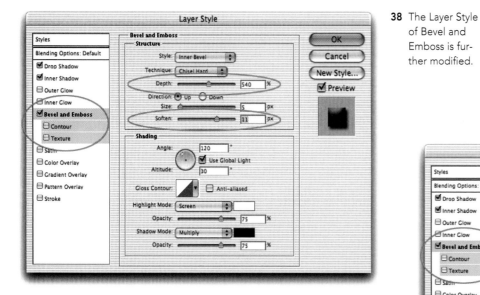

38 The Layer Style of Bevel and Emboss is further modified.

39 The Layer Style of Bevel and Emboss is further modified.

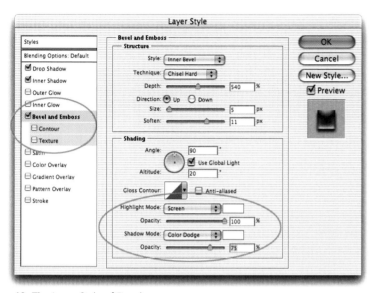

40 The Layer Style of Bevel and Emboss is given its final modification.

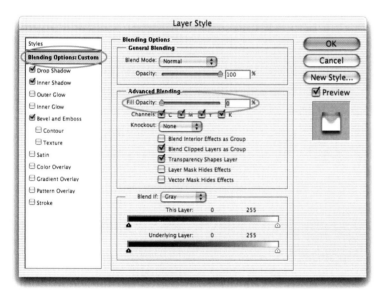

41 The blending options are modified in the Layer Style.

Now, to get that total liquid feeling a few more modifications were needed. I pushed the Highlight to 100%. The Shadow mode was another story. I already had shadows working in my drops. What I needed was the color intensification I had witnessed in the real drops I was studying. I changed the color to white and the mode to Color Dodge (Figure 40). This was going to have the affect on the underlying layers that I was looking for.

Finally, it was time to do something about the original black color used to make the drops. I went into the Blending Options: Custom, a section of the Layer Style window. Notice in Figure 41 that there are two opacity settings at the top. Opacity deals with the entire layer. Bringing down the amount makes the layer transparent, enabling you to see the layers underneath it.

Fill Opacity deals with the actual pixels that are in the layer, which in this case, are the black drops. Pulling back on this opacity setting will make the black of the drops fade while leaving all the Layer Styles untouched. I pulled it all the way back to 0.

The result was a realistic bunch of water drops sitting on top of the spigot as seen in Figure 42.

42 Several Layer Style modifications result in the final realistic water drops.

Creating Mold

The mold required a different approach. The power of the Brush palette, first introduced in Photoshop 7, gave me the tools to tackle this problem. For my intended use of the Paintbrush Tool, I chose a Spatter brush (Figure 43).

As you can see in the preview area of the Brushes palette in Figure 43, the brush in its default state would not work for the desired effect—a little modification was called for. First, I increased the Spacing setting to 25% to emphasize the irregularity in the brush stroke (Figure 44).

I went into the Shape Dynamics section of the palette for some additional modifications. I set an amount to the Size Jitter so that the brush tip would vary in size. The Control was set to Pen Pressure. The Minimum Diameter was not set, which meant that the brush could be very small. These three settings (Figure 45) would enable me to create a thin line when I pressed lightly on the tablet, which I use in preference to a mouse, and a large brush when I applied more pressure. Photoshop's pressure-sensitivity is a good argument in favor of using such a tablet for this type of work.

I also set the Angle Jitter to 100% so that the brush tip would twirl randomly as the stroke is applied, adding further randomization to the look of the stroke.

43 Spatter brush tip is selected from the Brushes palette.

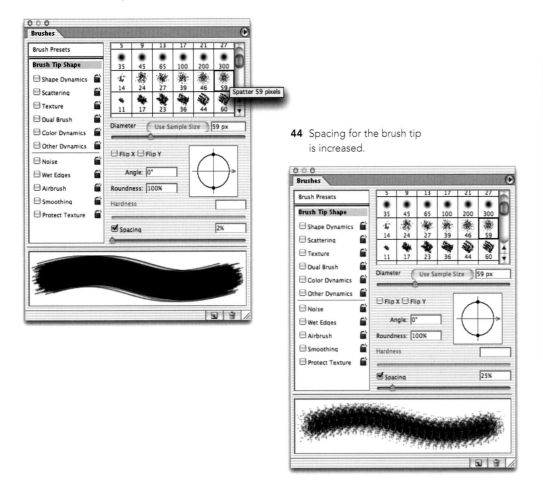

44 Spacing for the brush tip is increased.

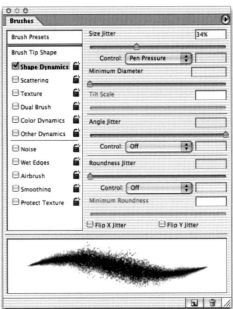

45 The Shape Dynamics are modified.

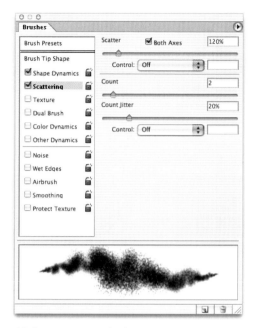

46 Scattering is applied to the brush tip.

Then I added Scattering to the brush (Figure 46). This moves the tiny brush tips in random directions away from the center of the stroke. I also increased the Count, which makes the stroke denser, but added Count Jitter to make the effect more random.

I created a new layer to contain the mold. With this brush, I started to apply the first touches of mold to the tiles on the wall (Figure 47).

For the extra-added touch of old, dry mold all over the tiles, I made one more modification to the brush—I went into Color Dynamics. Here I set the Foreground/Background Jitter to 100%. This meant the brush would switch between the two colors set for the foreground and background. I increased the Hue and Saturation levels to add randomization (Figure 48). Unfortunately, the Brushes window does not display the color settings in the preview at the bottom as it does with all the other settings.

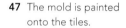

47 The mold is painted onto the tiles.

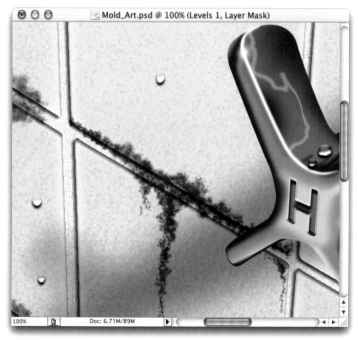

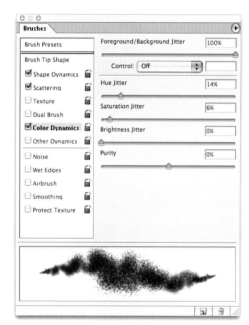

48 Color Dynamics are applied to the brush tip.

In a layer to contain the overall grime and mold, I applied large brush strokes with my customized brush (Figure 49). Pulling back on the opacity for that layer gave me the result I was looking for as seen in Figure 50.

49 In a separate layer, large areas of the walls are covered with what will eventually represent old stains and grime.

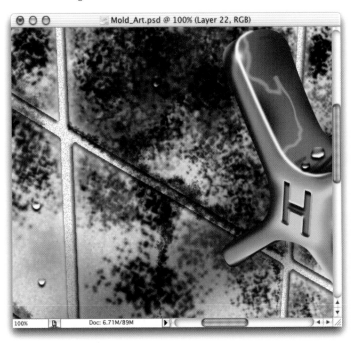

50 The layer with the large mold is lowered in opacity to look like stains on the tiles.

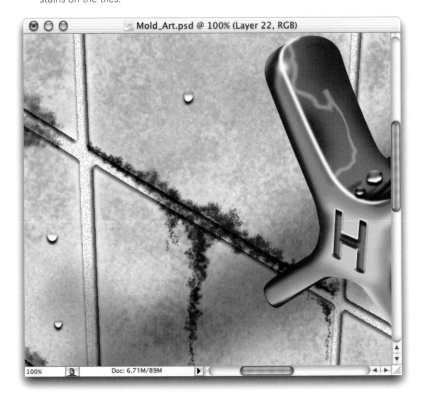

A Dangerous Place to Walk

Figure 51, a final photo-realistic illustration, is intended to show hazards for a pedestrian, such as standing water, cables, and other obstacles. The original thought was to show such hazards in an indoor setting. Figure 52 shows the original comp that I sent to the client.

The client decided to change the scene to one that was outdoors, such as a driveway. Based on this new direction, I created the new comp shown in Figure 53.

51 The final image.

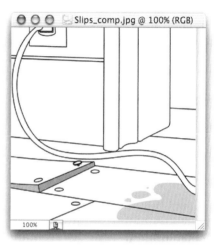

52 The original comp shows an interior scene with hazards such as a raised floorboard.

53 This new comp shows the hazards in an outdoor setting.

As I mentioned at the beginning of these exercises, I had to cobble together a layout from scratch, so I roughed out some paths in Illustrator. Then, saving a copy of the Illustrator document, I imported them into a low-resolution Photoshop file and incorporated some simple, low-quality B/W effects. Then I saved the file as a JPEG so that I could transmit it to the client for approval (Figure 53). When the approval came, I threw away the low-resolution B/W version and began the job again for real by copying and pasting the Illustrator paths into a new Photoshop document (Figure 54).

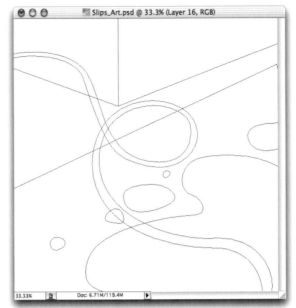

54 The paths were imported into Photoshop.

Creating Grass

My first target was the scraggly grass behind the driveway. Using the Photoshop Pen Tool, I started by creating three narrow stalk-like paths (Figure 55). I intended these to be a cluster of blades of grass, which I would then duplicate and modify as necessary. The paths were filled with black, selected with the Rectangular Marquee Tool, and defined as a brush (Edit > Define Brush Preset).

Just as with the brush I created earlier to apply the appearance of mold on tile, this Grass brush required a lot of adjusting in the Brushes palette (Figure 56). It was worth the effort, however, because after all these settings were loaded, I was able to create the entire grassy area with a single stroke of the brush. Figure 56a shows some variations in the color. The strokes were passed back and forth across the canvas twice. The change in foreground and background colors gave me the different tones in the grasses. This incredible brush-making flexibility was introduced in Photoshop 7, and its power still isn't widely recognized.

In fact, I did this job during the beta test period for Photoshop 7. The Photoshop 7 programming team was so impressed that they included my Grass brush as a default in Photoshop 7, along with a few other brushes that I designed.

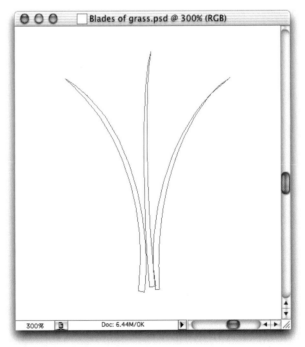

55 Three paths were created to form a cluster of blades of grass.

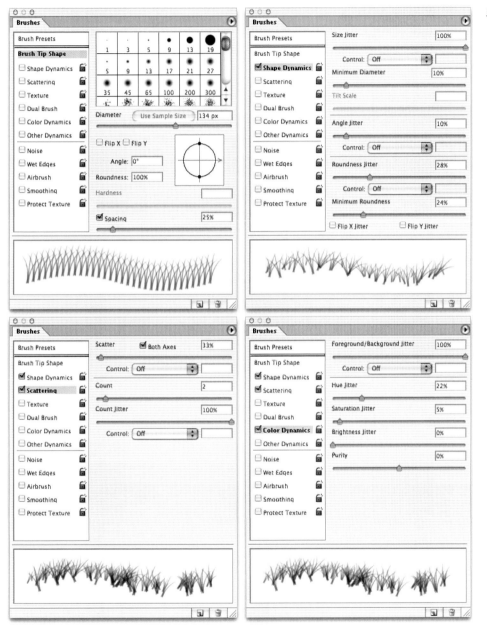

56 The Grass brush is modified to create an entire lawn in a single stroke.

56a The foreground and background colors are changed, giving the application of the grass a different look each time.

Dark and light shades of green were chosen for the foreground and background colors. In a separate layer, the grass was painted in, using the new Grass brush I created (Figure 57).

57 The grass was painted in a new layer.

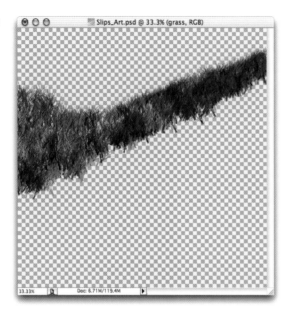

Planting a Leafy Bush

The bush behind the grass was created next. A simple leaf shape was created as seen in Figure 58. It was turned into a brush and modified in the Brushes palette with the settings seen in Figure 59. Note the new feature here: a texture, one of the Photoshop defaults. With it, I was able to add roughness to the leaves so that they would not appear too flat. Figure 60 shows a close-up of one of the layers that will eventually become the bush. The gaps in the leaves will be filled with other layers, as you will see as we continue.

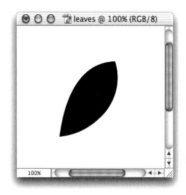

58 A shape for a leaf was created.

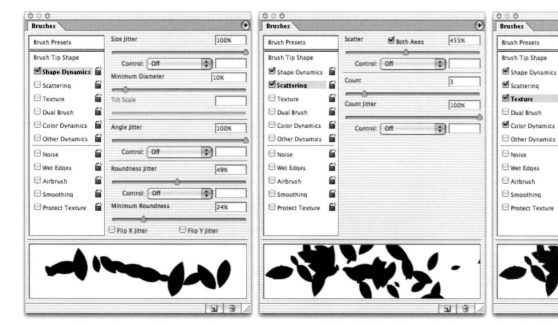

59 The brush modifications for the Leaf brush.

Using different colors, I created multiple shapes as in Figure 60 in separate layers. Darker tones toward the back created the effect of leaves being covered by the shadows of the leaves toward the front of the bush. Figure 61 shows two of the layers that make up the bush.

I merged the layers that made up the completed bush into a new, single layer. This was done by having all the layers of the bush visible and all the other layers turned off. A new, empty layer was created and made the active layer. Then Merge Visible was chosen

from the Layer palette submenu while pressing the Option button (Alt on a PC). This leaves the original layers intact, but merges a copy of them into the new layer.

I named this new, merged layer "bush shadow." The Transparency was locked and the layer was filled with black. Naturally, this filled the shapes of the leaves only, because Photoshop wasn't permitted to fill any areas that were previously transparent. At that point, I unlocked Transparency and then blurred the layer slightly with the Gaussian Blur filter (Filter > Blur > Gaussian Blur). Then I placed it behind the layers that made up the bush, as seen in Figure 62.

NOTE
The blur filters need to spread the edge of the image into the transparent area of the layer. If Transparency is locked, the filters will not do what you want them to.

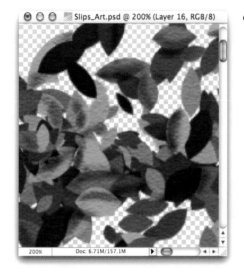

60 The leaves applied with the Leaf brush.

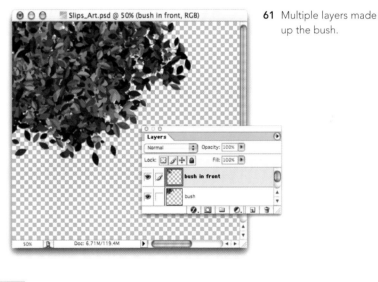

61 Multiple layers made up the bush.

62 The shadow for the bush.

Laying Down Fresh Soil

The soil under the grass and bush was next. A new layer was filled with a dark brown tone. I then filtered the layer to give it the feel of dirt. The filter that I used for this was the Texturizer filter (Filter > Texture > Texturizer) in Sandstone mode (Figure 63). The result was touched up in a few areas with the Dodge and Burn Tools to add further texture (Figure 64).

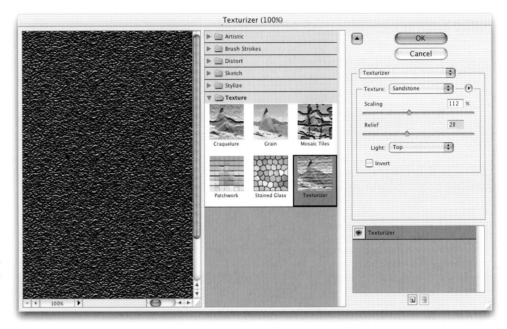

63 The Texturizer filter created the look of soil in the layer for the ground.

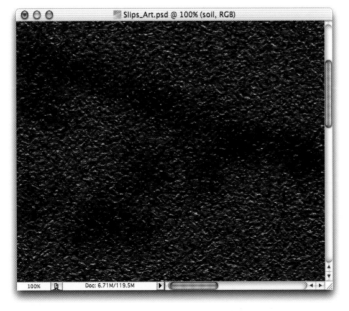

64 The soil texture was further modified with the Dodge and Burn Tools.

Building a Stone Foundation

Next, the two paths for the walls were turned into selections and filled with colors to represent the stone foundation corner of the house. A separate layer was used for each side of the building. The same filter used for the soil was used on the house but the Scaling setting was reduced to make the bumps less pronounced than in the soil. Figure 65 shows the finished walls.

Small indentations in the corner were added to make the stone look more realistic. The original edge was too crisp, too perfect, as shown in Figure 66. Using the Clone Tool with a small brush size, I cloned dark and light areas to simulate the imperfections seen in Figure 67. Using the Eraser Tool, I further roughened the rest of the edge by erasing tiny bits of the edge of the light-colored wall where it overlapped the dark wall.

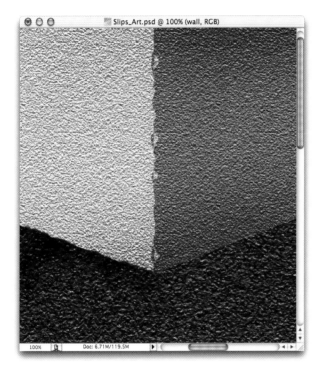

65 The corner edge of the building.

66 The edge was sharp because the paths that were used to create them were straight-edged.

67 Portions of the dark and light areas of the wall were cloned to simulate the dents in the corner.

Paving a Driveway

I now turned my attention to the driveway. In a new layer, the path for the shape of the asphalt was turned into a selection and filled with a gradient of grays as seen in Figure 68.

The layer was then given some texture with the Add Noise filter (Filter > Noise > Add Noise) as seen in Figure 69. As with the soil, the Dodge and Burn Tools were employed to add some stains and wear-and-tear to the asphalt (Figure 70).

In a new layer, a shape was created and filled with black to serve as a divider between the separate blocks of asphalt as you would find in a driveway. The Add Noise filter with the identical settings for the concrete was applied to the line (Figure 71).

A few simple Layer Style adjustments added the depth to the line to make it look like a depression in the surface of the asphalt (Figures 72, 73, and 74).

As a final touch to the driveway, I took a very small paintbrush and painted in some cracks at various places on the asphalt (Figure 75).

68 The asphalt area was filled with a gradient.

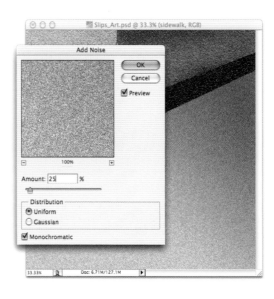

69 The Add Noise filter added texture to the asphalt.

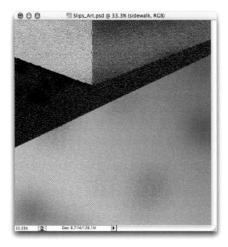

70 The Dodge and Burn Tools added random stains to the asphalt.

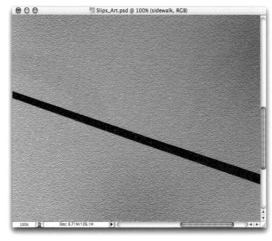

71 A simple black shape simulates the division found on asphalt driveways.

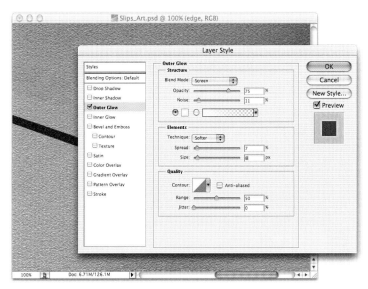

72 Outer Glow adds a light reflection to the outer edges of the asphalt division.

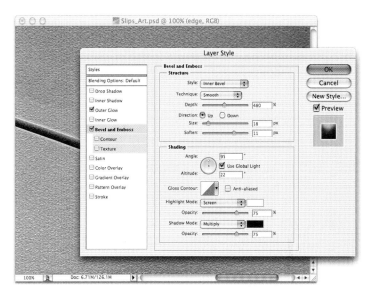

73 Bevel and Emboss complete the effect of the line in the asphalt.

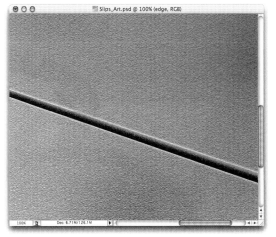

74 The finished line in the asphalt.

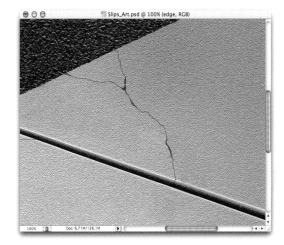

75 A few cracks were added with the Paintbrush Tool to complete the asphalt.

Stringing a Cable

The cable was a bit more involved than the other elements created up till now. For one thing, it curls over itself, which is guaranteed to make the lighting problematic. In a new layer, the path for the cable was filled with an orange color similar to the color found on outdoor extension cords (Figure 76).

Rather than relying on Layer Styles, the lighting and shadows for the cable needed to be created manually. A special mask had to be created to expose the edges in specific ways to get the look of a single cable curling over itself.

The layer with the cable was turned into a selection by Command-clicking it in the Layers palette (Control-clicking on a PC). I then saved this selection to an alpha channel (Figure 77) by choosing Save Selection from the Select menu.

I duplicated the channel by dragging it over the Make New Channel icon at the bottom of the Channels palette. This duplicate was blurred with the Gaussian Blur filter (Filter > Blur > Gaussian Blur) just enough to make it resemble the edge of a shadow traveling around the surface of the cable (Figure 79).

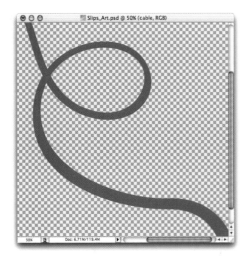

76 The paths for the shape of the cable were filled with an orange color.

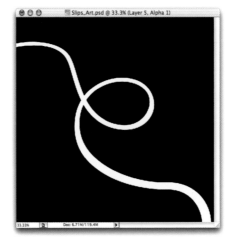

77 The alpha channel for the cable.

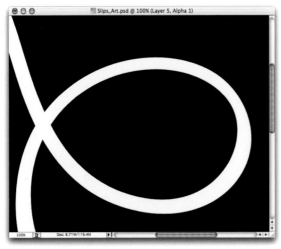

78 A close-up of the original, sharp alpha channel.

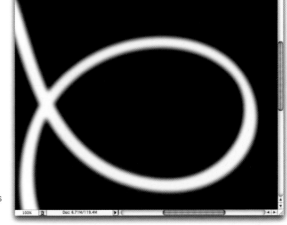

79 The duplicate alpha channel was blurred slightly.

I assigned display-only colors to the alpha channels so that I could differentiate them visually, and turned on the Eye icon for the first alpha channel where the original, sharp-edged cable resided. With the Move Tool, I moved the blurred channel to create the soft edge of a shadow or highlight overlapping the sharp channel as seen in Figure 80.

Based on where the two channels overlapped, it was now necessary to create a single mask that could be used to create the highlights on the cable. The Calculations command

(Image > Calculations), seen in Figure 81, is where the operation was performed. The blurred channel (Alpha copy 1) was put in Source 1. The original, sharp-edged channel was put in Source 2. I chose Subtract as the blending method. The results were sent to a new channel that is seen in Figure 82.

Because the cable loops over itself, it produced a gap in the mask. Zooming into the specific area of the overlap, as in Figure 83, we see the gap in the cable. This is also the problem that would arise if Layer Style were to be used to try and get this effect.

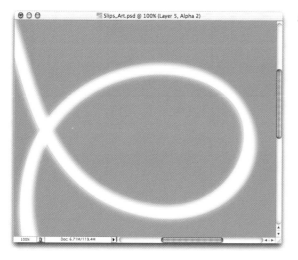

80 The area where highlights would be cast on the top of the cable are seen here where the blurred channel overlaps the sharp channel.

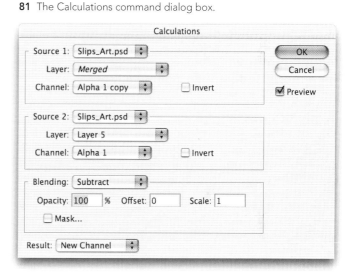

81 The Calculations command dialog box.

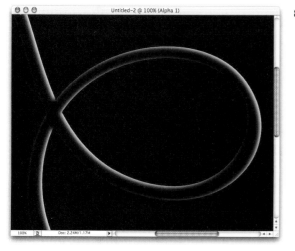

82 The result of the Calculations is a mask in which the edge of the cable is exposed to allow a highlight to be added.

83 This close-up shows the gap in the cable where it overlaps itself.

With the Pen Tool, I selected the area where the cable overlaps. With a soft-edged, white paintbrush, I painted in the edge of the cable as seen in Figure 84.

Back in the RGB channel, the completed alpha channel is made into a selection. In a new layer for the highlight, white is filled into the selection as seen in Figure 85. Note that the top portion of the edge is not filled with white. This is because the cable is bent, and at that point the light is no longer visible, so a shadow starts to

form. Because Layer Style only uses one color to create a glow or shadow, it will not work in this case.

The same procedure is followed to make a mask for the shadow edge of the cable. The blurred alpha channel is moved in the opposite direction to form the overlap at the backside of the cable. The gaps are filled, as seen in Figure 86. Figure 87 shows the shadow applied to the cable.

84 The gap is selected and retouched to fill the needed area.

85 The highlight is added to the cable.

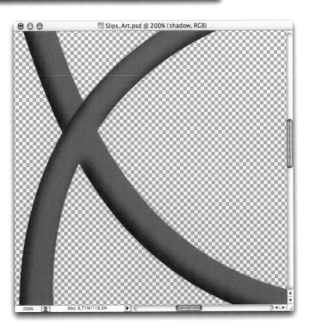

87 The shadow is applied to the cable.

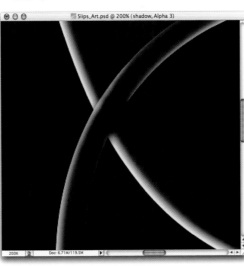

86 The alpha channel for the shadow.

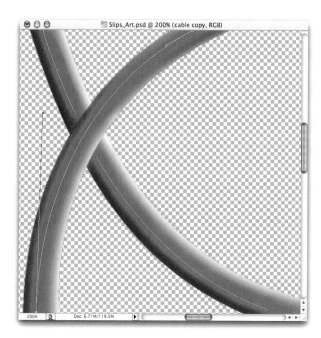

A highlight was needed along the central portion of the cable. I created a series of paths with the Pen Tool such as the ones visible in Figure 88a. Using a soft-edged paintbrush, the paths were stroked to add the highlight visible in Figure 88b.

The cable is coming from somewhere under the bushes by the house. The bushes cast a shadow over the cable in this area. The original layer created for the shadow of the bushes was duplicated as seen in Figure 89. This duplicate shadow layer was then clipped by the layer of the cable as seen in Figure 90.

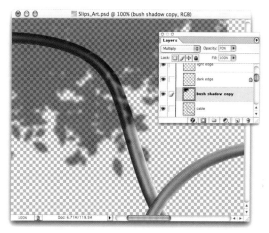

89 The layer of the shadow for the bush was duplicated.

88a Paths were created along the central portion of the cable where a highlight was needed.

88b The paths were stroked with the Paintbrush Tool to form the final highlights.

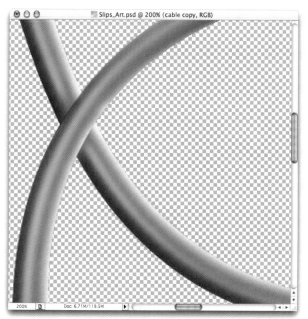

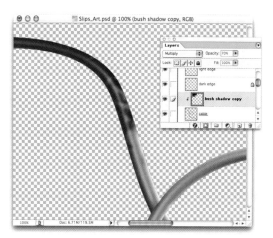

90 The duplicate layer for the shadow of the bush was clipped by the layer of the cable.

The Cable Casts a Shadow

The cable casts a shadow of its own on the driveway. Shadows are usually very easy to create. There is even a Layer Style for drop shadows. This particular shadow presents some challenges. Because we are dealing with a single light source, there should be only one shadow. The problem is that the cable is not flat against the ground—it is raised. Where the shadow is close to the ground, the shadow should be deep and sharp. Where it is further away, the shadow should be lighter and more out of focus. The trick is to create these transitions in a gradual manner so that the illusion is created that it is a single shadow changing over space. Here is a perfect example of why the alpha channel is so important.

In a new layer, to hold the cable's shadow shape, I used the Pen Tool to create the shadow shape and filled it with black (Figure 91).

I made a new alpha channel, filled it with black, and drew large white blotches in the approximate areas where the cable was off the ground (Figure 92). Then, using white and black as my foreground/ background colors, I selected each one of these blotches in turn and applied a gradient that faded each to dark gray or black where the cable was getting closer to the ground (Figure 93a). Figure 93b shows the channel viewed over the RGB image to ensure correct positioning.

The alpha channel was made into a selection and the Gaussian Blur filter was applied to the layer containing the cable's shadow. In Figure 94, note how the blurring effect is much stronger where the cable is further from the ground. This is the point of making the gradients in the alpha channel.

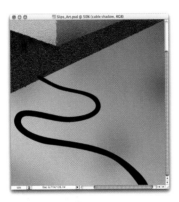

91 The basic shape for the shadow of the cable was created in a layer.

92 An alpha channel was created for the areas where the shadow was farthest from the ground.

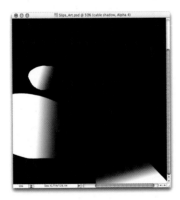

93a A gradient was applied to get the gradual effect needed for the blurring and lightening of the shadow.

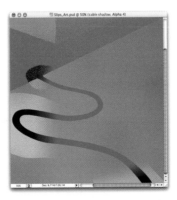

93b The alpha channel is viewed over the RGB channels.

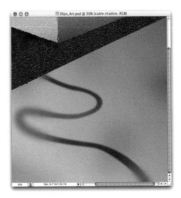

94 The shadow was blurred gradually precisely where it was needed.

95 The shapes for the puddle were created with the Pen Tool and filled with a solid color.

Spilling Some Water

The puddle, necessary to complete the hazardous driveway, was created in much the same way as the water drops were created in the bathtub example at the beginning of this chapter. One major difference is the reflection of the building.

In a new layer, I created a shape for the large puddle and a series of smaller shapes for the other wet areas that would surround it (Figure 95). Then I applied a series of Layer Styles (Figures 96 through 99) to simulate the effect of water.

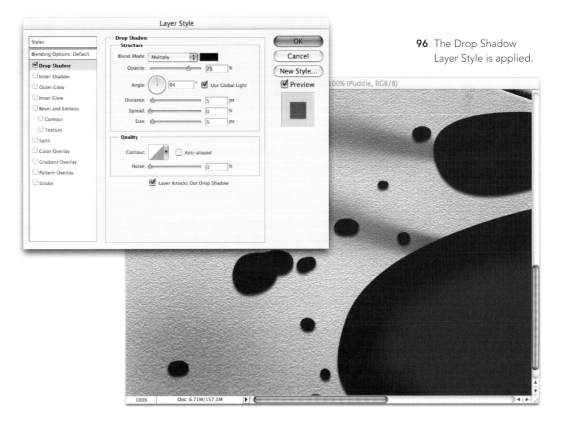

96 The Drop Shadow Layer Style is applied.

97 The Inner Shadow Layer Style is applied.

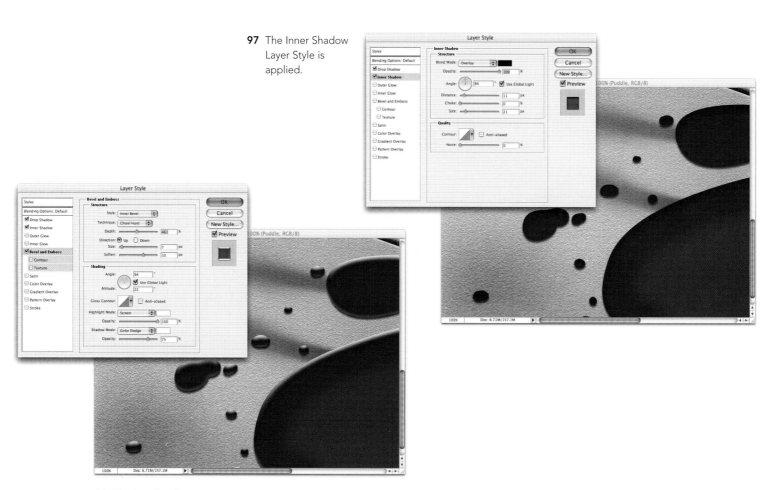

98 The Bevel and Emboss Layer Style is applied.

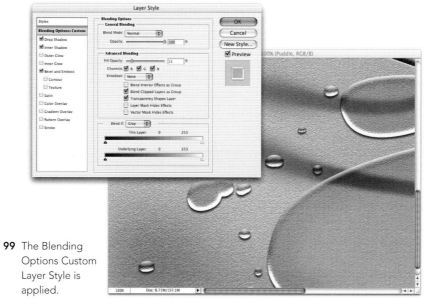

99 The Blending Options Custom Layer Style is applied.

The water drops in the bathtub scene were small. The puddle, on the other hand, covers a large area, thus acting as a mirror. Due to the viewing angle, we should be able to see the house reflected in the puddle.

Rather than spend the afternoon trying to create a house in Illustrator, I got out my digital camera and shot a few pictures of the corner of my own house (Figure 100). I imported the image into the illustration and flipped vertically (Edit > Transform > Flip Vertical). I placed the layer right in back of the layer with the puddle (Figure 101).

A puddle's edges are curved and will distort the reflections to some extent. The Liquify filter was perfect to make these distortions a reality, but first I made the layer of the puddle into a selection by Command-clicking it in the Layers palette (Control-clicking on a PC).

Because something was selected when I brought the layer of the house into the Liquify filter, it displayed the selected area as an orange-colored mask (Figure 102).

100 A picture of a corner of my house was shot to serve as the reflection of the house in the scene.

101 The layer for the reflection was flipped vertically and placed behind the layer with the puddle.

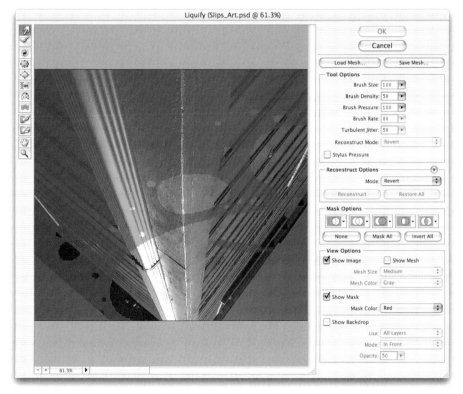

102 A selection of the puddle layer area appears as a mask in the Liquify dialog box with the house selection layer active.

With the edges of the puddle as a guide, I distorted the layer of the house reflections along the edges as seen in the circled areas of Figure 103.

I needed to clip the layer of the house reflection with the layer of the puddle. One problem: Because the Fill Opacity was lowered to 15% (Figure 99), making the original black shapes almost invisible, anything clipped by this layer would be equally invisible. To correct this problem, I duplicated the layer with the puddle and deleted all the Layer Style effects for it. I used this duplicate to clip the layer of the reflection.

The final touch for the puddle was a reflection of the cable. The layer with the cable was duplicated and darkened with the Levels command (Image > Adjustments > Levels). Sections of it were positioned where they would best appear as true reflections. This layer was then clipped with the layer of the reflection as seen in Figure 104.

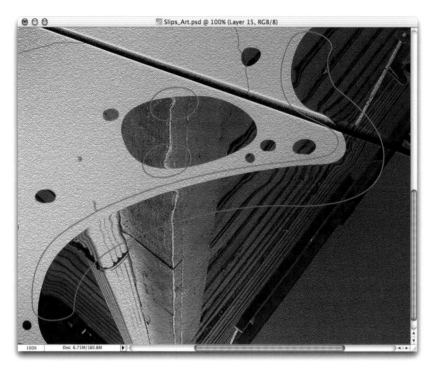

103 A distortion was applied to the edges of the reflection visible in the outlined areas.

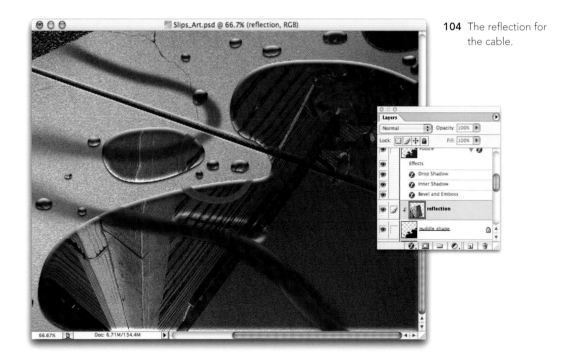

104 The reflection for the cable.

Nasty, Peeling, Lead Paint

Peeling paint is another one of those things to look out for when buying a house. Figure 105 shows the final art for this illustration. Figure 106 is the comp that I originally submitted to the client. As in the previous case studies, I imported the paths from Illustrator into Photoshop (Figure 107).

105 This illustration, shown here in final form, was to depict peeling lead paint along a window sill and frame.

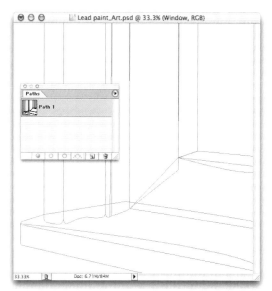

106 The comp submitted to the client.

107 The paths made for the comp were imported from Illustrator into Photoshop via Copy and Paste.

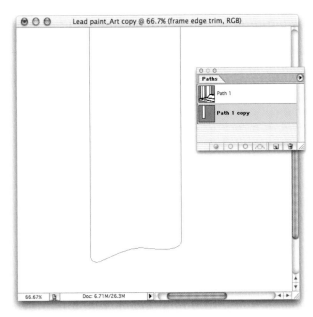

108 The path for part of the frame molding.

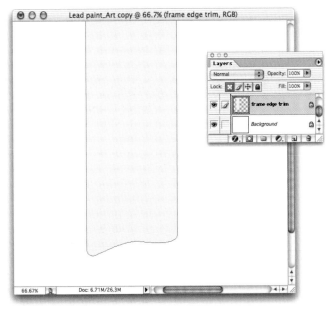

109 The path was filled with a color for the frame.

The paths were separated into individual paths for the separate elements in the image. Figure 108 shows the main section of the window frame's molding. In Figure 109, the path has been filled with the appropriate color for the frame.

The Transparency was locked for the layer. Using the Paintbrush Tool in various soft-edged sizes, I added tones to give the molding some dimension (Figure 110). I Shift-clicked from top to bottom to get straight vertical lines.

NOTE

You can create straight lines with tools such as the Paintbrush, Eraser, Clone, Pencil, and so on by connecting click to click with the Shift key. Try this to understand the concept. Click once somewhere on the canvas with any of these tools. Pressing the Shift key, click somewhere else on the canvas with the same tool. The result will be a line that connects the two clicks.

To add texture to the frame, I applied the Texturizer filter (Filter > Texture > Texturizer) as seen in Figure 111.

Making Wood

Next came the wood that was to be exposed by the peeling paint. In a new layer, I selected a large rectangle with the Marquee Tool (Figure 112).

Photoshop has now introduced a new filter that replaces the way I used to create wood. The new Fibers filter makes creating wood a much easier task (Figure 113). The only drawback is that it only works in one direction, but that can be easily overcome.

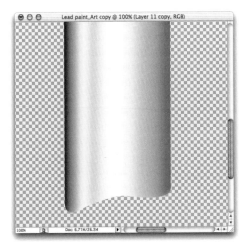

110 Tones were added to give depth and dimension to the molding.

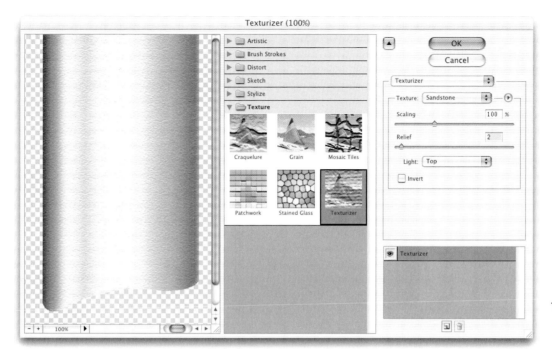

111 The Texturizer filter added texture to the molding.

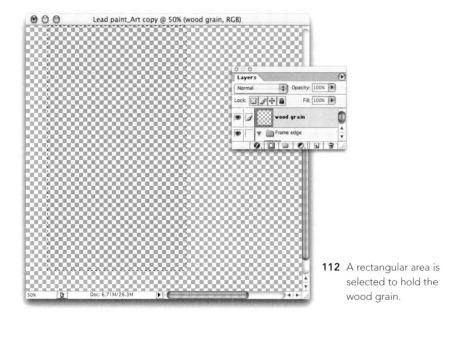

112 A rectangular area is selected to hold the wood grain.

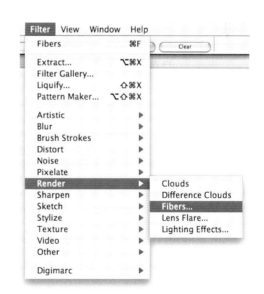

113 The new Fibers filter makes wood easy to create.

The Fibers filter uses the currently selected colors for the foreground and background as the basic colors for the fibers. I chose a dark brown for the foreground and a pale yellow for the background and applied the filter (Figure 114). I made some minor tweaks to the settings and came up with the wooden texture seen in Figure 115.

The layer was given a Layer Style of Inner Shadow (Figure 116). This would give the texture some depth, as you will see in a few steps from now.

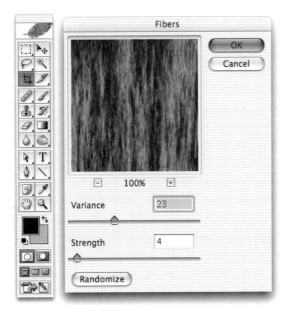

114 The dialog box for the new Fibers filter.

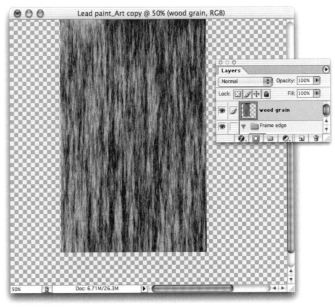

115 The rectangular shape was filled with the wooden grain texture.

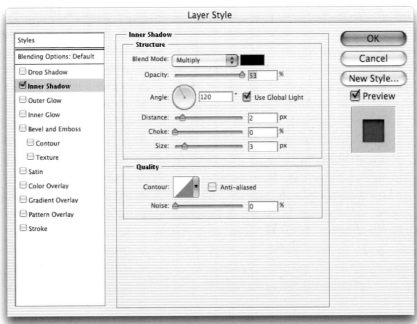

116 The Inner Shadow Layer Style was applied to the layer with the wood grain.

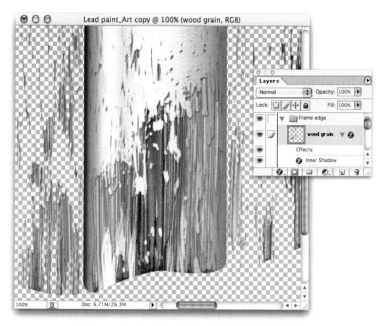

117 The wood texture is erased with a spatter-brushed Eraser Tool.

I chose the Eraser Tool and created a brush tip in much the same way as the one used to create the mold on the tiles earlier in this chapter. In this case, however, being the Eraser, it will use that brush to subtract detail from the image. In Figure 117 you see the effects of the Eraser Tool on the wooden layer as the molding layer beneath starts to show through. Note the slight shadow at all the edges of each section of peeling paint—that's the Layer Style at work.

The additional sections of the molding were created in the same fashion as the first section (Figure 118). In Figure 119 we see the paint peeled from the entire molding.

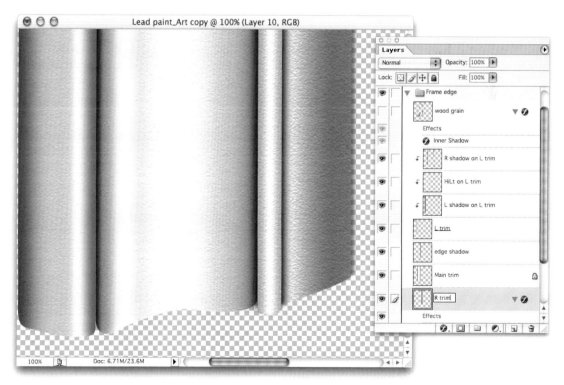

118 The rest of the molding.

119 The paint peeling from the entire molding area.

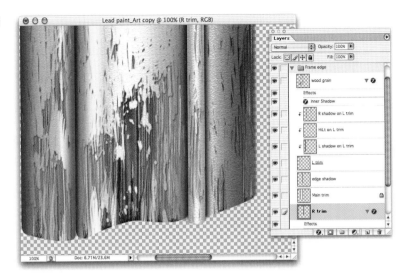

I created the other sections of the window frame with some shadows added here and there to give a sense of depth to the scene (Figure 120). These shadows were created with a large, soft-edged paintbrush and were black.

Figure 121 shows where a portion of the layer of the wooden grain has been rotated to follow the bottom portion of the frame. At the point where the two pieces of wood meet, I added a few extra dents and rot marks with the Burn Tool. These are visible within the red circle.

120 The completed window frame and sill.

121 Extra wear-and-tear was added to the edge where different pieces of wood meet.

7

Magazine Cover

I recently created art for a medical magazine, as shown in Figure 1. Close examination will show you that basically the entire image is a series of cylindrical shapes. Chapter 2 details the process of creating such cylinders.

I want to draw your attention to two details that are not covered elsewhere in this book: 3D letters and unusual shadows. Figure 2 shows a close-up of the small letters that make up the calendar on the top of the pill dispensers. The letters are raised from the surface.

1 This is the cover art for a medical magazine.

2 The letters are raised from the surface of the molded-plastic pill dispenser.

3D Extrusion

The technique I am about to show you is extremely useful when a three-dimensional look is needed and there is no time to rely on 3D software to do the job. In this case, creating a 3D effect in Photoshop is fast and easy.

For this exercise, 3D extrusion is applied to text, like on the cover. Figure 3 shows some text that has been distorted using the Distort command (Image > Transform > Distort) to simulate a 3D viewing angle. I obtained the text just by typing it into Photoshop with the Type Tool. To distort it in this fashion, it was necessary to rasterize it (Layer > Rasterize > Type). This command turns text into pixels. Make sure your spelling is correct; because after you rasterize, there is no text editing.

The layer with the distorted text was duplicated. The new duplicate layer automatically comes in above the layer that is being duplicated. The layer in back (original) was made active. The layer was filled with gray, but I had locked Transparency so that the fill would affect the letters only. Using the Move Tool, I lowered the new layer into position so that it rested just below the black letters (Figure 4). The distance chosen depends on the depth desired for the letters.

The Transparency was unlocked. Using the Lasso Tool and the Marquee Tool, the corners were selected as seen in Figure 5. Although I was still working on the layer with the gray shadow, I made sure that my selection stopped exactly at the corner of each black letter on the layer above.

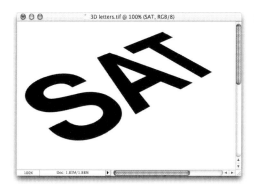

3 Text has been distorted to give it a three-dimensional look.

4 A duplicate layer is made. The original layer is then filled with gray and moved to give the letters depth.

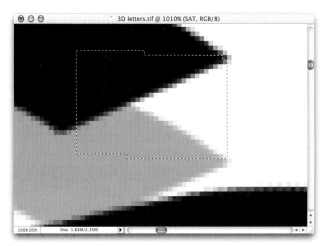

5 The edges are selected to form solid-looking blocks of letters.

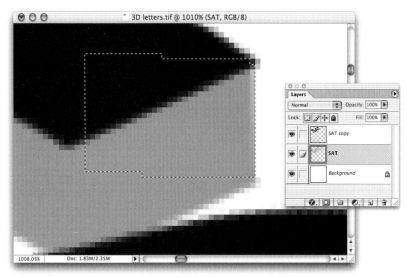

6 The selected areas are filled with the same gray.

The selected areas were then filled with the same gray to create the illusion that the letters are solid (Figure 6). Then I examined every edge carefully for imperfections. Figure 7 shows the side edge where the letter curves. A slight indent needs to be filled.

Figure 8 shows the completed extrusion of the letters. Just adding the depth is not enough. The very fact that the letters now have a shape means they will react to lighting conditions, casting shadows and picking up highlights.

Still working on the gray layer, I locked the Transparency again. With the Paintbrush Tool, using a soft-edged brush tip, and various shades of gray, black, and white, I painted these shadows and highlights into the letters as seen in Figure 9.

7 Extra care is taken to make sure all the edges have been filled.

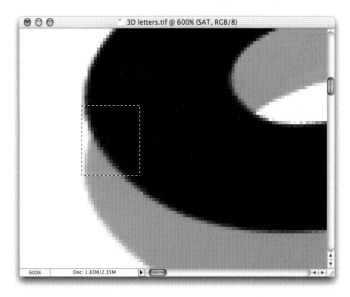

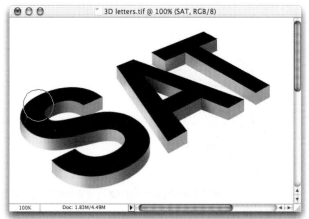

8 The letters start to look three-dimensional.

9 Tones are added to the edges to create shadows and highlights.

Sharp corners and sides are selected to add the appropriate tones to maintain the sharp appearance (Figure 10).

Because they are now blocks rather than flat shapes, the letters themselves must cast shadows. The layer that contains the black letters is duplicated. This duplicate is moved down in the palette so that it appears behind the other two layers. It is already black, so it needs no coloring. If the top letter layer had been in some other color, I would have needed to lock the Transparency of the third (bottom) layer and fill it with black, because it will be used to make a shadow.

With the Move Tool, I repositioned the shadow layer to simulate the shadow cast by the letters (Figure 11). Just like the extruded letters, these shadows need some alteration. At the corners of certain letters, an unnatural gap occurs between letter and shadow. To fix this, I made selections from tip to tip, as seen in Figure 12, and filled with black.

I then lowered the opacity for the layer with the shadow to simulate the look of a real shadow (Figure 13).

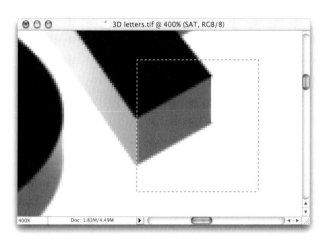

10 Hard edges are selected and filled to maintain the sharp quality of the edge.

11 A third layer is created and repositioned to serve as the shadow being cast by the blocks of letters.

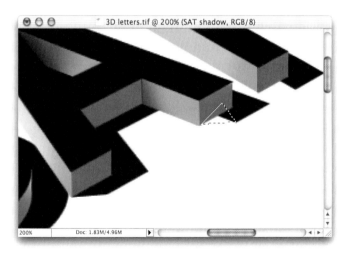

12 The corners are selected, and later filled with black to make a realistic shadow.

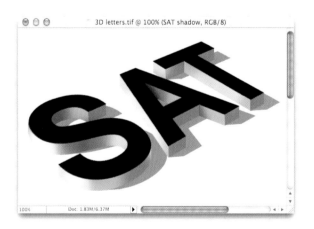

13 The opacity for the shadow layer is lowered.

Close inspection exposes a flaw that needs to be addressed. There is a small area between the *S* and *A* where the shadow is incorrect. The *S* should actually cast a shadow on one side of the *A*. Using the Pen Tool, I created a shape to serve as this extension of the shadow (Figure 14). In a new layer, I filled the path with black (Figure 15).

Finally, the layer with the extension of the shadow is clipped by the layer that contains the sides of the letters so that it is only visible where it should be, as seen in Figure 16.

Figure 17 shows the completed, three-dimensional letters.

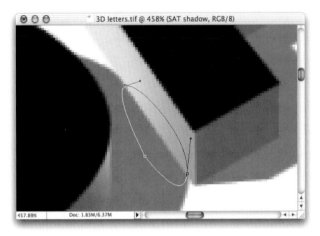

14 Using the Pen Tool, a path is made to serve as the shadow riding up the side of the letter.

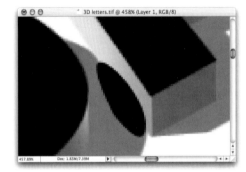

15 In a new layer, the path is filled with black.

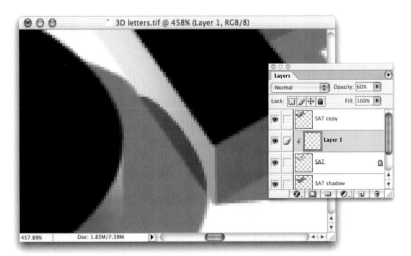

16 The shadow edge is clipped by the layer with the sides of the letters.

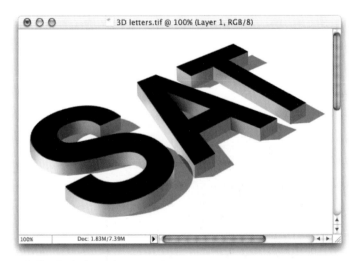

17 The final, three-dimensional blocks of letters.

Unusual Shadows

The second thing I want to point out about this illustration is the unusual shadow being cast by the pill dispenser (Figure 18). This is a single shadow, but it is being cast by three distinct elements. First, the white plastic of the pill dispenser is opaque. This will cause a solid shadow that is represented by the solid, dark, inner ring of the shadow seen in Figure 18.

Second, the top part of the lid is made of clear plastic. It, too, will cast a shadow, but one that is translucent, as seen in Figure 18 in the middle ring of the shadow. Finally, the corner of the lid will appear solid where the side of the lid meets the top, thus casting a solid shadow as seen in the outermost ring of the shadow in Figure 18.

I was not working with reference material. These dispensers are not real. The client wanted something generic that would not look too much like a particular brand. Knowing how light works is important in a situation such as this to ensure realism in the final image.

It is best to study objects and how they react to light to determine how you should realistically replicate these effects.

To get this effect, I created two black circles in two separate layers (Figure 19). Note that one layer darkens the other where they overlap. This happened because I lowered the opacity of each layer, but the bottom layer somewhat more than the top.

To get the outermost ring, I made the larger circle a selection (Figure 20) by Command-clicking the layer in the Layer palette (Control-clicking on a PC).

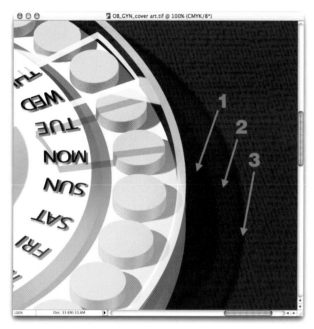

18 The shadow being cast by the pill dispenser reflects the different materials that the dispenser is made of: 1) The solid pill dispenser; 2) the clear plastic top of the lid; and 3) the corner edge where the side meets the top of the lid.

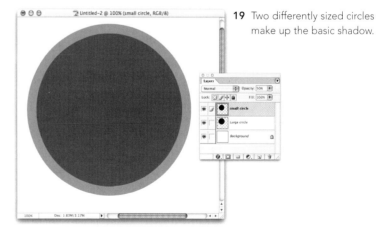

19 Two differently sized circles make up the basic shadow.

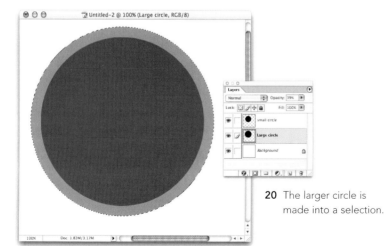

20 The larger circle is made into a selection.

In a separate layer, the selection was stroked with a thick black line (Edit > Stroke) as seen in Figure 21. I lowered the opacity for the layer with the stroke to match the effect created by the other two layers (Figure 22). Then I merged the three into a single layer.

Then I blurred the layer with the Gaussian Blur filter (Filter > Blur > Gaussian Blur) to complete the effect (Figure 23). Figure 23b shows the finished shadow.

21 The selection is stroked in black.

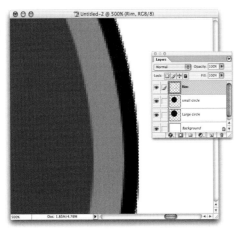

22 The opacity for the outer ring is lowered to match the inner shadow.

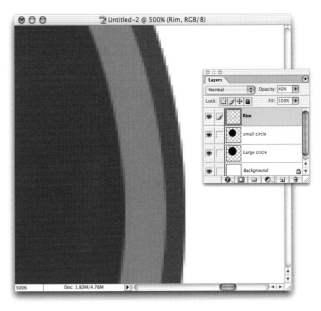

23 The composite layer is blurred to form the final shadow.

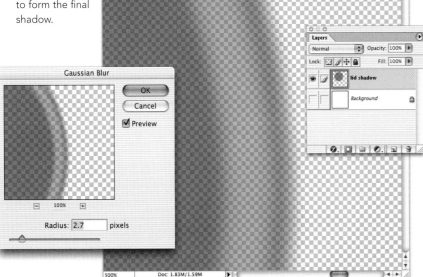

23b The final shadow.

Broadway Poster

Close to the end of writing this book, I was commissioned to create the poster art for an upcoming Broadway musical. Figure 1 shows the artwork that I created for the poster.

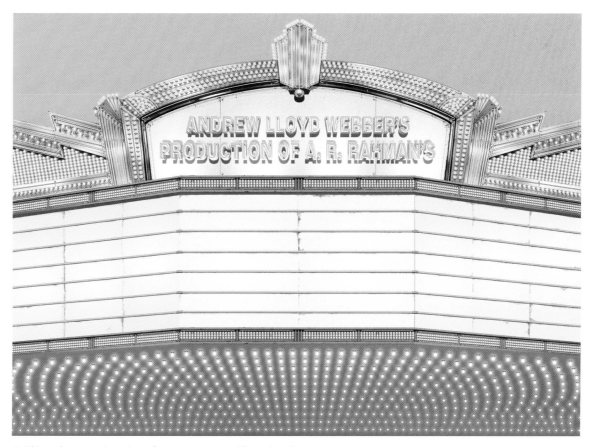

1 This is the central portion of a poster I created for a Broadway poster.

The Text

Figure 2 shows a close-up of part of the text. The reason I want to show it here is because the treatment and execution is similar to the raised, 3D text on the medical magazine cover. This text is also three-dimensional but with many additional levels. For one thing, this text is hollow.

The text started out very much the same as the text in the preceding exercise (the plastic, raised letters). Text was typed in the document. Spelling was checked and double checked. The text was converted to a path (Layer > Type > Create Work Path). This made the paths you see in Figure 3. Like the layer in the other exercise, the path was duplicated and shifted in position to form the back of the letters. One big difference is that these letters are in perspective. To create these additional angles, I slightly scaled down the duplicate path so that it was smaller than the original.

2 This is a portion of the text area in the poster.

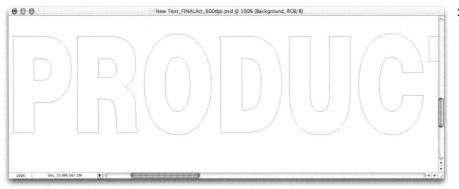

3 The text was converted into paths.

Figure 4 shows all the paths. Notice the slight difference in size for the path in back. Also, the connecting paths have been added and altered to form the solid shapes of the letter forms.

Figure 5 shows only the additional paths that were created to form side panels for letters where they were needed. Such panels are usually needed when the edge of the letter is straight.

These paths were individually filled in separate layers to start forming the sign. Figure 6 shows the backmost part of the letters filled with gray and additional tones added for highlight and shadows. The brighter tones used at the bottom of the letters are due to the spotlights shining upward toward the sign in the final image. I also applied the Add Noise filter (Filter > Noise > Add Noise) to add texture to the letters.

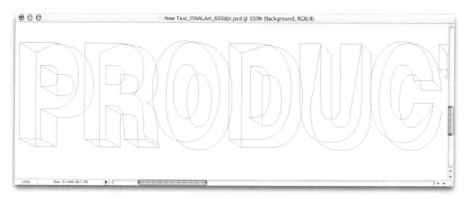

4 These are all the paths that would eventually be used individually to form the letters.

5 These paths were added to form the sides of the letters.

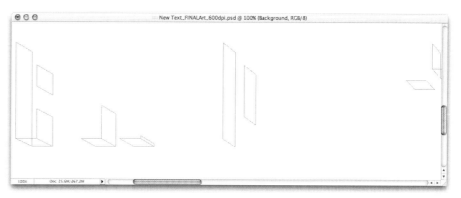

6 The paths for the back and sides of the letters were filled with different colors to simulate highlights and shadows.

Figure 7 had the front part of the letters filled with color.

Figure 8 shows the side panels of the letters filled with the appropriate colors.

The added twist to these letters is that they are hollow. Figure 9 shows the shapes that are filled to represent the inside portions of the letters. This inside space of the letters holds neon tubes.

I created a set of paths to represent the neon tubes (Figure 10).

7 The front of the letters were filled with color.

8 The additional paths for the side panels of the letters were filled with color.

9 The paths that formed the inside walls of the letters were filled.

Before the actual tubes were created, I set the glow that the neon cast inside the cavity of the letters. Using the very same paths that would eventually be used to make the neon, I created the glow. The neon was to be red in color. I chose the appropriate red as my foreground color. I chose the Paintbrush Tool with a tip that had 0 Hardness so that it would be very soft-edged. In a layer to contain the glow, I stroked the path with that Paintbrush. The mode for the layer was set to Overlay so that the red color would screen the colors of the letters, giving them a reddish glow as seen in

Figure 11. Another addition in Figure 11 is a layer containing the tiny holes where the neon is attached to the sign.

Figure 12 has two new layers added. One layer contains grime. The grime was created with a brush like the one used to create the mold in the bathtub in Chapter 6. In the second layer, the original path for the letters was stroked with a light gray tone (Edit > Stroke). This gave the letter shapes thickness (which metal letters on a sign of this type would normally have).

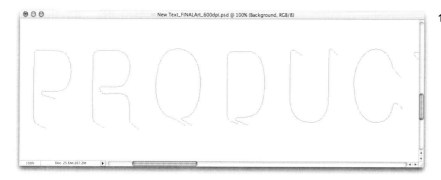

10 Paths were created to simulate neon tubes.

11 The glow from the neon and the connectors for the tubes were added to the inside of the letters.

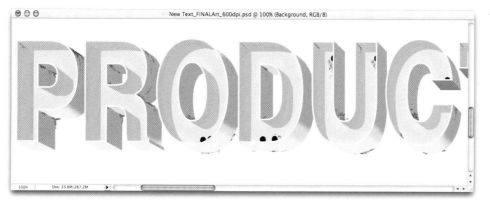

12 The main, outside shape of the letters were stroked to give them thickness. Grime was also added to the mix.

In Figure 13, the neon has been added. The paths for the neon were stroked with a hard-edged Paintbrush Tool. The technique for creating this neon is detailed in the next exercise.

Shadows for the letters were handled in a similar fashion as the shadows for the raised, plastic letters on the pill dispenser in Chapter 7 (Figure 2).

Unlike the preceding example, a second shadow is present. The light from above casts the shadow below the letters (Figure 14). There is a second light source in the image—the spotlight shining up at the sign. This second shadow is created the same way as the

first with a few exceptions. First, it is above the letters. Second, the effect of the spotlights is limited to the area where they are pointed. This causes a shadow visible only within the limited range of the light spread (Figure 15). To achieve this effect, I applied a Layer Mask to the layer. Using a gray tone, I drew shapes in the mask (Figure 15a) that toned down the areas where there shouldn't be a shadow.

NOTE

Creating a Layer Mask to hide these unwanted areas is better than actually erasing them because it enables you to make adjustments without ever losing information.

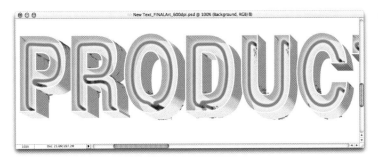

13 The neon tubes are created inside the letter shapes.

14 The light source from above the scene creates shadows cast by the letters.

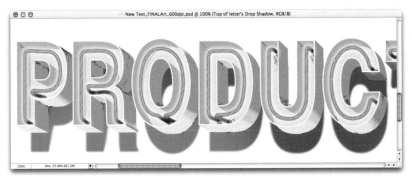

15 Spotlights shining up on the neon sign cast shadows onto the background.

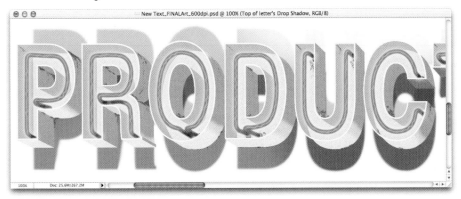

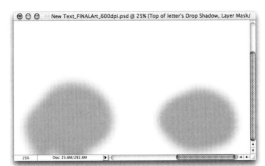

15a A Layer Mask is applied to make the shadows caused by the spotlights dim in areas where the light does not shine.

Make Your Own Neon

So that you understand how these neon letters were made, let's make one together. Start by creating a Photoshop file of any size and resolution you want.

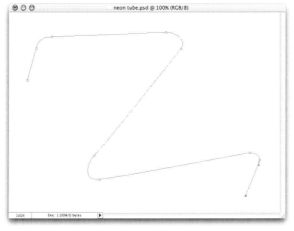

16 A path is created to serve as a neon letter.

With the Pen Tool, create a shape for your neon. It can be anything you want. Notice my shape in Figure 16 is the letter *Z*: It has extensions at each end where the neon tubes connect to the sign. You do not have to put them in if you just want a neon look. If you want it to look like an actual neon sign, however, these extensions are necessary for the sake of realism.

Create a new layer. Choose the Paintbrush Tool. Select a size for the brush tip that matches the thickness you want the neon tube to have. Choose a foreground color for the light, remembering that all neon bulbs emit relatively pure colors such as the orange I've chosen here. In the Brushes palette, set the Hardness to 100% and the Spacing to the lowest, which is 1%. Make sure you still have the Paintbrush selected as your tool. Make the path for your neon active in the Path palette and click the Stroke Path icon at the bottom of the Path palette. Your results should look like mine in Figure 17.

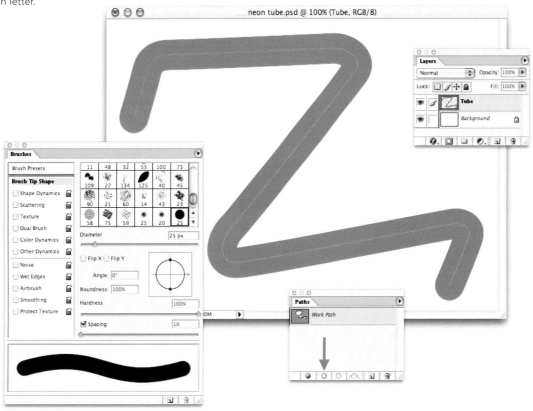

17 The path is stroked to form the neon tube.

Let's turn on the juice and give the neon some life.

Double-click the layer with the neon in the Layer palette to bring up the Layer Style window. Set an Outer Glow Layer Style to make the neon emit light (Figure 18).

Also choose Inner Glow, which in this case, despite its name, is not going to create a glow but rather a shadow. I chose a darker red than the neon and set the mode to Multiply to give roundness to the shape of the neon (Figure 19).

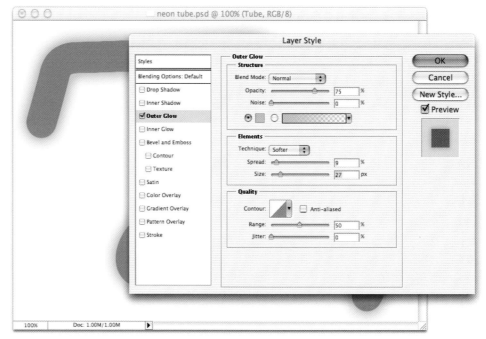

18 The layer is given a Layer Style to give the neon an outer glow.

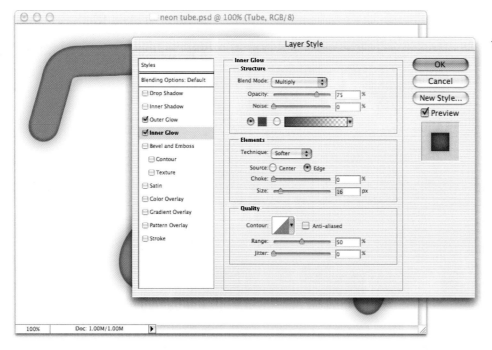

19 The layer is given another Layer Style to give the neon dimension.

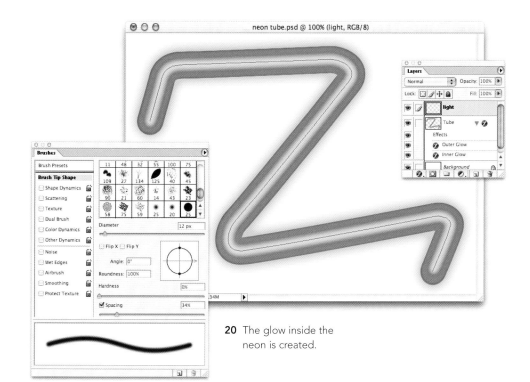

Neon signs have a glow inside the tube. To re-create this effect, choose the Paintbrush Tool. Because you have not used it since the step when you created the neon tube, the settings will be as they were then. Change the size of the brush to about half of what you had for the tube. Bring the Hardness down to 0 and increase the Spacing.

Choose a very light tone of the hue you used for the neon. Create a new layer. As with the neon, stroke the path again. Figure 20 shows the glow line of light inside the neon tube. Give the layer a Ripple filter (Filter > Distort > Ripple) to electrify the look of it, as in Figure 21.

20 The glow inside the neon is created.

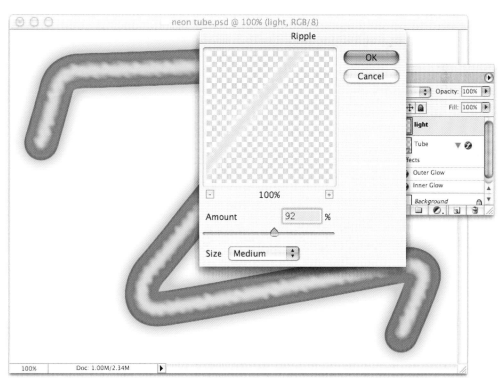

21 The glow is electrified with the Ripple filter.

The glow of this type is confined to the actual area of a neon sign that is the letter or symbol. The glow should not go to the end of the tube. Using a soft-edged Eraser Tool, eliminate the glow at the extensions of the tube as seen in Figure 22.

Create a new layer above the layer with the tube and clip it with the tube layer. Using a brush like the one made in Figure 43 in Chapter 6 for mold, paint in some tones at the ends of the tubes

(Figure 23). If you look at a real neon sign, you will see the ends of the tubes are usually painted with an opaque paint so the light will be seen only in the shape of the letters or symbols the sign is depicting. But, given the adverse conditions of intense light and heat, the paint is never solid but always a bit ratty-looking, as it is here.

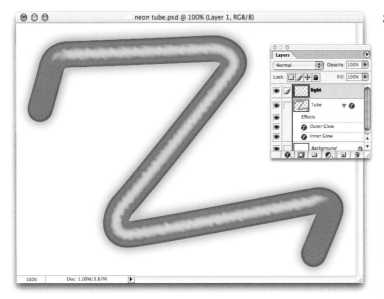

22 The glow is erased from the area where the neon is connected to the sign.

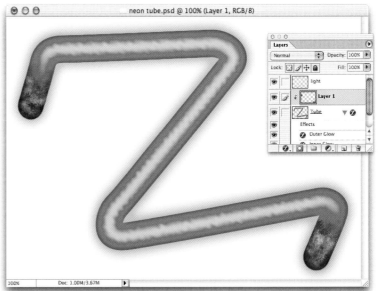

23 Paint is added to the ends of the neon.

The outer glow of our neon surrounds the entire neon shape. We just cut off the light at those neon connector ends. You need to eliminate the glow to these outer edges.

The glow is a Layer Style that you set back in Figure 18. Photoshop enables you to separate the layer styles from the layer that contains them into layers of their own. Create Layer (Figure 24), found under the Layer Style submenu of the Layer menu, enables you to do that.

With the outer glow in its own layer, it is easy to erase the portions of it at the ends where they should not appear. Figure 25 shows the completed neon.

24 Create Layer enables you to separate all the Layer Styles applied to a layer into separate layers for each style.

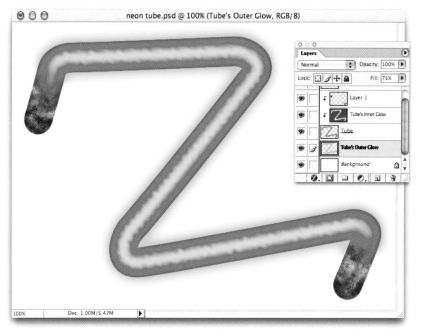

25 The completed neon letter.

Let There Be Light

The light bulbs under the marquee have some elements in them that use the same process to create a 3D effect in the 2D working space of Photoshop as the letters previously covered in this chapter. Figure 26 shows a finished light bulb.

In a new layer, I used the Pen Tool to create a shape and filled it with gray (Figure 27). This shape will be the top face of the socket where the bulb is inserted. I duplicated the layer and moved it up a slight distance (Figure 28). This is the same step that was used in the creation of the 3D letters in the previous exercises.

The edges were filled, and tones in various shades of gray were added with the Paintbrush Tool (Figure 29).

In a new layer, small shapes were created with the Pen Tool and filled with gradients (Figure 30). The gradients radiate outward with the lightest tones facing the center where the light bulb will eventually sit.

26 The completed light bulb.

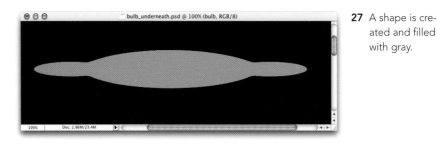

27 A shape is created and filled with gray.

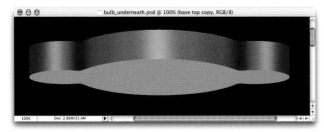

28 The shape is duplicated and moved up.

29 The edges are filled and stroked with shades of gray to form the edge of the base of the socket for the light bulb.

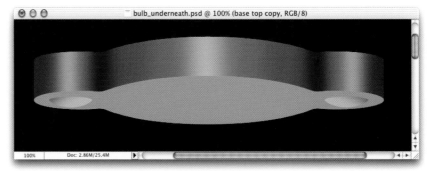

30 Small shapes to represent the screws that hold the socket in place are created and filled with a gradient.

31 A small shape is made to represent the socket.

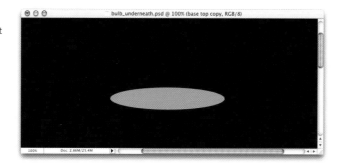

In Figure 31, a small ellipse has been created. For ease of viewing, the other layers have been turned off. This ellipse is the top of the actual socket where the bulb gets screwed in.

As with all the previous examples and using the same technique, the socket shape is turned into a 3D object (Figure 32).

In a new layer, a smaller elliptical shape is filled with black (Figure 33). This is to be the hole in the socket.

The shape for the actual light bulb was created with the Pen Tool and filled with a light gray (Figure 34).

32 The socket shape is extended to get a 3D look.

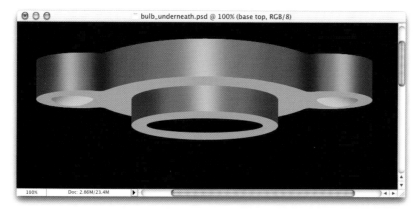

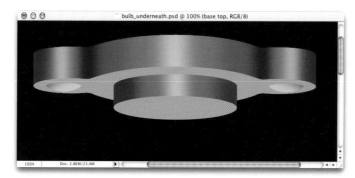

33 The shape for the hole in the socket is created.

34 The shape for the light bulb is created.

The layer with the light bulb was given a Layer Style of Outer Glow to give the bulb the glow that a light bulb would have when lit (Figure 35).

Finally, in a new layer, using a large soft-edged Paintbrush Tool, I placed a glow in the center of the bulb to represent the light within the bulb. Figure 36 shows the layer with the glow. For the sake of easy viewing, I turned the other layers off.

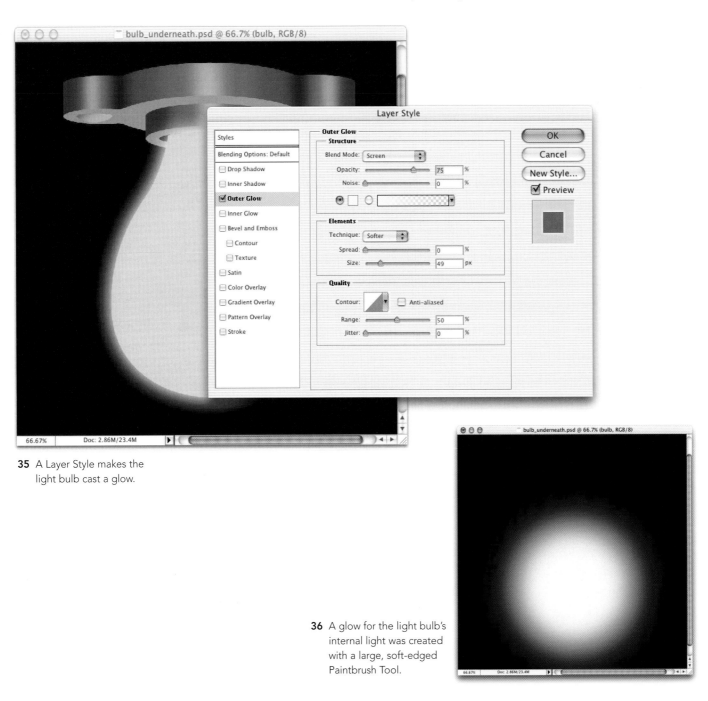

35 A Layer Style makes the light bulb cast a glow.

36 A glow for the light bulb's internal light was created with a large, soft-edged Paintbrush Tool.

Rows and Rows of Lights

The lights at the bottom of the marquee in Figure 1 are similar to the lights under the marquee on the magazine cover in Chapter 2.

A single light bulb is duplicated many times to form a row of light bulbs as seen in Figure 37.

The layer is duplicated and repositioned to make it appear as if there are many rows. Each successive row going back in space is scaled down slightly to give the foreshortening necessary to give the scene a three-dimensional quality (Figure 38).

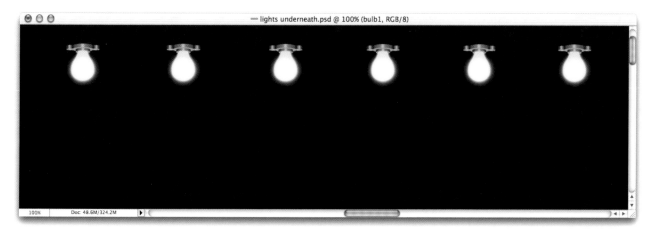

37 A row of light bulbs.

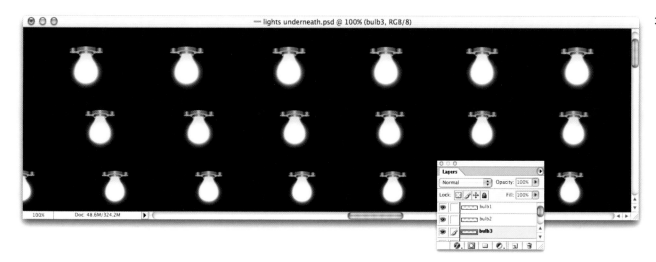

38 The row is duplicated to form additional rows behind. Each successive row is shrunk to add three-dimensional perspective

9

A Stitch in Time

Many of the jobs I do have some aspect that requires special thinking to meet a particular challenge. The shoe illustration in Figure 1 has stitching in its assembly that required a little creativity to re-create.

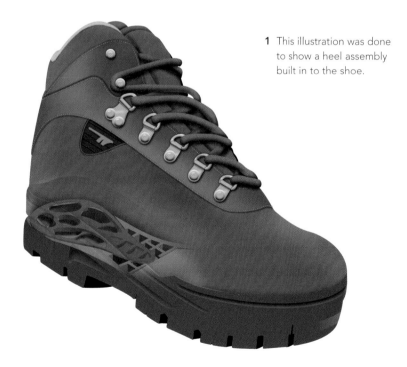

1 This illustration was done to show a heel assembly built in to the shoe.

The Stitching

Up until a few years ago, the stitching shown in close-up in Figure 2 would have had to be created in Illustrator or some other vector-art application. It's much easier now with the custom Brush Engine introduced in Photoshop 7.

2 Close up, we see the stitching on the shoe.

Let's do this one together. Create a new file in Photoshop.

Open the Brushes palette (Window > Brushes). Choose the Paintbrush Tool and a sharp-edged brush tip. Make sure Shape Dynamics is turned off in the Brushes palette. Make a dot on the canvas as seen in Figure 3.

Holding down the Shift key to connect clicks of the brush, click to the right of your original dot to make a dash like the one seen in Figure 4.

With the Rectangular Marquee Tool, select the dash and choose Define Brush Preset from the Edit menu (Figure 5). A dialog box will pop up that gives you the option to name the brush you have just created (Figure 6).

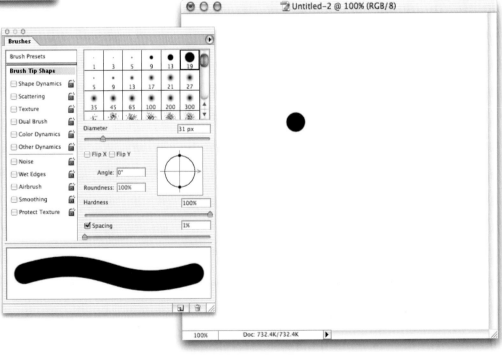

3 Create a single dot on the canvas.

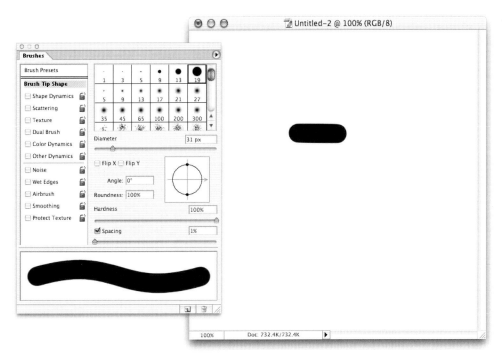

4 Shift-click to the right of your original dot to make a dash.

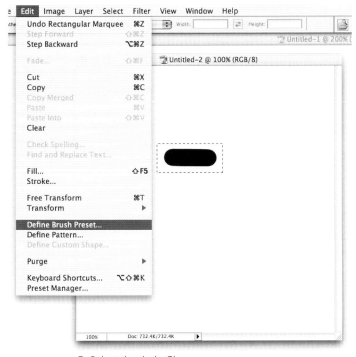

5 Select the dash. Choose Define Brush Preset.

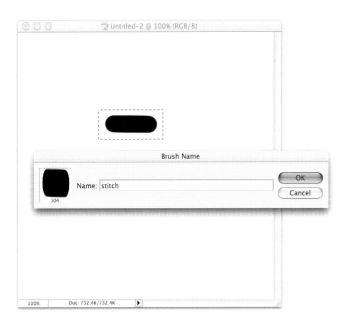

6 This dialog box enables you to name your brush.

7 Pick the brush you created from the picker in the options bar.

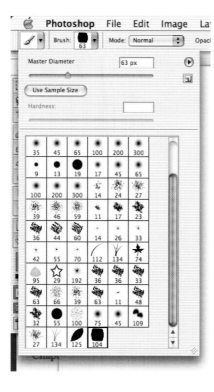

Choose the Paintbrush Tool and select the brush you just created from the Brush Preset Picker in the Options bar (Figure 7). It will appear as the last brush in the list. The viewing option for your Photoshop might be set to a different mode than the one I show in Figure 34 in Chapter 8 that is Small Thumbnail. The sub menu for the Preset Picker allows you to change your view.

Your brush will appear in the Brushes palette. In the Brush Tip Shape section of the palette, increase the spacing so that the stitches have some space between them as seen in Figure 8.

In the Shape Dynamics section of the palette, change the Control for Angle Jitter to Direction (Figure 9). Notice in Figure 36 in Chapter 8 that it is the only setting that has been adjusted. The other settings should match the ones in the figure. In the Brushes palette preview, you can see that the stitches now turn to follow the flow of the curve of the stroke.

Create a new layer (Layer > New > Layer). Make a stroke across the canvas like the one in Figure 10. If your stitches are too small or too large, you can change the size in the Preset Picker you see in Figure ???.

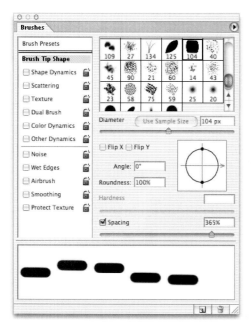

8 Increase the spacing to add some space between the stitches.

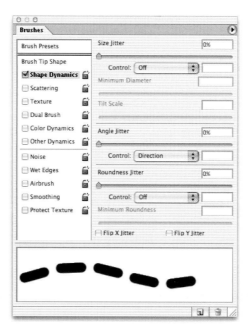

9 Set the Angle Jitter Control to Direction.

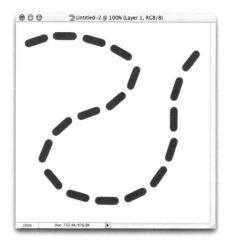

10 A stroke is made across the canvas.

Adding Dimension

To give the stitching some dimension, give the layer some Layer Styles. Double-click the layer with the stitches in the Layer palette. In the Layer Style window, choose Bevel and Emboss. Make some adjustments similar to the ones in Figure 11.

In the Outer Glow section, set the parameters to match the ones seen in Figure 12. The size you set will depend on the resolution and size of your stitches.

Final Touches

Finally, in the background layer, throw a little color and texture. Figure 13 shows a simple tan hue with noise added.

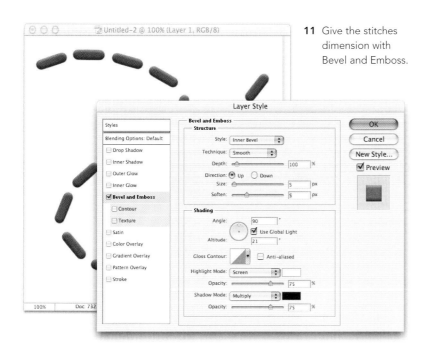

11 Give the stitches dimension with Bevel and Emboss.

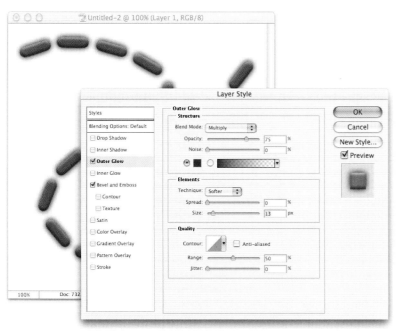

12 Add some shadows around the stitches with the Outer Glow Layer Style.

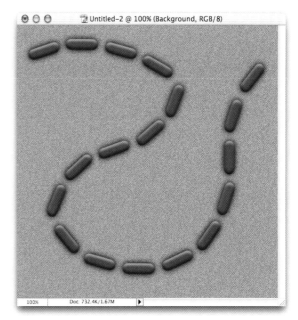

13 The final stitches

10

Taking a Dive

For this chapter, I want to turn to some of the work I have been doing for the past few years—my monthly appearances on TechTV's *The Screen Savers* show. I get a mere 6 minutes to teach a trick or two. I get to write up a brief tutorial on the TechTV web site, but I don't get to attach figures to the tutorials.

In this and the next chapter, I want to highlight two of the most popular segments and clearly outline the steps. I base the popularity on the number of emails that I received after these two shows.

The Underwater Scene

This first exercise creates an underwater scene.

Start with a photograph with rocks and gravel in the foreground to serve as the ocean bottom. Figure 1 is a sample of the type of image I mean. The gravel in the foreground of the image is what we need.

1 This image will serve as the basis for the ocean bottom in the underwater scene.

Using the Hue/Saturation control (Image > Adjustments > Hue/Saturation), push the Hue slider all the way to the left. Push the Saturation slider slightly to the right (Figure 2). Moving the Hue slider shifts the position of colors. The top gradient bar at the bottom of the dialog box represents the original colors in the image. The bottom gradient bar shows where the colors are being shifted to. Notice that the warm, red tones are now becoming cool, blue tones.

The shift to the plus side of the Saturation slider increases the intensity of the colors.

Create a new layer. Choose a dark blue for the foreground color and a bright blue for the background color. With the Gradient Tool, make a gradient with the light blue at top and the dark blue at the bottom as seen in Figure 3.

2 The hue/saturation for the image is adjusted to simulate the colors found under water.

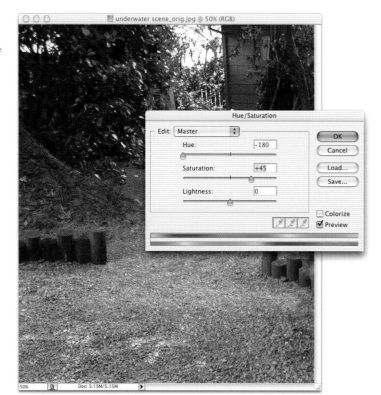

3 A gradient is applied to the layer.

4 The Glass filter.

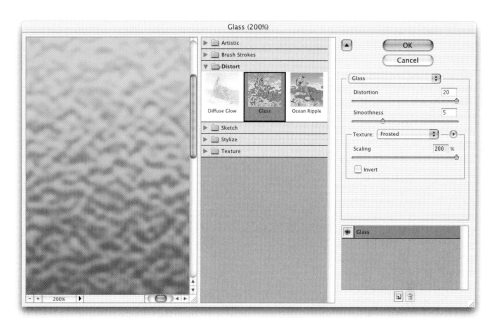

5 The settings for the Glass filter.

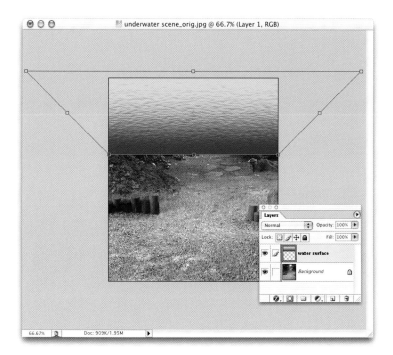

6 The gray work area is exposed.

To obtain a water-like texture, apply the Glass filter (Filter > Distort > Glass) to the layer with the gradient (Figure 4). Push the Distortion and Scaling all the way up (Figure 5). Click OK.

Zoom out so that you can see the gray work area around the image. Choose Edit > Transform > Distort to get the Distort function. When Distort comes on, you will see handles at the four corners and one handle centered on each side of the image. Grab the center handle at the bottom and raise it up to about the halfway point in the image.

Grab the upper-left handle and drag it out to the left of the image a couple of inches. Grab the handle at the upper right and drag it out to the right as seen in Figure 6. Press Enter to execute the distortion.

Create a layer in between the background and the layer with the gradient. Set the Gradient Tool to Foreground to Transparent. This is done in the options bar for the tool on the upper-left icon with the colored gradient visible (Figure 7).

In the new layer, create a gradient that connects the bottom of the layer with the top of the water and flows down into the scene (Figure 8). Note the neat effect where the new gradient intersects the rocks at bottom before fading out.

A Light from Above

Now you'll create the shafts of light penetrating the water from above. Make sure you are working at a low enough magnification that the gray work area outside the image is visible.

Create another new layer. Choose the Polygonal Lasso Tool and set the Feather to a large number such as 20. Draw a selection of a tall, thin parallelogram that narrows at the top as in Figure 9.

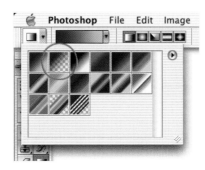

7 The Foreground to Transparent mode is chosen.

8 The abyss is created.

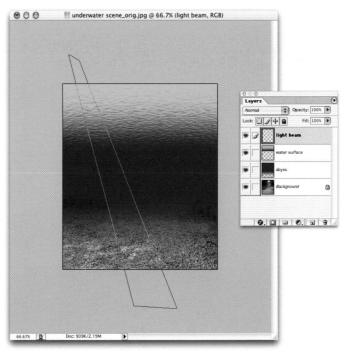

9 A tall, thin area is selected that narrows as it goes up the image.

10 The selection is filled with white.

Fill the selection with white (Figure 10). Note how the edges fade naturally into the water. This is the result of the heavy feathering you used when activating the lasso.

Bring down the opacity for the layer with the shaft of light.

Duplicate the layer with the shaft of light and skew it slightly (Edit > Transform > Skew). Move this new layer away from the original shaft of light so that the top of one shaft is close to the other (Figure 11). Change the opacity for this layer so that it looks slightly different from the other.

Duplicate these steps to create a third ray, or even more if it seems appropriate (Figure 12).

11 The shaft of light is duplicated and skewed.

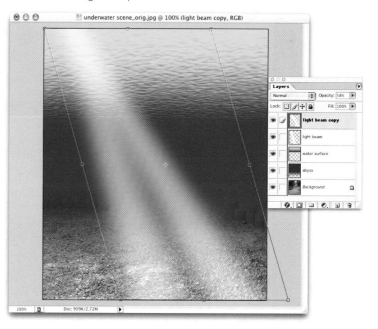

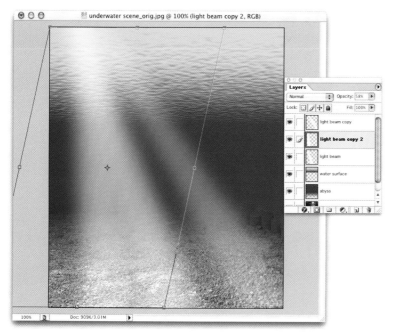

12 A light shaft of light is duplicated again and skewed.

13 The black layer is given some noise.

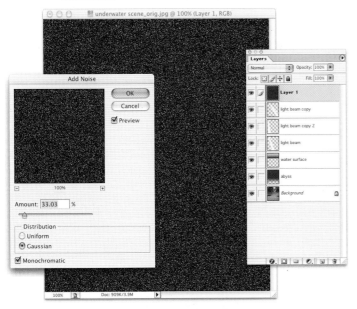

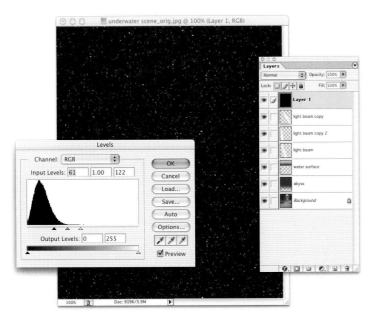

14 The blurred noise is adjusted to lessen the amount of noise.

The Little Things

Now you will create the particulate matter that floats around in the ocean.

Create another layer and fill it with black. Make sure this layer is at the top of all the other layers in the Layers palette. Add a little noise (Filter > Noise > Add Noise) in Monochromatic and Gaussian mode (Figure 13).

Duplicate the layer with the noise. Turn off the Eye icon for this layer. It will be used later for another effect.

Make the bottom noise layer active and blur it (Filter > Blur > Blur More).

Choose the Levels control (Image > Adjustments > Levels). When the dialog box appears, notice a high hill toward the left (dark tones) in the Histogram. Push the black slider in to line up with the point where the hill hits bottom on the right. Bring the white slider in toward the black just enough to expose some of the noise (Figure 14). Click OK.

Set that layer to Screen mode and reduce its opacity. Figure 15 shows the result of this last step. It created the particulate matter that floats around under water. Screen mode is the method of choice because it lightens the underlying layer—except in areas where, as here, the top layer is black, which is why we chose black to fill the layer in the first place.

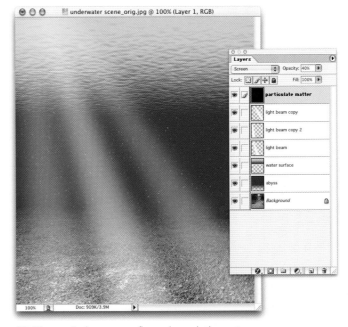

15 The particulate matter floats through the water.

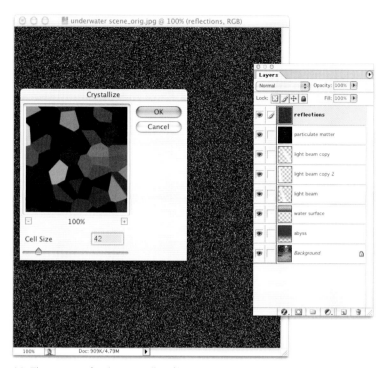

16 The settings for the Crystallize filter.

Reflections from the Surface

The waves on the surface of the water create a dappled reflection on the ocean floor. To re-create this effect, activate the Noise layer.

Choose the Crystallize filter (Filter > Pixelate > Crystallize). Set Cell Size to a size large enough to give you a distinct pattern at 100% as the one I got in Figure 16.

The Find Edges filter is applied to the crystallized layer (Filter > Stylize > Find Edges). Figure 17 shows the effect of the Find Edges filter. This filter has no dialog box. What it is doing is outlining areas of an image where abrupt color transitions occur.

Invert the layer by pressing Command-I (Control-I on a PC).

Choose the Ripple filter (Filter > Distort > Ripple) and roughen up the pattern as seen in Figure 18.

17 The result of the Find Edges filter on the layer with the reflections.

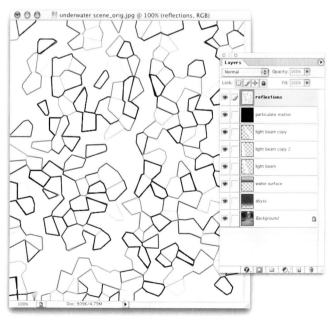

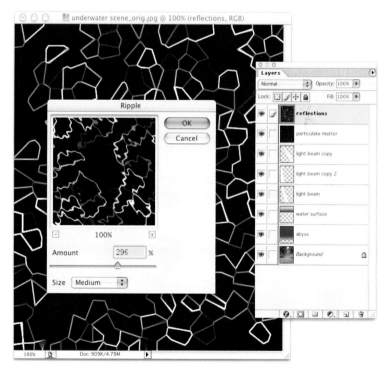

18 The Ripple filter is applied to roughen the pattern.

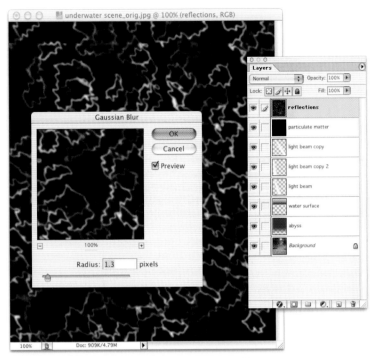

19 The pattern is softened with the Gaussian Blur filter.

Apply the Gaussian Blur filter (Filter > Blur > Gaussian Blur) to soften the pattern (Figure 19).

Set the layer to Screen mode. Just as you distorted the layer to form the surface of the water, distort this layer to resemble the reflections on the ocean floor as seen in Figure 20.

A Layer Mask with white at the bottom going to white at top is applied to the layer of the reflections to make them gradually disappear as they get further away (Figure 21).

Finally, we need some fish. Figure 22 might look familiar to you. It appeared in Chapter 4.

A small group of fish is outlined with the Pen Tool (Figure 23). You then convert it into a selection.

The fish are copied over to the main image and the scene is done (Figure 24).

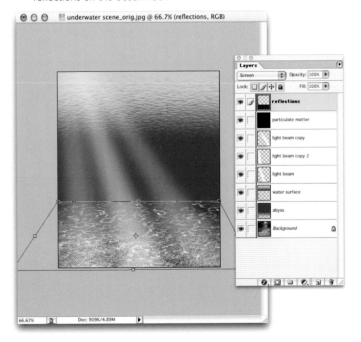

20 The layer is distorted to form the dappled reflections on the ocean floor.

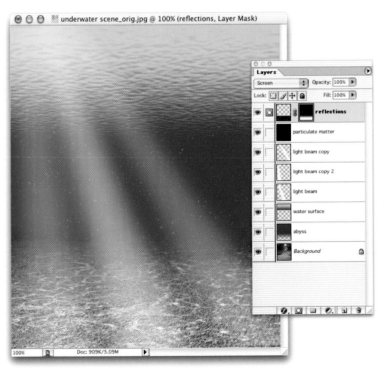

21 A Layer Mask is applied to the layer with the reflections.

22 The original photograph of fish.

23 The fish are outlined with the Pen Tool.

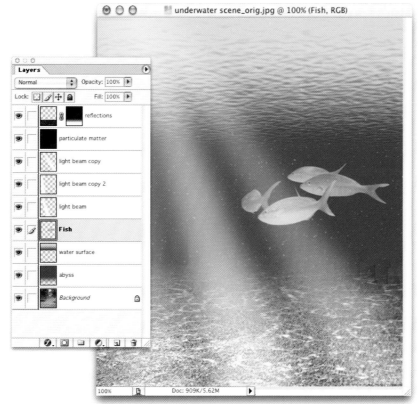

24 The final image.

Scanning and Colorizing Images

The exercise in this last chapter got more emails because of the image I was using than what I was doing with it. My son is a comic artist. This is one of his images, which I will use to show how to deal with scanning artwork when it is too big for your scanner.

There were many comments on the artwork, so I decided to show you another one of his pieces and how to colorize it.

Figure 1 is the final art.

1 The final art.

2 The scan of the top
section of the art.

3 The scan with the bottom
part of the art.

Scanning the Original

The original art was too big to fit on my desktop scanner, so it had to be done in sections. Figure 2 shows the file containing the top section of the art.

NOTE
It is crucial to scan an overlap between scans. This will be used to align them later.

Figure 3 shows the file containing the bottom section of the art.

Selecting the file that contained the top of the art, I increased the canvas size (Image > Canvas Size) to accommodate the bottom portion that was missing (Figure 4). Note that the anchor was set from top. This will set the new area of the canvas completely below the art. The result looks like Figure 5.

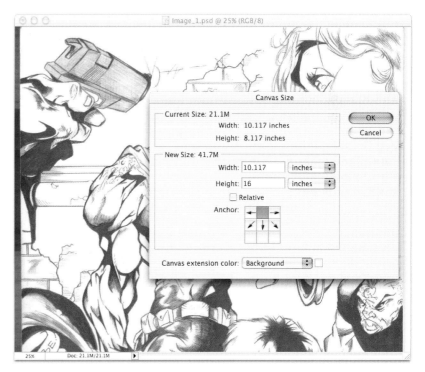

4 The canvas size is increased to accommodate the
missing, bottom section of the art.

5 The new, enlarged canvas.

With the Move Tool, I dragged the file with the bottom of the image and dropped it over to the enlarged file with the top of the image (Figure 6). Note the poor alignment of the two halves.

To align the two scans, the layer containing the bottom of the art is put into Difference mode (Figure 7). The result looks like Figure 8. Light tones indicate which parts of the layer differ from the layers beneath it. Black signifies no difference.

6 The bottom part of the image is imported into the file with the top of the image.

7 The top layer (which contains the bottom half of the artwork) is changed to Difference mode.

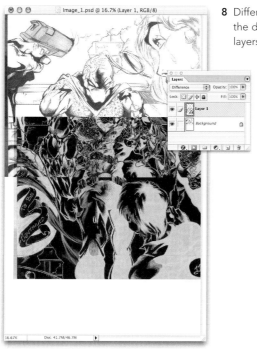

8 Difference mode displays the difference between layers in light tones.

9 The two layers are aligned when the overlap area appears black.

10 The file is flattened and cropped.

With the Move Tool, the layer is moved until the overlap area appears completely or as close to black as possible (Figure 9).

The mode of the top layer is changed back to Normal. The file is flattened (Layer > Flatten Image) and cropped to the edges of the art (Figure 10).

With the Levels command (Image > Adjustments > Levels), I darken the nonwhite areas of the image (Figure 11).

The background layer is duplicated and put into Multiply mode (Figure 12).

A new layer is created behind the multiplied layer of the background duplicate. This is where the colorization takes place (Figure 13).

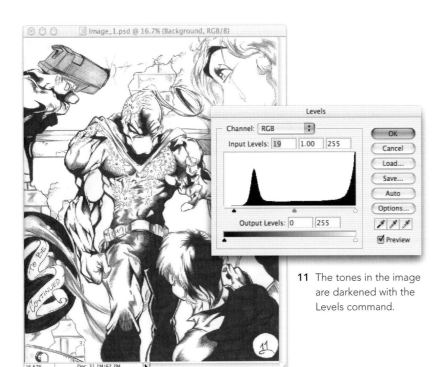

11 The tones in the image are darkened with the Levels command.

12 The background is duplicated and the resulting layer is put in Multiply mode.

13 A layer is created between the background and the layer containing the duplicate of the background. This is where the color is added.

Adding Color

This coloring process is a bit different from colorizing a black-and-white photograph. When colorizing a black-and-white (grayscale) image, gray values are replaced by colors. The lights and darks of gray turn into lights and darks of blue, for instance. Figure 14 shows a black-and-white image.

14 The original black-and-white image.

In Figure 15, the image has been converted to RGB (Image > Mode > RGB) to allow it to be colorized. Using the Paintbrush Tool with a green color, I colorized the leaves. Note that the luminosity values, or lights and darks, are preserved but the hue is changed from shades of gray to shades of green.

The process for colorizing the comic book image in this exercise is more akin to an art form called "reverse glass painting." The technique of reverse glass painting actually originated in China with oil-based paints. Toward the end of the Renaissance, the technique was adapted for use with water-based paints in Italy and subsequently grew in popularity across the rest of Europe. In colonial America, clocks were decorated with these glass paintings. A black line art was stenciled onto a piece of glass. Paint was then applied from the back. The view from the front shows black outlines with rich color showing through between the black detail.

The technique described here can also be compared to the paint by numbers we all did at some point in our lives—except you don't have to worry about staying inside the lines.

Figure 16 shows the black-and-white scan of the original art.

15 The black-and-white image is colorized replacing gray values with hue values but maintaining the light and dark values.

16 The original black-and-white scan.

17 The layer containing the color for the costume.

In the new layer created to contain the color for the costume, paint was applied in the two colors that the costume was made of. As you can see in Figure 17, the color is applied flat. Because the black lines in the art are so thick, the edges of the color are hidden, eliminating the need to be neat at the edges.

The additional tones for the shadows and highlights were done with the Dodge and Burn Tools (Figure 18). Using different-sized, soft-edged brush tips, the areas where the highlights appear were dodged. Shadows were burned. The original drawing was a guide to where these tones needed to be placed.

In Figure 19, the layer with the original ink drawing is visible over the color layer. The black ink defines the detail and cleans up the edges of the color layer.

18 Using the Dodge and Burn Tools, highlights and shadows are added to the color for the costume.

19 The layer containing the original black ink drawing is made visible over the layer with the color for the costume.

20 The color for the skin tones was selected in the Color Picker.

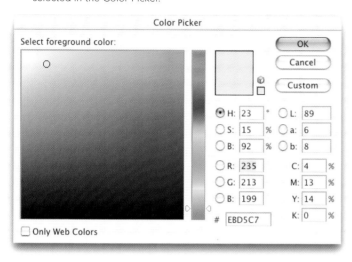

Skin tones were created using the same process. The color used was carefully selected. Figure 20 shows the Color Picker with the settings I chose for the skin tones.

Figure 21 shows the layer with the skin tones that have been dodged and burned to add the shadows and dimensionality to the body parts. Figure 22 shows the assembly of all the layers.

22 All the additional layers are made visible over the layer with the skin tones.

21 The skin tones were painted into the layer created to contain them. The Dodge and Burn Tools added the dimensionality.

23 The color for the hair is painted with the Paintbrush Tool. The highlights were created using a different color than the rest of the hair.

The hair was slightly different. Instead of relying on the Dodge and Burn Tools exclusively to add highlights and shadows, I painted in additional colors using the Paintbrush Tool. In Figure 23, you can see soft highlights added to portions of the hair color; these highlights contain more of a yellowish tone than the balance of the colors that make up the hair.

Figure 24 shows the hair color in place in the final art.

In some cases, I used filters to add additional texture to the art. The wall in the background of the scene was given a texture with the Texturizer filter (Figure 25). I did this the same way as I did when creating the building for the hazardous driveway exercise earlier in this chapter.

The wear and grime added to the wall in Figure 26 was done using the Paintbrush Tool with a modified spatter tip. This is identical to the method used to create the moldy bathroom wall at the beginning of this chapter.

The bricks visible through cracks in the plaster on the wall are another filter at work. I applied the color to a layer (Figure 27). Then I applied the Craquelure filter (Filter > Texture > Craquelure) to add the texture to the brick (Figure 28). Figure 29 shows the finished bricks.

24 The hair color in context with the rest of the image.

25 The wall texture was created with the Texturizer filter.

26 The grime on the wall was created using the same technique as the mold at the beginning of this chapter.

27 The layer with the color of the bricks seen here behind the layer with the line art.

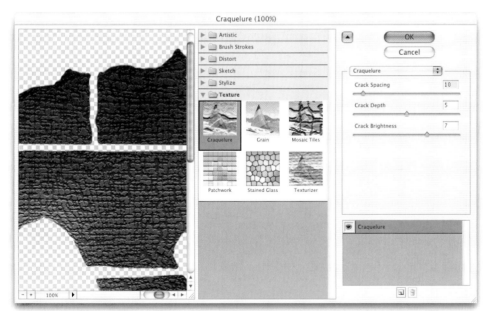

28 The Craquelure filter is used to add texture to the bricks.

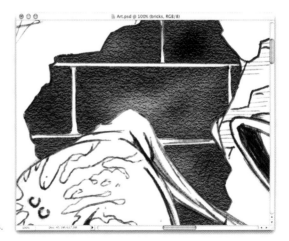

29 The finished bricks.

In other cases, a Layer Style was used to add dimension to the color. The blood visible in Figure 30 was colorized in the same way as all the other colors in the art—red paint was applied to a layer with the Paintbrush Tool.

Figure 31 shows a Layer Style applied to the Color layer to give it some depth. All that was needed was Bevel and Emboss.

These last few tricks reaffirm what I stated in my introduction—that the techniques outlined in this book should be studied for their process rather than the end result shown in this book. Your end result is of your own choosing.

In this book, a simple brush modification with the Paintbrush Tool became mold, grime, and the paint at the end of a neon tube; and, with the Eraser Tool, the same brush tip was used to create the peeling paint off a window sill. That same brush will do something entirely different for you to help you solve some problem you face.

I have given you tons of techniques in this book. Now the job is up to you to master all I have shown you and put it to good use creating your own images.

I sincerely hope this helps to set you on the road to imaging bliss.

Have fun!

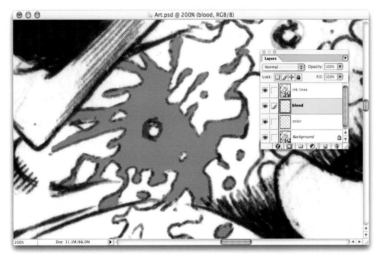

30 Red is painted into a layer to contain the color for the blood.

31 A Layer Style is applied to give depth to the Color layer.

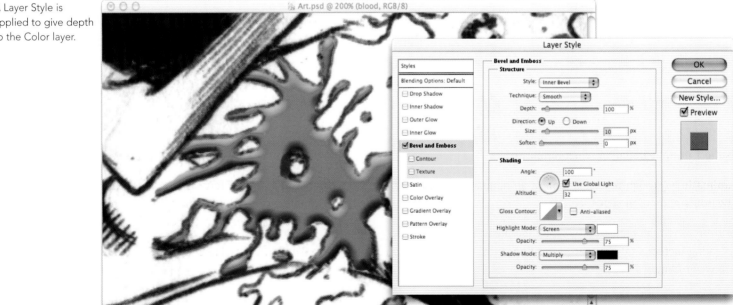

Glossary

A

additive primary colors Red, green, and blue; combinations of which are used to create all other colors when direct or transmitted light is used. They are called additive because when all three are superimposed on each other, the resulting color is white.

address The exact location in computer memory where a particular piece of data is stored.

algorithm A set of instructions for solving a computer problem by setting up a series of step-by-step programming commands. An algorithm is independent of the language being used to program.

alpha channel A grayscale channel used for masking techniques.

alphanumeric Computer data that is made up of numbers and letters.

analog An electronic signal consisting of varying voltage levels. The quality of analog signals is much lower than digital signals and suffers from degradation when duplicated.

animatic A rough representation of an animation. Used for storyboarding animation sequences.

animation The process of creating the illusion of movement by creating incremental changes in position, form, color, and so on between frames.

antialiasing The process of blending the color of adjacent pixels to eliminate the "jaggies" or stair-stepping associated with pixel-based images.

application A computer program.

arbitrary map The pencil function in the Curves dialog box. By changing the shape of the curves with the Pencil tool, you can very specifically control brightness and density values along any part of the spectrum of the image. It's also used to control the amount of black in a color separation.

architecture The overall structure of computer software and hardware in terms of how they interact.

ASCII Acronym for American Standard Code for Information Interchange. It assigns a unique binary number to each character and control character.

aspect ratio The ratio of height to width.

attribute Computer term that relates to characteristics of an image such as its color and size. In word processing or page layout programs, it denotes the size, font, and style of characters.

axis The imaginary line around which an object rotates.

B

background color   The color that represents the canvas when using the Eraser tool. Also the ending color when creating blends or gradients.

Bézier curve   A path that relies on a series of mathematical curve definitions. Named after Pierre Bézier.

bicubic   An interpolation method used to generate intermediate pixels (during operations such as resize and arbitrary rotate) that yields highest quality at the expense of increased processing time.

bilinear   An interpolation method used to generate intermediate pixels (during operations such as resize and arbitrary rotate) that combines relatively high quality with faster processing times.

binary   The numbering system based on the concept of a memory location, or bit, being either on or off.

bit   Abbreviation for binary digit. The basic unit of information that is the foundation of all computing.

bit depth   The amount of information contained in a single pixel.

bitmap   In computer graphics, it refers to an image made up of pixels, each having a specific size (which is expressed in terms of resolution), distinct color, and brightness value. In Photoshop it specifically refers to an image having a single channel with 1 bit of information per pixel, in which all colors are represented by either black or white.

black generation   The amount of black density in the black plate of a separated CMYK file.

black ink limit   The maximum amount of total ink coverage that a specific printing process (or press) can accurately handle.

bluescreen   A process used to isolate foreground images from a pure blue background (devoid of any red or green values). Bluescreen extraction and compositing is used to facilitate the creation of masks, especially for objects with complex edge characteristics (such as hair).

blur   The process of reducing contrast between adjacent pixels to deliver the perception of smoother intermediate tones and increased image softness.

brightness   One of the three attributes of color; hue and saturation are the other two. It is a term used to describe the intensity of light.

buffer   Temporary storage area in a computer or output device used to store data until it is required for processing.

bug   A defect in computer software or hardware. The term came from an insect that wandered into the circuitry of the vacuum tube of the first electronic hardware and caused a short-circuit.

bull's eyes   Marks that appear on the individual films of a separation used for alignment.

bump map   In 3D graphics, the technique of adding surface roughness or bumpiness to an object without actually changing or affecting the geometry of the shape; the effect is seen only when the image is rendered.

burn   The process of overexposing an image, which makes it lighter.

C

calculations   Photoshop operations that compare the pixels of two images and apply discrete logic testing to yield a resulting set of pixels.

calibration   The process of equalizing and balancing the color values of different steps of a production process, including scanning, display, and output devices.

calibration bars   A set of swatches on the side of a printed image to denote the 11-step grayscale on the black plate.

canvas size   The dimensions of a file.

caption   Descriptive text that appears below an image on a printed page.

CCD   Charged-coupled device. A light-sensitive electronic chip used as a temporary image storage device in scanners and video cameras. When light hits a CCD, the color and brightness information is converted to digital information that the computer understands.

CD-ROM   Compact Disc-Read Only Memory. A type of optical disc used to store large quantities of data. The information is stored in a series of plateaus and valleys. When a laser light bounces off these plateaus, it is converted into binary code.

channel   The discrete components of an image. The colors red, green, and blue each reside in their own channel. Images saved in Photoshop can have up to 24 channels. Besides brightness and color information, additional document channels are used for masking.

characteristic curve   A plotted curve that demonstrates the change in density of an image as the exposure is increased. The slope of this curve is the measure of gamma, or contrast.

clipping groups   The technique of "grouping" multiple layers together which uses the bottom-most layer as a mask for all other layers grouped with it.

clipping paths   Vector-based selection masks that can be embedded into an EPS image for silhouetting bitmap images with resolution-independent masks in external programs such as Illustrator, PageMaker, and Quark XPress.

cloning   The process of copying portions of an image into other areas of an image.

CMYK   Cyan, magenta, yellow, and black, which are the four process colors in printing.

CMYK image   An image made up of four channels. Each channel contains the information for the individual process colors cyan, magenta, yellow, and black.

chroma   The intensity of color in an image.

color correction   The process of manipulating the color information of an image to optimize the printing process.

color difference matte   Any of the matting processes that use the color of the image as a base for separating the image from the background. Any color can be used provided the image is devoid of that color. Bluescreen and greenscreen are color difference mattes.

color lookup table (CLUT)   A special palette that stores the colors used in an image.

color map   A table of information used by the computer to adjust the color and brightness of an image.

color separation   An image that has been broken down into the four process colors of cyan, magenta, yellow, and black. Each channel contains the individual color information, which is translated onto plates used in the printing process.

comp   In the graphic design industry, it stands for a rough representation of a finished product used for client presentations and such. In imaging, it is an abbreviation of composite.

composite   The result of taking two or more images and combining them to form one image.

constrain   To restrict the movement of a tool or the proportions of a selection tool or image.

continuous-tone image   An image containing gradient tones.

contrast   The relative difference, or "spread" between the dark and light values of an image.

crop   To select a portion of an image and delete the unselected areas.

crop marks   Marks printed with an image to indicate the outer edges where the image will be trimmed.

D

database   An organized collection of data capable of being searched or cross-referenced easily.

DCS   Desktop Color Separation, the file format used to export pre-separated CMYK images in EPS format for inclusion in full-color pages in PageMaker or Quark XPress. DCS produces five files—four for the CMYK plates, and a screen file for placement in the page layout.

debugging   The process of identifying and correcting errors (bugs) in computer hardware or software.

defringe   The process of removing the edge artifacts created when an object is isolated from a background and placed (composited) into a new background with different color or brightness values. The antialiased pixels from the first background are removed, and the edges are mixed with the colors in the new background, to create a more seamless edge.

degradation   The loss of quality of an image when duplicated or manipulated.

densitometer   An instrument used to measure the density of printed halftones by taking readings from the calibration bars. Also an instrument for measuring the opacity of a film image. This reading plays an important part in the determination of proper bluescreen exposure and matte density.

density   The opacity of a film image. An opaque image that transmits no light has the maximum density, whereas a totally transparent one has no density.

density range   In printing, the range from the smallest dot (highlight) to the largest dot (shadow) a press can handle.

depth of field   The range of focus in front and behind the principal subject of an image.

desaturation   The loss of color intensity.

difference matte   The mask created when applying difference matting techniques.

difference matting   The process of separating elements of an image by comparing the difference in color values between them. The foreground elements are separated from the background by calculating the difference between the background and the image pixel values.

digital   Format of information that is converted and stored as numeric sequences of 1s and 0s that are deciphered by a computer. Any device or process that manipulates digital information.

digitize   The process of converting 2D or 3D static or dynamic visual or audio forms into binary information.

digitizing pen   Also called a stylus, is an electronic pen used in conjunction with a digitizing tablet to control the position of a cursor on the screen.

digitizing table/tablet   A drawing pad that is relative to the computer screen. Passing a digitizing pen over the pad moves the position of the cursor.

dithering   The process of creating patterns of colors to simulate colors absent in an image or unavailable for display. Examples include the patterns of black and white pixels in a bitmap image to simulate grayscale values and the screen patterns created when viewing a high-quality image on a low-quality computer display.

displacement map   One image whose pixel values are used to distort another image. Lower pixel (darker) values result in less distortion, whereas higher pixel (lighter) values distort the image more.

displacement mapping   The process of distorting an image to form a surface texture.

dodge   The limiting of exposure of an image to cause it to appear darker.

dot gain   A defect in printing causing dots to print larger than intended. Often caused by the ink absorbency of a particular paper.

download   The process of transferring data from one computer to another. Usually refers to transferring data from an online network to an individual computer.

DPI   Dots per inch; a measure of resolution. The number of dots that a printer will produce within an inch. The higher the number, the more detail will be visible.

dubbing   The process of duplicating data onto different media, be it computer storage media or audio/video tape.

duotone   An image printed with only two standard, often Pantone, ink colors.

dupe   Short for duplication. A duplicate of the original. The process of making a duplication.

dynamic range   The range of colors and values a computer is able to represent based on the number of bits used to record each color. The higher the number of bits, the higher the dynamic range.

E

edge characteristics   The appearance of the edge of an element that has been composited into another image.

eight-bit color   The color depth of an image that has 8 bits of information per pixel. The 8 bits allow for each pixel to contain 1 of 256 colors.

element   A single image that is being composited into another.

EPS   Encapsulated PostScript; graphics format for bringing images into object-based drawing and page layout programs. It is resolution independent, meaning the output resolution is based on the output device, not the image file. Besides the image description data, an EPS file also carries a preview PICT or TIFF file, used in displaying the image on the screen.

export   A file is exported when another version of it is needed in another file format or for a specific purpose, such as output.

external memory   Any memory storage device connected to a computer to augment its internal storage hard disk.

F

fade-out rate   The rate at which the Paintbrush or Airbrush tool runs out of paint to simulate a real brush stroke.

feather   Gradually fades out the edges of a brush or selection, giving variably soft edges.

fill   To paint a selected area with a color or pattern.

fixed hard disk   Any disk drive that is permanently attached to a computer.

flare   A visual effect to simulate a bright light source being distorted and accentuated as if seen through a real optical lens.

flatten   Taking an image with layers and merging the layers into a single background layer.

flip   The process of making a mirror image of the original or reversing the facing of a selection or image.

foreground color   The color used by all the tools that utilize a color (Paintbrush, Pencil, Line tool, and so on).

foreshortening   In drawing, painting, and so on, to represent the lines of an object as shorter than they actually are to give the illusion of proper relative size, in accordance with the principles of perspective.

fractal   A visual algorithm that when repeated forms a greater image of essentially the same character.

frame grab   The process of digitizing a single frame of video into a digital image file.

frame grabber   A device for making frame grabs.

fuzziness   A means of controlling the amount of antialiasing that will be applied to the edges of a selection. Similar to feathering.

G

gamma   The objective measurement of contrast in an image.

gamma curve   See *characteristic curve*.

gamut   The range of colors a given color system can visually represent.

generation   The reference given to the number of copies made of an original. In film or analog duplication, this is an important factor that will determine the level of degradation.

generation loss   The loss of quality of an image due to duplication.

gigabyte   One thousand megabytes or one billion bytes.

grain   A noise texture that appears on film images. This is due to the silver halide particles that make up film emulsion. The grain is microscopic but becomes visible when an image is enlarged. The grain increases with each generation of reproduction.

gradient fill   A fill method that consists of the gradual transition of multiple colors.

gray-component replacement (GCR)   The removal of CMYK and replacement of their values with values of black.

gray ramp   A graph representing the density of equal amounts of neutral colors (equal amounts of cyan, magenta, and yellow) in an image. Used in color separation.

grayscale image   Often referred to, incorrectly, as black and white. A single channel image that consists of 256 levels of gray.

H

halftone   The reproduction of a continuous-tone image made by using a screen to break up the image into dots of various sizes. The proximity and location of these dots on the printed page gives the illusion of continuous colors.

handles   The extension of the points made by the Path tool that allows for the manipulation of the Bézier curve between two points.

hard copy   Images viewed in printed form rather than on the monitor.

hard disk   A metal disk coated with magnetic material used to store computer data.

Hard Light mode   This mode, like Overlay, multiplies dark areas and screens light areas. The process is based on the color or tone in the layer set to Hard Light rather than the layers beneath it.

highlight   The lightest parts of an image. In a halftone, this area is represented by the smallest dots or the absence of dots.

histogram   A graphic representation of the number of pixels with a given color value. It shows the breakdown of the tone gamut and color occurrence in an image.

horizon   The eye level of a person viewing a scene.

horizon line   In perspective, the eye level where sky and land meet. All vanishing points meet at the horizon line

hot   An area of an image that is too bright.

hue   The main attribute of a color that distinguishes it from another color.

I

icon   A picture or symbol used to represent a tool, command, and so forth in a computer.

image enhancement   To improve the quality of an image by reducing noise, increasing contrast, and so on.

image mapping   The process of placing an image over a three-dimensional shape in 3D programs.

imagesetter   An output device for plate ready art.

indexed color   A single-channel image with 8 bits of color per pixel. Unlike a grayscale image, it contains color rather than levels of gray. The index is a color lookup table that contains 256 colors.

interactive   The process of providing real-time response or feedback to the user.

interpolation   A mathematical operation that averages nearby pixel values together; used when resizing an image or selection.

J

jaggies   Stair-stepping caused by pixels on the edge of the elements of an image.

JPEG   A lossy compression system used to compress color images. JPEG stands for Joint Photographic Experts Group.

JPEG 2000   A mathematically sophisticated recent update to the JPEG spec. The JPEG 2000 format ordinarily results in slightly smaller files and elimination of certain boxy artifacts that were characteristic of the former spec.

K

kern   To adjust the space between characters in type.

keyword   A word given as a database search parameter.

L

lab color   A color model that interprets color as one lightness component, ranging from black to white, and two color components, the first ranging from green to red, the second ranging from blue to yellow. This is the native color space for PostScript Level 2.

laser printer   An output device that uses lasers to set ink onto paper.

layer   A component of object-based raster imaging, wherein a set of pixels can be separately addressable from the rest of the pixels in the image.

layer mask   A grayscale component of a layer that determines its opacity.

layout   The arrangement of all the elements (for example, headline, copy, pictures) within an ad, book, and so forth.

leading   The space between lines of text.

light value   The degree of brightness or darkness in an image.

linear fill   A fill that is projected from one point to another in a straight line.

low res   Short for low resolution; an image that has insufficient information for final reproduction. Low-res images are used for presentation of work in progress or can be set to the monitor resolution and used for onscreen presentations.

lpi   Lines per inch; refers to how many halftone screen lines can be measured within a linear inch.

luminosity   A color parameter that measures the brightness of color.

LZW compression   An image compression scheme used with the TIFF file format.

M

marching ants   The term used to describe the animated lines that indicate a selected area of an image.

marquee   The area of a selection is outlined by a series of traveling dashes (marching ants).

mask   An area used to protect a portion of an image while exposing others for manipulation. Often based on an 8-bit grayscale component that varies the mask's opacity based on levels of brightness, black being opaque and white being transparent.

matte   The portion of a mask that protects the image from manipulation.

meg   Short for megabyte (one million bytes).

menu   A list displayed on the computer screen of commands available to the user.

menu bar   A strip along the top of the computer screen that contains the menu items.

mid-tone   A range of tones whose value is approximately halfway between the lightest and darkest value of an image.

moiré pattern   An undesirable pattern in printing caused by incorrect angles set to overlying halftones.

monotone   An image printed with only one nonblack ink.

morph   The process of progressively transforming one object into another. The name derives from metamorphosis, and usually is a hybrid process of cross-fading and distorting.

morphing   The process of creating a morph.

multichannel image   An image consisting of more than one channel. In Photoshop, it most often refers to a grayscale image with more than one channel.

Multiply mode   A layer set to Multiply mode literally multiplies its pixel brightness values with those of the layers beneath it. This has a significant effect of darkening the layers below it. The result is then divided by the maximum range of brightness values to prevent large areas from clipping to solid black.

N

neutral density   A value that allows all wavelengths of light to be absorbed equally. With a neutral density, an image can be lightened or darkened without a shifting of color.

noise   A randomly distributed color and tonal shift among pixels, resulting from scanning of photographic source material or the Photoshop noise filters.

NTSC   Acronym for the National Television Standards Committee; refers to the standard colors of video broadcast. NTSC frames have a television resolution of 525 lines.

O

offline   Any equipment that is not directly communicating with the computer and its components.

online   Any equipment that is directly communicating with the computer and its components.

opacity   The opposite of transparent. The level at which light is blocked.

output device   Any device that can display computer data, from computer monitors to color printers.

Overlay mode   Light areas in a layer set to Overlay mode are screened onto the layers below it, whereas dark areas are multiplied to dark underlying areas. As brightness values in the upper layer reach 50% gray, the screening and multiplying effects lessen. A value of 50% gray has no effect on the underlying layers.

P

path   A vector-based Bézier curve made with the Pen Tool that can be edited at any time. It is used to make masks and clipping paths that require very little storage space.

pattern   An image that repeats in tiles to form a regular design.

PAL   Acronym for Phase Alternating Line; the television broadcast standard of most of Western Europe, which uses 625 lines of resolution.

palette   The floating window containing the options for the various tools. Also refers to the colors available to be applied to an image or the colors that exist in that image.

perspective   The appearance of objects or scenes as determined by their relative distance and positions.

pixel   Acronym for picture element; the smallest subdivision of a digital image, which has a set of values that describes its color and tonal qualities (see *pixel depth*). Also used to refer to a single dot or phosphor element on a computer display device.

pixel depth   A measurement of how much information is carried in a single pixel.

PostScript   Page description language used to transfer the information of an image to a printing or output device.

process color   The system of four-color printing that describes each color as a mixture of four ink colors: cyan, magenta, yellow, and black.

Q

quarter-tone   Tonal value of a dot or pixel whose value is approximately halfway between the highlight and mid-tone values of an image.

quick mask   A method of viewing a mask over an image to facilitate adding to subtracting from the mask.

R

radial fill   A fill that is projected from the center out in a circular fashion.

RAM   Random-access memory; the part of the computer that stores instructions and information temporarily. Applied to the running of applications and the execution of commands.

raster-based image   An image described as an array of pixels. *See* Bitmap.

rasterize   The process of converting vector information to bitmap or raster based.

raytracing   A feature of 3D programs used to accurately create the surfaces of reflective and refractive objects.

real time   The amount of time in which an event would actually occur, as opposed to "slow motion." In interactive media, the feature of having immediate response to user intervention and action.

reflection map   An image that is mapped onto a 3D object that acts like a reflection of the surrounding environment of the scene.

registration marks   In printing, marks used to properly align the individual plates.

rendering   The process of creating the final detail and color of a 3D computer-generated image.

resample   To change the resolution of an image.

resize   To change the dimensions of an image.

resolution   The number of dots or pixels of an image contained in a given area. It also refers to the number of bits per pixel. In a printer, it refers to the number of dots per inch.

RGB image   A three-channel image made up of the additive colors of red, green, and blue.

rotoscope   To trace onto paper an image that is projected from a piece of film. Also used to describe the act of manipulating, drawing, or painting directly onto individual frames of a film.

S

sample rate   The frequency with which a computer takes a data sample. Sampling takes place when scanning or digitizing any media into the computer.

saturation   The intensity or the degree of purity of a color.

scanned image   An image that has been digitized on a scanner.

scanner   An electronic device that digitizes images into the computer.

scratch disk   The hard drive volume where the Photoshop temporary files are stored.

screen angles   The angles at which halftone screens are set in relation to each other.

screen frequency   The density of dots in a halftone screen.

Screen mode   A layer set to Screen mode adds together the values of it and the layers beneath it. This has the effect of lightening the layers below. The result is constrained to the maximum brightness of all the layers.

selection   A part of an image that has been segregated from the rest for the purpose of modification or duplication.

separations   The individual four-color-process films used to make the plates used for CMYK printing.

seps   Short for separations.

shadow   The darkest values of an image.

sharpening   A selective contrast enhancement used to increase contrast between edges in the image, making images sharper and more "in focus"; edges are determined by the degree of contrast between light and dark pixels.

sixteen-bit color   Color depth capable of approximately 65,000 colors per pixel.

spacing   The distance between the pixels that are affected by each painting and editing tool.

storyboard   A series of drawing, used to describe a sequence of motion in film or video.

T

texture map   An image used to give the look and feel to a 3D object.

three-quarter-tone   Tonal value of a dot or pixel whose value is approximately halfway between the shadow and mid-tone values of an image.

tolerance   A parameter that specifies the color range of pixels to be selected.

transfer function   A method of calibration for imagesetting devices to control, or compensate for, dot gain.

trap   An overlap that prevents gaps from appearing along the edges of two objects of different colors caused by misalignment of plates in printing.

tri-tone   An image printed with three inks of different colors.

U

undercolor removal (UCR)   The technique for reducing the cyan, magenta, and yellow inks from the darkest portion of an image and replacing them with black.

V

vanishing lines   In perspective, the horizontal lines of an object that are going off in the distance and meeting at the vanishing points.

vanishing point   In perspective, the point on the horizon line where all the vanishing lines meet.

vectors   Programmed coordinates that are connected in a dot-to-dot fashion to create a shape.

vignette   The softening of the edges of a selection to create a gradual transition. *See* feather, fuzziness.

virtual memory   The use of unused hard disk space as RAM for the storage of temporary memory.

Z

zoom   To magnify or reduce an area of an image to see detail.

Index

www.informit.com

YOUR GUIDE TO IT REFERENCE

New Riders has partnered with **InformIT.com** to bring technical information to your desktop. Drawing from New Riders authors and reviewers to provide additional information on topics of interest to you, **InformIT.com** provides free, in-depth information you won't find anywhere else.

Articles

Keep your edge with thousands of free articles, in-depth features, interviews, and IT reference recommendations—all written by experts you know and trust.

Online Books

Answers in an instant from **InformIT Online Books'** 600+ fully searchable online books.

POWERED BY

Safari

Catalog

Review online sample chapters, author biographies, and customer rankings and choose exactly the right book from a selection of more than 5,000 titles.

www.newriders.com

VOICES THAT MATTER

VISIT OUR WEB SITE

WWW.NEWRIDERS.COM

On our web site, you'll find information about our other books, authors, tables of contents, and book errata. You will also find information about book registration and how to purchase our books, both domestically and internationally.

EMAIL US

Contact us at: **nrfeedback@newriders.com**

- If you have comments or questions about this book
- To report errors that you have found in this book
- If you have a book proposal to submit or are interested in writing for New Riders
- If you are an expert in a computer topic or technology and are interested in being a technical editor who reviews manuscripts for technical accuracy

Contact us at: **nreducation@newriders.com**

- If you are an instructor from an educational institution who wants to preview New Riders books for classroom use. Email should include your name, title, school, department, address, phone number, office days/hours, text in use, and enrollment, along with your request for desk/examination copies and/or additional information.

Contact us at: **nrmedia@newriders.com**

- If you are a member of the media who is interested in reviewing copies of New Riders books. Send your name, mailing address, and email address, along with the name of the publication or web site you work for.

BULK PURCHASES/CORPORATE SALES

The publisher offers discounts on this book when ordered in quantity for bulk purchases and special sales. For sales within the U.S., please contact: Corporate and Government Sales (800) 382-3419 or **corpsales@pearsontechgroup.com**. Outside of the U.S., please contact: International Sales (317) 428-3341 or **international@pearsontechgroup.com**.

WRITE TO US

New Riders Publishing
800 East 96th Street, 3rd Floor
Indianapolis, IN 46240

CALL/FAX US

Toll-free (800) 571-5840
If outside U.S. (317) 428-3000
Ask for New Riders
FAX: (317) 428-3280

New Riders

VIEW CART 🛒   [   ] search ⊙

▸ Registration already a member? Log in. ▸ Book Registration

OUR AUTHORS

PRESS ROOM

| web development | design | photoshop | new media | 3-D | server technologies |

EDUCATORS

ABOUT US

CONTACT US

You already know that New Riders brings you the **Voices that Matter**. But what does that mean? It means that New Riders brings you the Voices that challenge your assumptions, take your talents to the next level, or simply help you better understand the complex technical world we're all navigating.

Visit **www.newriders.com** to find:

▸ **10% discount** and **free shipping** on all book purchases

▸ Never before published chapters

▸ Sample chapters and excerpts

▸ Author bios and interviews

▸ Contests and enter-to-wins

▸ Up-to-date industry event information

▸ Book reviews

▸ Special offers from our friends and partners

▸ Info on how to join our User Group program

Ways to have your Voice heard

WWW.NEWRIDERS.COM

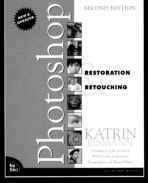

073571133X
Suzette Troché-Stapp
US$39.99

0735713502
Katrin Eismann
US$49.99

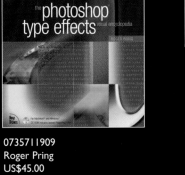

0735711909
Roger Pring
US$45.00

0735713561
Scott Kelby and Felix Nelson
US$39.99

0735713537
Scott Kelby
US$39.99

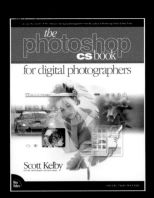

0735714118
Scott Kelby
US$39.99

VOICES
THAT MATTER™

New Riders

WWW.NEWRIDERS.COM